An Indiana Tragedy

A True Story of Crime and Devotion

Dixie Distler

Copyright © 2025 Dixie Distler
1-15012875321

All rights reserved.

ISBN: 978-1-7329695-9-9

First Edition

ACKNOWLEDGMENTS

I am grateful for the editorial assistance of
Willy Mathes
www.bookeditorcoach.com

And for the cover design by Robin Johnson
Florida Girl Design Inc.
www.gobookcoverdesign.com

I also thank my husband, family, and friends who encouraged me to keep writing so Edward Leyer's story could finally be told.

Introduction

What you have before you is a true, thought-provoking account of a German immigrant named Edward Leyer. The circumstances of his life and death were chronicled in newspapers across the United States, but none more so than *The Evansville Courier-Journal and Press* and *The Evansville Journal*, both of Evansville, Indiana. Within the articles of these and other periodicals of the time, the dialog, names, places and events have been preserved, and are set forth here as part of a genuinely historical accounting of one of the most troubling, eye-opening stories ever recorded in the state of Indiana.

Some conversations and characters have been added to present a cohesive chronicle of events, but the people and places that came together to impact Edward Leyer's troubled existence are described herein as truly and accurately as possible.

"Never, in all my years, have I seen a wife and children as devoted and loving as Mrs. Leyer and their children have been."

- Sheriff Wunderlich, Evansville, Indiana

Prologue

At the onset of the Civil War, James Shackelford assembled and equipped the Twenty-fifth Kentucky Regiment of Infantry and was made colonel of the same. Although engaged at Fort Donelson with that regiment, he lost his health through exposure and was obliged to resign his office in 1862.

Sometime afterward, President Lincoln issued Shackelford special orders to raise a regiment of cavalry for the Union service, which he accomplished in four weeks, choosing from among sixteen hundred first-class men who embodied what was known as the Eighth Kentucky Cavalry.

About this time, a man from Kentucky, William Davenport, went to visit his friend, President Lincoln, and on gaining an audience, stated his business: "Abe, I have come to know if you would like to have General Morgan captured."

"I know of nothing that would suit me better."

"Then, we have a boy in our neighborhood, Colonel James Shackelford of the Eighth Kentucky Cavalry, and if you'll make him brigadier general, I guarantee he *will* capture Morgan inside of six months."

The President not only heard, but heeded, and on the 17th day of March 1863, Shackelford was promoted to the rank of brigadier general.

In June 1863, General John Hunt Morgan, along with nearly 2,500 of his rebel soldiers, started upon his memorable raid through Kentucky, Indiana and Ohio, and General Shackelford, in command of the First Brigade, Second Division, Twenty-third Army Corps, began his pursuit.

Very little resistance was offered to the rebels until Morgan and his brigade reached the Ohio River on July 19. A half mile away, in the direction of Buffington Island, Shackelford heard artillery fire from a battle raging on the river. His officers and men—notwithstanding the immense fatigue they had undergone—seemed to be inspired with new life and energy, and rushed forward. The river had risen unexpectedly, and it was possible for Captain Le Roy Fitch of the Union Forces to place his gunboats in advantageous positions to guard the crossing.

Union Generals Edward Hobson and Henry Judah, too, had established their forces nearby, and though tired and weary from days of pursuit, were still in good spirits and anxious to fight. Morgan was pinned in from all sides, and in the fight that ensued, Shackelford captured seven hundred prisoners, their horses and arms, and two hundred more were either shot dead or drowned.

The following morning Shackelford sent a flag of truce to the rebels and their commander, demanding their surrender. Forty minutes for consultation were granted, at the end of which between 1,200 and 1,300 Confederate cavalry soldiers surrendered and turned over all their arms and supplies.

However, with about five hundred of his men, Morgan slipped away before the surrender, turned back from the river and headed toward Pennsylvania, hoping to join General Robert E. Lee.

The Federals were not sufficiently well prepared for further pursuit. At Lebanon, Kentucky, Hobson's force was nearly decimated by the Confederates, with only five hundred horses left in the command. Nevertheless, Shackelford, along with five hundred of Hobson's men, mounted their horses and, followed by Major George W. Rue of the Ninth Kentucky Cavalry and Major William B. Way of the Ninth Michigan, undertook the capture of Morgan.

On July 26, they succeeded in hemming Morgan in on all sides near Salineville, Ohio, on the New Lisbon road. When General Shackelford came up, Morgan surrendered himself with 350 men, although a small remnant escaped.

The officers were consigned to the penitentiaries of Columbus and Pittsburg and the other prisoners to Camps Chase and Morton. Ironically, Morgan and Shackelford had been boyhood friends and fellow officers in the Mexican War, and on this occasion, Shackelford addressed him with the following words, "General Morgan, I am glad to see you, sir!"

General Morgan replied, "I have no doubt of it. But damn it, I'm sorry I can't return the compliment."

Upon finally being captured, the Confederate leader stepped forward to surrender his sword, but Shackelford refused to accept it, allowing his former comrade to maintain his dignity. However, Morgan desired to give his saddle and mare to Shackelford. By order of General Ambrose Burnside, he was allowed to do so, the saddle and horse remaining in possession of Shackelford… until a forged order was presented for the saddle one day. Shackelford's family, believing the document to be legitimate, relinquished it – no trace of it ever being discovered afterward.

General Shackelford's wife died in 1864, and being left with four small children, he felt it his duty, at the termination of the war, to resign, although offered by President Lincoln the rank of Major General.

Consequently, he resumed the practice of law, hanging his shingle in Evansville, Indiana.

Part 1

The Land of Opportunity

In 1855, I immigrated from Germany with my wife Helena and infant son Herman, eventually settling in Evansville, Indiana. Here we found a German community that filled the cultural void we left behind. Little did I know I would be called to arms in my adopted country.

- Edward Leyer

Chapter 1

Nestled on the northern bank of the mighty Ohio River sat the booming town of Evansville, Indiana. Once, this had been home to ancient Native American tribes, the Miami, Wea and Piankashay, who were relocated in the 1800s as the English settled the territory. Over the years, as the town's popularity spread and the Evans and Crawford Railroad came online, more immigrants, predominantly Germans, found their new beginnings in this growing Midwestern municipality.

***

Helena Leyer sat on a wooden bench, watching the horse-drawn carriage slowly meander down the dusty city street toward her modest home. As he passed the front porch, the driver tipped his hat respectfully and nodded a greeting toward her.

After the wagon disappeared from view, Helena frowned and turned her attention toward the thin figure of a man sitting on the front steps across from her. Angry, hurt and bewildered, she narrowed her eyes in contempt at him. "I don't understand why you must go," she finally said, breaking the silence. "This isn't *our* war. Leave the English to fight amongst themselves. I didn't sail with you from Germany to lose you in a war I don't understand!"

After lowering his pipe, Edward blew a ring of grey smoke upward, watching it gradually dissipate in the crisp morning air.

Even after six years, he and Helena were still struggling to adjust to the newness of the land and the complex English language, so most of their conversations were in their German language. "Lena, America is our adopted country. It's our home now. All able-bodied men have been called to arms. It's my *duty* to fight."

"Is it your duty to *die*?" she snapped, angrily turning away from him. "Is it your duty to leave your wife without a husband and your children without a father? You're thirty-five years old! Leave the fighting to the younger men!"

With a sigh, Edward stood and walked over to the bench. Sitting beside his wife and seeing tears welling up in her large blue eyes, he gently lifted her chin in his hand and turned her face toward him. "I will come back to you, and it's only for three years." Wiping a tear from her cheek, he whispered, "Besides, if I volunteer, there's a good chance I'll be in a support role, like a blacksmith or cook. That way, I won't have to fight."

The couple fell silent upon hearing the sudden patter of small feet on wooden planks as five-year-old Herman scampered across the porch and climbed onto the bench beside his mother. Edward tousled the boy's curly dark hair. "Such a blessing you are, our little cub."

"Please, Edward, promise me," Helena pleaded, then pulled Herman closer to her side. "Promise *us* you'll come back alive."

Edward stretched and began rubbing a kink out of his neck. Turning to respond, he paused and watched his son playfully tugging at his mother's apron string. But then he saw the concern in Helena's face, waiting for his reply. Forcing a smile, he laid his hand on her shoulder and said, "This isn't an easy thing I do."

Just then, Edward heard a faint "coo" coming from inside the house as their baby son, Eddy, stirred from sleep in his bassinet. Stepping through the front door to attend to the infant, Edward knew much would be at stake with his departure to the Union Army.

Lifting Eddy into his arms, he carried him out onto the porch and again sat down beside Helena and Herman. Studying his wife's still anxious face, Edward leaned over and tenderly kissed her on the cheek, followed by the same for Herman. "Don't be afraid, my dears. From what I hear, the Southern army will refuse to fight. This whole thing will be over in a matter of months. Then you'll see me walking through our front door, a soldier who served a good cause in the American war."

***

On October 8, 1861, Edward Leyer mustered into Company A of the 28th Regiment in Louisville, Kentucky. The line moved quickly as each man signed his name, or made his mark, on the roster in front of a corporal seated behind the open-air table. The morning fog mixed with smoke from numerous cooking fires to create a heavy haze that hovered over the muddy ground. Edward stared back at his enlistment papers, mesmerized at the notion of now being a newly inducted volunteer foot soldier in the Union Army.

After stepping away from the table, a slap on his back suddenly shook him from his thoughts. "Come on, Private," the fellow recruit said, pointing to their right. "We're supposed to go to that tent to get our uniforms."

Edward stood still for a moment, looking a bit bewildered by the encounter. "I am German," he finally blurted out, smiling as he motioned his hands at himself.

The recruit laughed and patted him on the back, "Ah, German! Still learning the language." Snickering, he gestured for Edward to follow him, then started walking away quickly. "Come!"

Lagging behind at first, Edward picked up his pace so as not to lose track of his newfound comrade in the commotion.

Upon arriving at the tent, with Edward right behind him, the young soldier turned and extended his hand. "Garner."

Reaching out and shaking his hand, the German replied, "Leyer."

Within the hour, Edward stood shoulder-to-shoulder in a row with other recruits, tightly holding his uniform and accessories, as a lieutenant rode on horseback up and down the line. The German was overwhelmed by the officer's shouted instructions, of which he understood only a few words.

As the men were dismissed, he asked Garner, "Where go we now?"

"To our sleeping quarters," he replied, pointing toward the rows of dingy, grey tents. "We change into these uniforms and then fall out for chow."

"Chow?"

"You really don't know much English, do you? Lunch... food."

Grabbing the puzzled foreigner by the arm, Garner pulled him along toward the tent with the number 22 hanging above the entrance.

Beginning to feel a part of something bigger than himself, Edward looked down at the uniform he now proudly wore, fingering its shiny brass-colored buttons, as he stood in the chow line. They moved quickly, with other privates serving spoonfuls of food onto each passing tray. Observing his plate, Edward stared curiously at what the server called potatoes, a grayish-white gooey mass that created a thick creamy puddle in the dish's center. Floating atop that mass was a lumpy, brownish piece of meat that looked like the worn bottom of one of his old boots. Feeling a bit queasy, Edward looked up and shuddered, thinking, *Never would anything like this appear on our dinner table at home.*

The next line server, an enormous soldier with two missing front teeth, snarled at Edward, "You want kawn?"

"Kawn?"

The hulking brute leaned in closer to Leyer, staring him straight in the face. "You makin' fun o' me, little man?" Tiny droplets of saliva spewed from his mouth as he spoke.

Backing up a step, Edward blurted, "Nein, no, no…"

"Please excuse my friend," Garner interrupted, pushing his way in front of Edward. "He's German and is still learning the language."

"Well, ya' better learn faster if yo' gonna' make it here, Dutchman!" the private sneered, plopping a spoonful of watery corn on each of their plates. "Move along!"

A week passed before Company A arrived at their first duty station, guarding the Louisville-Nashville rail line as it ran through Shepherdsville, Kentucky. Although most of the soldiers were patient with Edward's poor English comprehension, higher-ranking soldiers were not as tolerant of his inability to follow the simplest instructions. As a result, his lot was to spend night after night on guard duty, during which he'd stand for hours on the outskirts of camp, holding a rifle in the cold rain and bitter wind.

One morning, upon returning to his tent after many late-night hours of bone-chilling guard duty, Edward felt Garner pulling his shoulder from behind. Turning his German friend around and studying him up and down for a few moments, he said, "You're not looking too good, Leyer." Frowning and shaking his head, he added, "Your face is as red as a beet!"

The next three nights were sleepless for both men, given Edward's horrific hacking cough kept them both up, with only brief periods of one or the other drifting off from sheer exhaustion. Finally, Garner spoke to his company sergeant about his friend's illness, who relayed the message to Lieutenant Meyers, who in turn sent for Private Leyer.

Edward shuffled slowly into the tent, his face drawn and eyes displaying a haunting emptiness. Standing before the officer, he weakly saluted.

After taking one look at Edward, the lieutenant handed him a slip of paper and said, "Go see the doctor, Private. You're not well."

Nodding his acknowledgment, Edward again feebly saluted. Then, stumbling out of the tent, he wheezed a deep, rattling cough he'd been struggling to suppress in the lieutenant's presence. When his cough suddenly became even more intense, Edward grasped a tent pole to steady himself, then doubled over and violently spit bloody mucus on the ground. Without warning, he collapsed into an unconscious heap. Seeing him go down, a group of soldiers standing nearby rushed over to gather up his thin, motionless body, and quickly carried him to the infirmary.

That evening, the company doctor had him sitting on the back of a wagon headed north toward Louisville.

When Edward arrived at the hospital in Louisville, he drifted in and out of consciousness, still waylaid by his affliction. Several hours later, during one of his rare awake moments, he weakly pleaded to a German-speaking nurse, Gretchen, to assist him in writing a letter home, fearing his end was near:

My Dearest Lena:

I find myself in a military hospital in Louisville. I suffer terribly from pain in my breast and a congested cough. Please pray to God for his mercy upon this, his faithful servant. Yesterday, a man in the bed next to mine with a similar affliction was taken to his grave. I will fight this disease with all of my strength, so that I may touch your face and hold you in my arms once again. If this is my last letter, let it be known that all I have, I leave to my wife, Maria Helena Leyer. As for my inheritance from my father and brother, I leave that to my wife, as well. She is the sole heir of all that I have and all that I am.

Your loving husband,
Edward

Chapter 2

For eight days, Edward laid there in his hospital bed fighting a high fever and severe, persistent cough. At the close of the eighth day, he awoke to the touch of a soft hand stroking his forehead. Squinting, he tried to focus on the figure sitting on the edge of his bed.

"Edward, my love."

The voice was familiar, having heard it daily in his fever-induced dreams. Slowly, he opened his eyes to see Helena sitting by his side. But the excitement of the moment sent him into a coughing fit.

"Shhh...," she said, patting his hand. "Don't try to talk."

"Am I dreaming?" he gasped, still finding it difficult to breathe. "How?"

Smiling as she tried to hide her genuine concern, Helena explained, "I received your letter saying you were ill and had been moved to Louisville. I was given permission from the captain to care for you, on the condition that I agree to help the other soldiers when I'm not by your side. They even gave me a bed in a room two floors down!"

"The children? Herman? Eddy?"

"I left them with our neighbors, Mr. And Mrs. Lienau. They're in good hands."

Standing beside his bed, she reached over, pulled his shoulders forward, and helped prop him up by placing a second pillow behind his back, "This should help you sit up to eat, but also help you breathe easier."

Then, moving a chair next to his bed, she sat and took a spoon and warm bowl of bone broth from a table. "Now eat, my dear. You can't fight this sickness without your strength."

He closed his eyes, notably exhausted from the excitement. "Open," she whispered, carefully lifting the spoon of broth to his lips.

The hospital's minor ward was fitted with ten beds, only four of which were occupied. Over the coming days, Edward watched as a few men were brought in with battle wounds, but most were there with natural diseases. Given what Helena conveyed to him from what she'd heard staff nurses report, cases of pneumonia and diphtheria, had been running rampant throughout the regiments, sending many soldiers to their deaths without ever having fired a shot.

Two physicians were in charge of the entire ward, Dr. Keegan from Indiana and Dr. Flora from central Kentucky. Helena served both doctors by splitting her time between Edward and the other men, especially helping those who could not feed themselves. But as often as possible, she appeared at her husband's bedside, with encouraging words and tender care, if not a fresh bowl of broth to offer him.

Though working tirelessly, day after day, assisting in the hospital, Helena made arrangements to take one quick trip back to Evansville to check on their home and two young boys. Upon her return, however, she saw Edward had continued to slip further into the grasp of his agonizing illness.

While perched on the edge of his bed, she held his hands in hers and spoke forcibly to Edward, even though he lay there barely conscious. "You're still a soldier. Your battle has just begun. I want you to fight this with all of your might. You have a wife and children who need you. Hold onto your promise to come back to us, Edward. Now, you fight!"

Several days later, Dr. Keegan stood at the foot of Edward's bed, watching Helena help him lean over the bedside while he coughed profusely into a rag, which was already soaked red with his blood.

After the coughing fit, she helped him lay back in bed. "Mrs. Leyer," the doctor said grimly, "we should talk."

With her head hanging low, Helena followed Dr. Keegan out of the ward.

"The tests I've performed indicate Private Leyer has phthisis pulmonalis, which is a pulmonary consumption. Unfortunately, I'm sorry to say your husband is too far gone."

"No, Herr Doctor," she protested. "He is over the worst. My man, he is a strong man. He will be good. I know he will."

"Sometimes, Mrs. Leyer, we must accept the things we cannot change. Your husband bleeds from his lungs. He's dying, Mrs. Leyer. You'll take him home now. I'll give you a letter that permits him to resign from the Army."

Putting her face into her hands, Helena wept and quietly sobbed.

A few moments later, she sniffled and said, "Nein, he will be better."

Dr. Keegan wrapped his arms around her, and patting her on the back replied, "Pray hard, Mrs. Leyer. Pray for his healing. Miracles do happen."

***

While sitting in his makeshift office, Dr. Keegan was visited by his colleague, Dr. Flora, who strode in and asked, "So you're sending him home, are you? Private Leyer?"

"Yes. A man this far gone should die at home in his own bed. Who knows, with God's grace and the love of a good wife, he may pull through this yet. But it won't happen here."

Shaking his head, Dr. Flora replied, "So many of these brave men die, leaving widows to raise their children. Hopefully, the Leyers will not add to the disparity."

"Amputations, bullet wounds and disease," Dr. Keegan added. "I'm so weary of the conditions in this slapdash hospital. But if we can save just one soldier from the meat-grinder, it'll be a good day."

As he returned to the ward, Dr. Keegan saw Edward's wife helping Nurse Gretchen change Private Garner's bandages, a double leg amputee, as he slept. "Mrs. Leyer, here!" he called out.

After taking the envelope from him, she asked, "I can take him home? Now?"

"You may, but please, be realistic. He may not make it home. I'm so sorry, Mrs. Leyer, so sorry. God's mercy on you both."

***

After Helena had wrapped Edward in thick, woolen blankets and made him as comfortable as possible in the back of their flatbed wagon, she slowly drove their horse, Hilda, away from the Army hospital. Mile after mile, the two endured a long, bumpy ride on the dirt road leading to the ferry used for crossing the Ohio River, and then on to Evansville. In the darkest of night, led only by a single lantern and Hilda's instinct to stay on the road, Helena stared up into the night's sky and prayed, *Please God, let me get him home. Let me lie next to him just one more time.*

In time, she found the steady clip-clop of the horse's hoofs on the hard ground to be a soothing rhythm. But in the midst of a brief reverie, she thought, *If I lose Edward, I'll have to take Herman and Eddy back to Germany. Oh my God, I can't go back!*

As dawn broke, and with a renewed sense of urgency, Helena snapped the reins to push Hilda into a trot.

After finally arriving and stopping in front of their home, she hurried to the back of the wagon to help Edward down. "We're home, my love! We made it!"

Helping him to his feet, Helena kept the blanket around him, but freed his right arm to wrap around her neck, as she supported him from his waist. Carefully walking him through the front door, she then helped her husband up on to their bed.

The following afternoon, with Helena's approval, Mrs. Lienau brought Herman to the bedroom window, where he could stand on an old crate to see his father through the window and watch as his mother cared for him. For two solid hours, Helena saw the concern and love in her son's face through the closed window.

Day after day Edward seemed unable to muster the strength to even talk, but Helena's beef bone broth and rich chicken broth kept his heart beating. Once every hour, she sat next to him on their bed, cupped her hands, and pounded his back, as the doctor had shown her, to break loose the thick mucus that formed in his lungs, so he could breathe more freely.

Helena also gave him a concoction of whiskey, honey and lime, one spoonful at a time, to help suppress his cough. But soon it became clear she wasn't alone in her efforts to help Edward recover. Every day, caring friends and neighbors brought remedies, and her husband was urged to try them all. Onion soup, garlic soup, vegetable broth, cabbage soup, chicken soup, mustard wraps, various liniments and tinctures, all of which were proclaimed to have helped heal respiratory disorders. Nothing was too farfetched or outlandish, and Helena expressed sincere appreciation for the kindness.

"More soup?" Mr. Lienau asked as his wife walked to the front door carrying a crock.

"Day and night Helena cares for her husband," his wife replied. "She feeds him, comforts him, bathes him, cools his brow and warms his feet. I've never known someone so determined to save a life as Mrs. Leyer."

Herman's eyes widened one afternoon while standing on the wooden box and peering in, when his father first noticed him at the window and summoned the strength to wave at him. With a huge grin, Herman jumped from the box and ran to tell Mrs. Lienau.

Finally, two weeks into his struggle to recover, Edward's fever began to drop, his cough subsided, and his appetite returned. Slowly his vitality reappeared, and eventually, the boys were allowed to see their beloved "Papa."

Helena thanked all who had cared for both her and Edward, baking them some of her special *lebkuchen* for Christmas, a cherished German treat that took two days to prepare, in order for the flavors to meld together before baking.

The aftermath of the illness left Edward extremely frail and wobbly, but happy to be alive. Each day, he would push himself a little bit more to do things around the home, even to the dismay of his concerned wife, who regularly feared he was overexerting himself.

When Christmas Eve arrived, after Herman and Eddy were fast asleep, Helena and Edward sat together on the small, overstuffed sofa in their living room, watching the bright red and orange flames in the fireplace dance and swirl around the burning logs, adding warmth to the room and playful shadows to the walls.

Edward took Helena's hand in his and whispered, "I should never have gone to war. Fighting is a younger man's game." Putting his arm around her back, he pulled her to him and tenderly kissed the corner of her eye. "I love you."

Outside, the road glistened like diamonds, as the moonlight reflected on the newly fallen snow. The euphonious sound of caroling neighbors filled the moment with the traditional Austrian Christmas song, "*Stille Nacht, Heilige Nacht.*"

Seven months later, Edward received his medical discharge papers from the Army of the Union Forces.

Chapter 3

A gentle southwesterly wind blew a greying blond lock of Helena's hair across her face. With a slight grunt, she pulled it back and secured it under her hair bonnet. Picking up her wooden knitting needles and yarn, she once again attempted to work on a scarf she was making; but after losing stitches three times from the jarring of the bumpy road, she sighed and tossed the supplies back into her knitting basket.

Edward and Helena sat next to one another on the wagon bench, behind their sprightly nag, Hilda, on the road to Greenbrier.

"Impossible," she mumbled, before hearing her husband's snicker. Pushing his arm, she playfully chided, "So you think that's funny?"

Over her left shoulder, Helena checked on her six children, who were resting quietly, rocked by the soothing movement along the rugged road. Herman rested an arm on their old steamer trunk.

I can still see myself sitting on that trunk, she thought, *on the dock in Boston Harbor. Back then, I held Herman in my arms, waiting for Edward to find us. After three harrowing weeks at sea, what an anxious, exciting day that was! Starting over in this new land. Dear Lord! And look at Herman, now, practically a man himself!*

"We're starting over, again," she said to her husband. I thought Evansville would be our home, but now we're leaving it behind."

"I didn't want to leave either, but you saw how those people treated me, how they treated all of us. I've been accused of everything from stealing to murder. When we lost our home in the fire, they even accused me of starting the fire! I work hard for men who promise to pay, and then they disappear like the wind. Those who *do* pay cheat me with some fruit or a chicken, instead of the money they owe me."

Edward looked back briefly at the town that had been their home for seventeen years, then continued, "Two weeks ago, after I threatened to take some of those thieves to court, they formed a mob and came to our house to drag me into the street to beat me, or maybe worse. If it hadn't been for the kids watching from the front porch, they would have had their way. I could be dead now."

Scanning the horizon, she sighed, "So much empty space." She continued to gaze from her wooden perch as they passed by countless fence rows surrounding cultivated fields and barren pastures.

"I'd just started getting used to city life," she began, "with neighbors and shops nearby. And though this country is lovely, with its fields of wildflowers and butterflies, there's no one around, with only occasional farms or homes scattered here and there."

"Patience, my dear. I believe we're getting near Greenbrier. *Now*, you'll see houses."

Edward snapped the reins slightly to quicken Hilda's pace, and soon, as they rounded a corner, a small building appeared up ahead. Upon their approach, however, it turned out to be a dilapidated hay barn.

A little more than half an hour later, the Leyer family found the Village of Greenbrier *actually* consisted of two farmhouses, a country blacksmith shop, and some three thousand acres of alluvial mud.

"Houses, you say?" Helena scoffed.

Staring blankly at the few time-worn wooden structures comprising the "village," she frowned as Edward urged Hilda forward, and Greenbrier disappeared behind them as quickly as it had appeared. While they continued down the straight and narrow road, she remarked, "I didn't even see a store."

Soon, as they came to a crossroads, he tugged on the reins and turned the wagon to head down Dittany Hill Road. Edward kept Hilda moving forward a while longer, finally pulling her to a stop in front of a farmhouse. "Greer Township, Warrick County, here we are," he announced.

Helena noticed their wagon sat in two muddy ruts where others had worn deep. "We're near the end of the road, Edward, and it's-... a *wasteland*. This is it?" she nervously asked, looking toward the weatherworn structures ahead of them in the distance.

"Is this our new home?" August asked, his innocent enthusiasm countering his mother's cheerless tone.

"The entire farm is ours," Edward proudly answered, waving his arm from one fence row to another. "You kids go explore!"

One-by-one, the children jumped off the back of the wagon, Herman lifting his young siblings above the mud to land in the grass.

Albert stayed by the wagon as the rest of the children darted down the lane. From her bench seat, Helena yelled, "Stay out of the house and barn until we know it's safe!"

"Don't let first impressions fool you," Edward said. "Please try to keep an open mind."

"My mind can't imagine a more desolate farm in all of Indiana," she said, wringing her hands in her lap. "I've seen it. Now, please take me back to Evansville."

While Helena surveyed the landscape from her seat, Edward climbed down and stepped in ankle-deep mud. As the thick goo seeped into his shoes, he sloshed around to her side of the wagon. "Come, my love, let me show you. It has possibilities."

Rolling her eyes, Helena climbed down to the single step before leaning into him. From there, he lifted her to the side of the road onto the tall grass. Then, knocking off some of the caked mud from his shoes, Edward took her hand and held it, as they carefully proceeded through the grass, walking toward the small farmhouse, while four-year-old Albert walked closely behind his mother.

"The fields are *completely* overgrown," she said. "How long has it been since anyone lived here?"

"I'm not sure. Several years, at least."

"But it's so far away from everything," she noted, looking around at the vast fields and dense forest in the distance. "Where will we go for supplies when we need them?"

"We're about ten miles from Boonville, twenty back to Evansville."

Together, they approached the rustic, weather-worn barn as Albert scooted beside his mother and slipped his tiny hand into hers. "This barn has seen better days," Helena said. "Some of the siding planks are missing."

"I can fix these things," Edward replied. Peering inside, he inventoried aloud, "Six stalls, a shop, and a large pigpen out front."

They eventually made their way over to the farmhouse. "Let's look inside," he said, pushing open the front door, which barely clung to its rusty hinges. Helena winced when two large mice scurried across the wood plank floor and disappeared through a hole in the wall, though she noticed this left the numerous spiders sitting upon their massive webs seemingly undisturbed.

"The floors creak with each step," Helena complained, releasing Albert's hand, "and the air is thick with the smells of moldy, wet wood and dead rodents."

After slowly evaluating each corner, nook and cranny of the house—especially noting the many rotted floorboards—she declared, "This will take a lot of work, Edward."

When Albert picked up a dead mouse by the tail, Helena barked, "Drop it!"

Moving over to one of the broken windowpanes and peering out, she saw Mina and Richard holding hands and running toward the corn crib, a seemingly never-ending field of tall grass in the background. "Albert, go find your sister and stay with her."

"I'm not afraid of work," Edward replied after the young boy ran out of the house. "Look at the opportunity. There's plenty of room for our children, and you'll have a nice kitchen, yes?"

"I'm trying." Turning around to face her husband, with tears in her eyes and voice strained, she added, "But aside from all the work, I see only a life of isolation."

Edward stepped forward and took Helena's hands. "Don't you see, my love? This farm will sustain us. We'll have horses, pigs, chickens and goats. I'll fence off a garden for you to grow vegetables. Besides, we aren't isolated. We have neighbors, farmers, just like us. They'll help us get things started here, because neighbors help neighbors."

Gently dropping her hands, he whirled around and hurried to the door, "I'm going to set up my kiln in front of the barn and make all the tools we need."

But before leaving, he spun back to face his wife, poked his thumb at his chest, and declared, "When our neighbors need metal work, they'll come to *me*."

Following behind her husband, Helena noticed a welcoming light breeze cooling her face when she stepped outside the moldy house and back into sunshine. The couple walked a few yards from the house and looked around in every direction. Helena asked with a smirk, "From here, can you see any other farmhouses? And how many of these farmers do you think speak German?"

"I don't know, but I'm sure some do."

Edward gestured for her to follow him toward the barn. "We need to keep improving our English, though. There's a school just a couple of miles from here," he pointed toward the tree line across the overgrown field, "There, our children will learn to read and write English, and we will learn from them."

"How much did you pay for this place?"

Edward didn't respond, but with a head gesture invited her to join him as he began wading through the sea of tall grass. After a short distance, the couple paused and regarded the farm for a brief moment listening to a meadowlark twitter loudly in the nearby field.

"You see, we're not alone, my dear. God's creatures are with us," Edward cheerfully said, though he saw she wasn't amused.

When they were again standing in front of the porch, Edward spoke up. "I've been saving what I could, Helena, and still had some inheritance from my mother's passing. The former owner was asking $1,900, and that included four horses. I offered him $1,600, and he accepted it."

Turning away from him, she walked toward an old well not twenty feet from the front door, picked up a stone and tossed it in. Eventually, upon hearing it make a splash in the water below, she smiled slightly and shared, "It's a deep well."

"Good. We'll never be want for water, and it will never freeze."

Stepping back through the front door, she slowly strolled around the house again, noting various bits of damage, including a gaping hole on the far side of the roof. "Can you fix that?"

"I'll have it patched by tomorrow, and will start working on the bad floorboards below it, too."

When she'd concluded her second inspection, Helena sighed, "I'll miss my friends in Evansville."

With as encouraging a tone as he could muster, he replied, "We'll get back to Evansville often, my dearest. Besides, you'll make wonderful friends here. I was told the people who originally settled this township wanted to name it *Happy Valley*."

"Happy Valley," she dreamily whispered, gazing out on the fenced pasture.

"I remember you telling me how much you enjoyed your childhood on your grandparent's farm," he said. "Look how happy our children are," pointing to the boys as they ran around in front of the barn.

"Since the war," he continued, "I've worked as a blacksmith, a clerk in a hardware store, and a caregiver in the Pest House. I know how to work and I'm committed to seeing this through."

After taking a deep breath, she nodded her approval.

Edward called out, "Wonderful!" and leapt forward to embrace her. "You'll see, Lena. Life will be good here. We can raise and grow everything we need."

"The first thing I want is a dozen chickens."

Kissing her on the cheek, he laughed. "Then chickens you shall have!"

Chapter 4

Edward and Herman worked diligently, day after day, making repairs to their new farmhouse, while the rest of the children helped Helena clean and tidy up the home.

One morning, Helena complained, "Two weeks we've been on this farm, and we have yet to meet a single neighbor." After pouring two ladles of milk soup into Herman's bowl, she added, "I noticed a path through the woods that leads to the farm next to ours. After breakfast, I'd like all of us to go over there to introduce ourselves and make some new friends."

Edward nodded, "Good... yes."

With breakfast aside, the family of eight strolled down the trail, with Edward at the front of the single-file line and Helena holding little Albert's hand at the end. Their hike through the woods soon brought them to their neighbor's perimeter fence, then across a wide yard, and eventually to a house that was easily twice the size of their own and in far better condition.

Somewhat cautiously, Edward approached the front stoop. Instantly, a stocky young man with bright red hair and a beard only slightly more brown than red stepped through the front doorway and stood on the porch, sizing up the uninvited visitors.

"Good morning, neighbor," Edward said, moving forward and extending his hand in greeting.

Leaning over the porch railing, the red-headed man shook Edward's hand, and then straightened back up, with no discernible expression on his face.

"I'm Edward Leyer. We bought the farm next to yours," he said, motioning back toward the path through the woods.

Cocking his head as he studied Edward, the neighbor then looked over Helena and the row of various-sized children standing quietly at the foot of his porch. "You sound like a Dutchman," he said in a seemingly condescending tone.

"My wife and I are from Germany, but most recently, we're from Evansville. This is Helena, and these are our children."

The man turned his gaze back to Helena and nodded, "Ma'am."

Helena responded with a polite nod and faint smile.

Then, without taking his eyes off the Leyer family, he called back toward the open front door, "Liz, honey, come out here for a minute."

A young woman in a flowery cotton dress appeared at the door before stepping onto the porch, her face bright and unblemished, like a porcelain china doll, and her golden hair was neatly tied in a bun behind her head.

Helena thought, *Such an attractive, young couple. Never have I seen such a pretty dress.*

Following closely out the front door behind the young blond woman were three small girls, all with fine blonde hair like their mother's, each wearing a tidy pinafore dress. The girls paused and looked curiously at the strangers standing in their yard, and then started to whisper and giggle amongst themselves.

"Children, behave!" their mother scolded, immediately causing the girls to become sullen and jump behind her.

Stepping forward and taking her place beside her husband—with the girls still peeking from behind her—she looked up into his face, as though motioning for him to introduce them. "I'm Fred Cook, and this is my wife, Elizabeth."

Helena returned the greeting toward Elizabeth, "I'm Helena, and this is my husband, Edward Leyer." Then, turning to face the children behind them, she started with the oldest, "This is

Herman; he's 18, Eddy is 13, August is 10, our little girl Mina is 8, Richard is 6, and this is our youngest, Albert, who is 4." Helena smiled as she watched Albert scamper to be near his siblings.

Elizabeth chuckled. "That's quite a family you have there!" Pulling the girls to the front of her, she said, "These are our three girls."

Instantly, Fred stepped in front of his family and scooted them backward, nearly causing his wife to lose her footing.

"What brought you folks to this place?" Fred asked. "There aren't many of your kind around here." His face had become serious as he made eye contact with Edward, "This is mostly an English settlement. I imagine you were around more Germans back in Evansville."

Shifting nervously on his feet, Edward smiled politely. "We wish to start a farm. Here, a hardworking man can feed his family. I'm a blacksmith and can do metalwork for our neighbors."

Fred looked down from his porch at the Leyers and rubbed the back of his neck as he spoke. "As I said, aren't many of your kind here. And that farm you bought sure needs work."

Edward narrowed his eyes. "English or German, we're all farmers. I'm a good worker, and in time the farm will get better."

Albert wandered behind his siblings and parents toward a cistern, not ten feet from where the family stood. Fascinated by the still water, he picked up a small stone and tossed it in, listening as it landed with a plop. He clapped his hands joyfully while watching the small ripples on the water's surface.

"You there! Stop that!" Fred yelled, pointing his finger at the boy, who swiftly pivoted toward the intense voice.

"He's just a child," Edward said. "He meant no harm."

"We drink from that water," Fred barked, his face now red with anger. "How would you like it if I came to your place and threw mud in your drinking water? You should teach your children some *respect*!"

Helena rushed over and scooped Albert into her arms. The other children ran behind her and gathered close to their mother.

"Good day to you," Fred said abruptly, waving his hand and dismissing the visitors. He then turned and shooed his family back into the house, closing the door quickly behind him.

Edward glanced over at Helena and shrugged. Then he joined his family by the cistern, "Let's go home."

The Leyers walked somberly through the woods toward their home, no one saying a word.

Upon arriving at their farm, Edward mumbled, "Well, *they* didn't seem very friendly."

"Maybe our other neighbors will be more hospitable," Helena said uneasily. "I'll bake some bread in a few days and take it to Mrs. Cook. Everyone likes a nice loaf of homemade bread!"

As time passed, the rapport between Edward and Fred grew cooler and tenser. And as the wives dutifully followed their husband's sentiments, any hopes for good relations between the two families quickly faded. "No thank you," Elizabeth said, as she handed the cloth bundle back to Helena.

"I baked this loaf of bread for you and your family," Helena explained. "To be a good neighbor; I want us to be friends."

Elizabeth stepped from her porch to confront Helena face-to-face in front of her home. "Please don't take this the wrong way, Mrs. Leyer, but we don't accept food from strangers. Besides, we don't care much for the German way of cooking."

"Not everyone is as rude as the Cooks," Edward explained after listening to Helena's most recent encounter with Elizabeth as he poured a bucket of slop in the pig pen. "Just this morning, I met Mr. Ebenezer Day. He's a well-preserved and honest old gentleman of the old school who's not caught up in the politics of the community. He seemed genuinely interested in our German heritage, and even gave me the names of other German immigrants living nearby."

Chapter 5

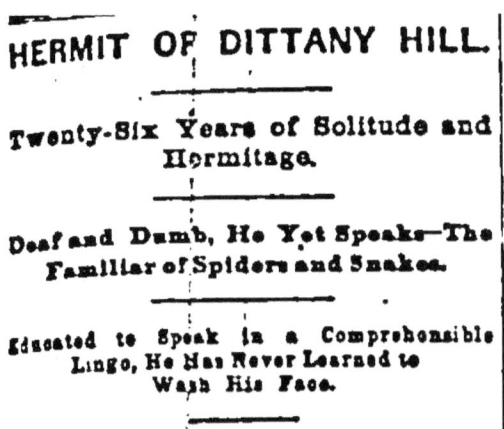

Edward and Herman rode along Dittany Hill Road on their old flatbed wagon with Hilda pulling it along toward Boonville, in order to procure feed for the horses.

However, upon seeing Mr. Ebenezer Day emerge from a barn beside the road, Edward slowed their horse to a stop and set the handbrake.

"Good morning, Edward," Ebenezer said, stepping forward and greeting him with a handshake, as father and son stepped down from their wagon.

"Good morning to you, Ebenezer. I wonder if I might ask you a question that weighs heavily on my mind."

"What might that be?"

As the two men moved to the back of the wagon, Herman hoisted himself up on the flatbed.

"Minutes ago, and not for the first time, Herman and I believe we saw something watching us from the woods. Strange as it sounds, it looked like a white bear."

Herman added, "But it runs away like a wolf when we turn toward it."

Ebenezer burst into laughter at their descriptions and asked, "Near Dittany Hill?"

"Yes, in the thicket," Edward confirmed.

"You just gave the best description I've ever heard of Benjamin Talbert, 'Old Ben,' as we call him. He's well known in these parts as 'the Hermit of Dittany Hill.' You really should meet him, what with you being practically neighbors and all."

"I suppose I should, but I don't see how that's possible, as he runs from us whenever we're near."

"I can introduce him to you now, if you like, but I'll need to bring my son, for reasons you'll understand upon meeting him."

When Edward nodded, agreeing to go meet Old Ben, Ebenezer walked across the road to his son's house and not two minutes later returned with William Day at his side. Together, the four of them headed back down Dittany Hill Road, riding the wagon on which Edward and Herman had first arrived.

"You see the hills about a quarter of a mile to the south," William said as he began describing their destination. "Dittany Hill rises like a miniature range of mountains. There are two of them, but not distinctly defined, and they rise to a height of about three hundred feet, sloping away to the farms below. The summit and the southern side are covered with dense wood, but on the east and north, the sides are cleared and farmed. In one of these, and within a hundred yards of the forest, is the hut in which Benjamin Talbert has spent twenty-six years."

"Old Ben's existence is just too strange for ready belief," Ebenezer added. "Even in the country, which is rich and well settled, there are few acquainted with his *unusual* story. And by the way, you'll find no mention of him in the county seat records of Boonville."

"Does he live alone?" Herman asked.

"Indeed, he does," William said. "The hermit is deaf, and nearly dumb. He's friendly enough, but he dislikes meddling and doesn't trust strangers. I need to be here to introduce you."

After another fifteen minutes traveling over roads deep with ruts, Edward steered Hilda down a narrow, muddy lane, then over a smooth meadow along the hill slope. "Do you see the two large chestnut trees to the right?" William asked, pointing the way.

"I do," Edward replied.

"You want to drive right between them. I know it's tight, but it's the only way in."

Before the wagon came to a full stop in front of a pitiful-looking shed, William hopped to the ground and said, "Let me see if he's about, before we intrude."

"He's not here," William declared after noticing the rusted latch on the front door. "We should wait for him, because he's going to know someone was here by the hoof prints and wagon ruts. I'll keep an eye out, if you want to look around his place."

Ebenezer, Edward and Herman hopped down from the wagon, and all three approached the hermit's home. Looking at the rickety old structure, Edward mused, "It can't be more than seven feet from the floor to the comb of the roof."

"And the front door is only three feet high," Herman added.

"You're right," Ebenezer explained. "Ben's hut is certainly crude and slapped together into such a *frail* shape. The walls are barely four feet tall and the whole is probably twelve feet square. We believe it was once a dog kennel, or perhaps it was built for hogs."

While the men were peering about, William hollered, "He's coming," and they all scampered to the front, trying *not* to look like they'd been peeping.

With quick and long strides, an old man could be seen moving over the wind-rippled meadow, and soon he stood squarely in front of the small group.

Edward openly stared at the gaunt figure, roughly five-and-a-half feet tall, with the stoop of age in his shoulders. Dressed in dirty gray jeans without buttons, a pullover shirt made of weatherworn burlap, a pair of rough brogans on his feet, and on his head something between a conical liberty cap and a small wash basin. Beneath this "headdress," the old man's white curls were cropped off at the neck straight around, while his beard and mustache were unkempt and of moderate length.

Herman stared at the hermit's face with some concern. "His right eye."

"Yes," William acknowledged. "His eye has been a cloudy grey one for as long as I have known him. One can't help but wonder if it offers him any vision. I have noticed he sights his rifle with his left eye, though."

Turning toward the old-timer and then back to the others gathered, William said, "Although Old Ben here was born deaf and dumb, he was taught at a school in Danville, Kentucky to imitate the movement of the lips and tongue. He can, with effort, speak sounds that some of us, over the 20-plus years he's been out here, have learned to translate, though *some* of his words are plain and easily understood. He reads the lips of those who talk to him, and understands quite well."

Turning to the hermit, William introduced the strangers, "Ben, this is Edward and Herman Leyer. They're new to the neighborhood and came to meet you and to see your house."

Old Ben stepped forward, shook hands all around and threw open the door covering the hole leading into his abode.

Stooping awkwardly, each visitor took three steps and was hence put in the middle of Ben's diminutive shack, with all of the hermit's belongings exposed to the gaze of his curious guests.

Edward stood silently, noting to himself, *The floor's hard-packed soil is worn smooth and solid, and his bed is simply a compressed pile of filthy rags of every color and shape.*

On one side of the small, solitary room was a rock-built fireplace a few feet wide, in which some embers were smoldering.

Edward also noticed that in front of Ben's fireplace were two thick logs of wood covered with rags laid across them, which he presumed to be a makeshift seat cushion. Seeing two deep-worn indentations in front of one of the logs and almost in the ashes of the fireplace, he thought, *Those were likely made by Ben's feet being placed constantly in the same spot, as though he'd sat on his log-chair with his elbows on his knees, musing and reflecting in his silent world of deafness for thousands of nights in solitude. What a lonely life this man must live.*

In the corner of the bed area, Edward spotted a perfect den for spiders, their webs hanging in thin, tattered veils from the ceiling.

Ebenezer suddenly spoke up, saying, "Mr. Lynn, Ben's neighbor, said that some time ago he was riding past Ben's place here at daybreak and saw him coming to the road with something in his arms. He waited to see what it was, and, Lordy, he claims it was a huge black snake coiled in his embrace. Says Old Ben had found it in his bed when he woke up, then carried it tenderly to the strip of woods over yonder and released it unhurt."

William turned to face Edward and said, "When the woods 'round here were cleared away several years ago, the snakes disappeared with them. At the same time, Old Ben took up with a big ol' handsome cat with a tortoise-shell saddle. And as most people know, cats are the enemies of snakes and rats. So with that cat's presence, those other critters have entirely vanished. But he keeps a large trap, and whenever rats are captured, he takes them into the woods and lets them go."

Looking back over in Ben's direction, William concluded, "The good news is, with the clearing away of the forest, his solitude was broken. He began to connect with his neighbors and, by degrees, became known and rather liked. Ben saws stove-wood and does odd chores occasionally, and is regularly furnished with food by them."

Soon, the visitors became overwhelmed by the fetid smell inside Old Ben's shanty, and they beat a rather hasty retreat to the outside air and sunlight of the day.

Following the group out, the hermit, with the delighted look of a child, watched and waited for an exhibition of his guest's impressions of his home.

William looked to the others and, recognizing their uncomfortable sentiments about Ben's shabby dwelling, immediately asked them, "So, do you have any questions for him?"

Edward promptly asked, "How old are you?"

William, who was more practiced at interpreting for Ben, supplemented Edward's effort, to which the hermit, by signs and in a gibberish-like tongue, answered, "Come next sow of oats, I ya' born," with extended fingers, counting, "tane, twainty, terty, fotty, fity and twainty-six yares."

"Seventy-six years?" Ebenezer asked.

The old man smiled and bobbed his head rapidly, appearing proud of his achievement.

"How long have you lived in this house?" Herman asked.

"Tane..." Ben began counting aloud again. "Twainty and six yares come, corn drop, drop, drop," making the motion of planting corn.

In his primitive manner, Old Ben fielded the questions from each member of the group, revealing his name was Benjamin Talbert, he was born in Butler County, Kentucky and was taught to spell with his fingers, read the lips of others, and imitate language forty-two years earlier.

"He can't read print," William said, "but Ben *can* read the finger alphabet like lightning."

Ebenezer turned to the hermit and asked, "Ben? Can you show us your rifle?"

Ben lifted his hands as though he was carrying an invisible gun, to which Ebenezer confirmed his request with a nod. "Gun, shooty, shooty!" Ben gleefully exclaimed, as he ran back through his front door.

While the old man stepped away, Ebenezer said to the others, "His father was a preacher, and fought in the War of 1812. His brother was a soldier in the Mexican-American War, and Ben still has his rusty old flintlock rifle, with a bore like a twenty-five-pounder, which he threatens to use to kill anybody who talks of taking him to the poorhouse."

Upon his return, Old Ben handed the rifle to Ebenezer, who in turn passed it on to Edward, who smiled when he felt the weight of the antiquated weapon. "My father had a rifle very similar to this back in Germany, but the barrel was shorter. I haven't fired a flintlock since I was younger than Herman."

Edward then carefully placed it in Herman's hands.

"Ben moved to Warrick County with his mother and that brother thirty-six years ago," Ebenezer said, watching Herman lift the rifle to point at an imaginary target. "They're both dead now. In the neighborhood, it was believed Mrs. Talbert buried large sums of money in the woods. She lived frugally, and said she would save enough to leave the afflicted son comfortable, yet she died suddenly, and left no sign of her hidden wealth. As far as any of us know, Old Ben is penniless."

William took a few steps away from the group and leaned against the wagon, continuing, "With little to his name, unable to pay rent or taxes, he came to Dittany Hill to begin his life of solitude. He built this place for himself and has become somewhat of a living legend to those of us who've come to know him."

After Herman handed the gun back to the hermit, Edward reached in his pocket and pulled out a silver quarter. "Thank you for meeting us, and showing us your home," he cordially said, handing the quarter to Ben.

"Quatty, quatty," Old Ben said with childish glee, holding it out in the open palm of his hand and showing it around to the rest for them to see.

Ebenezer said to Ben, "Edward lives at the end of the road, next to Fred Cook's place."

A scowl came over the old man's face, his grayish-blue eye nearly closed and his forehead scrunched into a river of lines. "Frey Coo!" he shouted, before turning his head and spitting on the ground.

"The fact is," Ebenezer interjected, "twice, Fred has chased Old Ben from his property with a shotgun. Apparently, he believes Ben steals from him."

Seeing the name uttered again on Ebenezer's lips, the old man reiterated his disdain for Edward's neighbor. "Frey Coo!" followed by an even *more* aggressive spit.

Edward turned to Ben with a sympathetic scowl on his own face, and bellowed, "Fred Cook!"… then spit on the ground, as well.

Herman joined his father. "Fred Cook!" he hollered, followed by a similar spit.

Before parting, and with William's help, Edward told Old Ben, "You will always be welcome on my farm."

As they drove off, Edward turned to see the colorful hermit standing out and waving his conical hat to the group.

After Edward steered Hilda between the two tall chestnut trees, Ebenezer said, "If you need to contact Old Ben, best to do it in the morning. It's 1:00 in the afternoon, now, and he'll likely go to his den, lie down, and sleep until tomorrow morning at daybreak."

Chapter 6

The white bear, or *ghost*, as Mina had come to believe, was much less frightening once the explanation of Old Ben was made around the dinner table. Herman told the story to his siblings and mother of his encounter with the hermit of Dittany Hill.

While the elder siblings were working in the garden, Eddy approached his older brother and whispered, "Herman, I just saw him. He's watching us from over there along the tree line."

Herman stopped turning the soil, looked in the direction Eddy indicated and laughed. "There's no need to whisper. I told you, he's deaf!"

"Oh… right," Eddy said in a louder voice.

Taking a few steps toward the trees, Herman saw Old Ben had removed his hat and was waving it as he had seen him do when they'd first met. Moments later, the old man stepped out of the woods and stood beside a fence.

One by one, Herman's siblings came forward and stood next to their oldest brother. Even Helena took note of the legendary figure from the window and came outside.

"Everyone wave," Herman said.

Those with hats waved them, and those without waved their arms. But it wasn't until the old hermit saw Helena waving that he scaled the fence and meandered toward them.

"He won't hurt us, will he?" Richard asked.

"No, Old Ben's very nice. He can't hear you, but he'll know what you're saying, if he watches your lips when you talk."

When the hermit arrived at the group of young spectators, Herman reached out and shook his hand. "These are my brothers and sister," Herman explained as he named them individually.

Ben shook each hand as they were introduced.

As Helena approached the group and studied the hermit, she felt a warm kinship for the kindly old man. *I don't find his tattered appearance, long white hair, and beard repulsive at all,* she thought. *On the contrary, he has a certain mystique, like a mystical creature of the forest. He resembles one of the bearded gnomes from the nursery rhymes I used to read as a child. And his cloudy gray eye, I believe, can see right into my soul.*

When Herman introduced her to Ben, she wiped her hands on her apron before reaching to shake his, but instead of greeting her with a handshake, Old Ben put his hands over his face and turned to the side with a childlike giggle. Then, he pointed at her and said, "Purdy lady," followed by his immediately hiding behind his hands again.

Helena withdrew her hand, slightly embarrassed he would single her out this way, especially in front of her children. Hoping no one would notice her blushing, she said, "Would you wait here a moment?" raising a finger toward him. She then ran to the house and quickly returned with a brown paper package, which she handed to him.

Motioning for Ben to open it, he did, and found inside a loaf of warm, freshly baked bread. His face glowed as he cheered, "Brey! Brey!" showing the loaf to each of the children. "Tankie, tankie!"

As Ben wrapped the loaf back up, Helena stepped forward and hugged the elderly character. "Waldhart," she said as she released her hold.

"Waldhart?" Mina asked.

"Yes, that's the name of a woodland magician from a fable my mother told me as a child. Ben reminds me of Waldhart."

She saw in Ben's face, though, her warm embrace was more precious than the gift of bread, a beaming grin emerging there, just before he quickly turned and ran toward the woods while singing, "Purdy lady, purdy lady," over and over until his voice faded in the thicket.

Soon, Old Ben became a regular fixture on the Leyer farm, and though never asked to work, could often be found chopping wood, mucking stalls, slopping hogs or whatever needed attention at the time.

One evening, during dinner, August pulled a small figurine of a crudely carved horse, sat it on the table, and said, "I really like Old Ben. He was showing me where the best walnut tree is, and carved this for me from a walnut branch."

"I think he's the grandfather we never knew," Mina added.

"He may be like a grandfather, to you," Edward said, "but your mother seems to have really touched his heart."

"Oh stop it," Helena responded. "He only likes me because I keep his belly full."

"I think there's more to it than that, *Purdy Lady*," Edward said with a wink.

Chapter 7

One morning in mid-July of 1875, Edward walked alone past the barn and the corn crib to check on the field of corn and summer squash in the garden. He was startled to find the stalks of ripening corn that had stood strong and proud the day before were now flattened on the ground! Only a handful of the plants remained standing, where there was previously a quarter acre of tightly packed rows. Amid the carnage, Edward saw a lone sow greedily devouring the broken stalks and scattered ears.

He turned back and angrily called for his dog, "Mikey! Mikey, come here, boy!" In seconds, sprinting around a corner of the house came a barking black mutt with flopping brown ears. Edward gave his order, "Get that pig, Mikey! Kill it... kill it, Mikey!"

The adrenaline-charged canine bolted through the open gate and barked relentlessly, charging at the engorged pig when she turned to face her aggressor. Just as the dog lunged toward the sow, she spun around in retreat and darted across the field toward Fred Cook's property. Edward trailed the spooked creature, which Mikey closely pursued, nipping at her hindquarters between barks.

As she approached the fence that separated the Leyer and Cook properties, the frightened sow scampered to an opening where a missing plank had made it possible for her to get through and into Edward's field.

"Good boy, Mikey! Stay on her! Kill that pig!"

Edward spun around and rushed back to the house where, immediately upon entering, he grabbed his rifle and proceeded to load it with buckshot.

"What's wrong?" Helena asked, sensing his anxiety as she stood at the wash basin scrubbing dishes.

"One of Cook's sows got into the garden last night and pillaged the corn. So I'm going to kill that pig and teach Cook a lesson he won't soon forget!"

Helena's eyes widened and she dropped a plate into the water. "No, Edward. Please, no! Give him a chance to make things right. Killing his pig won't fix anything."

"He's gone too far this time, Lena! He's been trying to drive us away since we got here. Now he's attacked our farm, our livelihood. Payback is the only thing a man like Cook can understand. So now I'll make things right *my* way."

The Leyer children, who were all gathered for breakfast at the table, stopped eating and watched their father as he pointed toward his two older sons, "Herman, Eddy, come with me!"

Dropping their spoons in their bowls, the two boys jumped up immediately from the table and followed him in the direction of their neighbor's property, all three sprinting through the grassy field.

Helena stood in the open doorway, watching as they raced away and disappeared from view. Stroking Mina's hair, who stood next to her, she sighed and whispered, "Not again."

Hurrying past the ravaged garden and back toward the broken fence, Edward and his sons could clearly hear Mikey still yapping at the sow.

Suddenly, a gunshot from Cook's farm silenced the barking. Stopping in their tracks twenty yards from the opening in the fence, they all listened attentively, but heard nothing.

"Let's go!" Edward suddenly hollered, and the three Leyers ran to their neighbor's fence. Edward gasped for air as he struggled to scale the wood rails, but Herman and Eddy made it over the fence with ease. After pausing to wait for their father, the two boys dashed across a grassy pasture toward the sound of the gunshot. In the distance, they heard Mikey had resumed his barks, but from the sound of them, he was retreating toward his home.

Satisfied their dog was alive, Edward and his sons continued toward Fred's pigs. But to their utter surprise, there stood an angry, scarlet-faced Fred Cook, who strode quickly forward and stopped not two steps away from them.

"Why are you dogging my sow?" Fred demanded, waving his hands in the air.

"Because your sow broke through my fence and destroyed my corn!" Edward roared back, pointing his finger at Cook's face. "And did you just shoot at my dog?"

"If I'd shot at your dog, he'd already be dead, you stupid Dutchman!"

Enraged, Fred grabbed Edwards's finger and pushed it aside forcefully.

"You owe me, Fred Cook, for the damage your sow caused in my cornfield."

"I owe you, alright. The next time I see that mutt of yours on my property, he won't be walking home. This is your only warning, Leyer! If you don't quit dogging my hogs, I will make you suffer like you've never known."

"I'm not afraid of you, Cook."

Fred glared vehemently at Edward, and then looked toward the two boys who were watching from behind their father.

"You'll get afraid," Fred whispered back to Edward with a nod, giving him a dark, sinister smirk.

Rage boiled in Edward's blood as he pulled back the hammer on his rifle. But Herman leapt forward and grabbed Edward's arm, just as he was swinging the gun to point at Fred.

"Smart boy, Leyer," Cook taunted. "He may have just saved your life. Now get off my property."

Edward stared his adversary straight in the eyes and, even though Herman had hold of his arm, he slowly stretched his finger across the trigger. With the rifle pointing skyward, Leyer pulled the trigger and let a load of buckshot fly, the blast startling Cook, who jumped backward. Edward scowled at him, as he stood his ground.

Then, shouldering his rifle and nodding to the boys, Edward turned and walked back toward the path without saying a word.

As they approached the broken fence, Edward put his arm around Herman's shoulder and said, "You boys fix this, alright?" motioning toward the plank lying on the ground. "And be sure to put some nails through the board toward Cook's side. If that sow tries to push her way through the fence again, I want her to get a head full of nails."

"You're not a young man anymore," Helena said from the open doorway as Edward returned to the house.

"I know," he said, struggling to find the strength to walk up the steps to the back door, before handing her the rifle.

"Go lie down and I'll bring you some broth. There was a better way to handle this problem than by threatening a neighbor."

"I made my point. He won't be giving us any more trouble, if he knows what's good for him."

***

Later that same afternoon, all of the Leyers were in the ravaged corn field, picking up and saving what they could of the good corn, while also piling the broken corn stalks beside the garden for animal feed.

"Will we have time for another planting?" Helena asked, breaking the silence as she wiped the sweat from her brow.

Edward sighed and looked skyward, after tossing yet another half-eaten ear of corn into the basket. "I don't know. We can try. Maybe a smaller crop this time."

Glancing around the field at the devastation, he walked over to his wife and said, "Watching all six children working hard to salvage what we can of the crop gives me some solace."

He pointed to Albert, their youngest, who shuffled around the dusty field, giggling as he picked up an ear of corn. Hurrying to his mother, he held it high for her approval. She gave him an accepting nod and gestured to the basket, then laughed as he scampered over to it and tossed the ear in.

Edward closed his eyes and lifted his face to the sun, then whispered, "Thank you, God, for all your blessings, for Lena and for our family."

Wandering across the field, Edward stood next to Herman, who while throwing an immature ear into a basket angrily said, "The corn needed several more days, maybe a week, before it fully matured, but that time was stolen from us."

Only one fence separates Cook's corn field from his cattle," Edward said in a hushed tone, slightly tilting his head toward Cook's farm. "Maybe he should get a taste of what it feels like to lose a crop."

Herman stopped shucking an ear and looked at his father.

Nodding to his son, Edward picked up an arm full of broken stalks and carried them to a pile that would later be chopped into horse feed.

***

The following afternoon, Fred rode up to Edward, who was working his forge outside the barn. After dismounting, he approached and sharply asked, "Leyer, did you or your boys throw down my fences?"

Edward kept hammering the red-hot steel spike with hard blows, followed by short bounces, repeating the same strikes as the glowing piece of metal took shape. Staying focused on his task at hand, but pausing briefly, he loudly replied, "I don't know what you're referring to, Cook."

"Now listen, Leyer, someone threw down my fence and let my cattle into the corn field!"

Edward stopped hammering and glared at his neighbor. "It sounds to me as though your animals have a habit of walking through fences to take what doesn't belong to them. Perhaps you need to train them to stay on their side of the fence." Turning away to resume hammering, he growled, "Now, get off *my* property!"

"You haven't heard the end of this, Dutchman!" he yelled, shaking his fist at Edward, then stomping over to his horse and riding away, leaving a trail of dust behind him.

Chapter 8

In September of 1875, August and Mina strode along the dirt road on their way home from school, when they came across an untidy young boy standing off to the side of the road, whacking a tree limb with a long stick. August nudged Mina's arm and tilted his head toward the boy, who appeared to be about August's age. With a nod from his sister, they walked over and stood by the boy.

"Hello. What's your name?" August asked.

Looking suspiciously toward the children, the boy with a grimy face and dirty, tattered clothes didn't answer.

"I'm August. You have a name, don't you?"

Continuing to ignore August, he began hitting the tree limb harder.

Mina asked, "Do you live around here?"

Finally, the boy turned around and, throwing the stick away, bitterly responded, "What do you care?"

"Where are you from?" August asked.

Looking down at his own worn shoes, he muttered, "Nowhere in particular."

"I'm Mina," she said, smiling at him.

Reluctantly he replied, "I'm Ed… Ed Haddenbruck."

"Are your parents around?" August wondered aloud, gazing up and down the road.

"Ain't got no parents."

"You're an orphan?"

"Yep, no parents, no family. Just me. You ask too many questions. I ain't hurtin' no one."

"Where're you living?" August stubbornly asked again.

"No wheres! I ran away from school a few days ago, and I ain't never going back!"

"Don't you like school?" Mina asked.

"Not *my* school. They're *mean* there. They whip us… a lot!"

"Our mama and papa whip us sometimes when we don't listen, but not so hard as to hurt us," Mina said.

Unexpectedly, Ed turned his back to them and pulled up his shirt. Mina and August gasped at the multitude of ugly scabs and embedded scars cut into his skin.

"I'm so sorry!" Mina cried out, looking away quickly, with tears forming in her eyes.

"Why would they do that to you?" her brother asked.

"That's how they *punish* us kids," Ed snapped, kicking hard at a stone on the road, sending it to the other side. "And I ain't never going back!"

After glancing over at August, Mina replied, "Are you hungry?" Do you want to come home with us?"

"Yes, come to our home," August said. "Our mother will help you."

Studying their faces for a moment, Ed humbly answered, "I could eat."

Later that afternoon, while Helena fed him and her other children, she noticed their new friend ate with a voracious appetite. Upon filling up his plate a second time, she asked, "What was the name of the school you left?"

"Fulton Avenue School."

"Do you have family who can take you in?"

"No, ma'am, just me."

When Helena left the room, Ed continued shoveling potatoes covered with gravy into his mouth, but then made eye contact with Mina. "Your mother talks strange."

Laughing, she said, "Our mama and papa are both from Germany."

Ed shrugged and continued eating.

Two minutes later, pausing to drink some milk, he candidly told Mina, "Your mama's a real good cook. Can't say I ever had food this good!"

Upon returning to the dinner table, Helena overheard the boy's words and said, "Thank you for the compliment, Ed. I'm glad you like it."

A moment later, the door to the house swung open and Edward stepped in. "Papa!" Mina called out, and excitedly began introducing him to their guest. "This is Ed Haddenbruck," she said, gesturing in his direction.

Surprised to have a young visitor in the house, Edward briefly looked him over and asked, "Does he live around here?"

"No, Papa," August said. "He has no home, no parents or family. We met him on our way home from school. We were hoping you'd let him stay here for a while."

Edward looked at Helena and asked in German, "For how long? We don't know anything about him."

"He's a nice boy," Mina pleaded, as the whole family began conversing in German.

Edward laughed sarcastically, "I don't need another mouth to feed."

Mina implored him, "Oh, please, Father, he has nowhere else to go!"

Ed nervously set his spoon down and watched the family carrying on a conversation he couldn't understand.

"Come, dear!" Helena whispered, as she walked past Edward to step outside. Following her out, he was startled at her intensity. "Edward, this boy has been beaten and starved. I have seen the scars on his back with my own eyes."

"I'll take him to the Sherriff," Edward said. "He'll get him in an orphanage, where he belongs."

"An orphanage is what *did* this to him. He was in Fulton Avenue before he ran away."

"Fulton Avenue, in Evansville? That's a home for troubled boys! We already have enough troubles, don't we?"

"We know that's where he's from. But we don't know he's a troublemaker, Edward! In fact, over supper he's seemed very mild and, well, *grateful*. I think we should let him stay here, at least for a while. He was near starvation when the children brought him home."

"Lena, you would bring a stray bobcat home if you thought it was hungry. How can we afford another child? You've seen how much older boys eat."

"Edward, is it really in your heart to turn away an orphan?"

Scratching his head and uttering a deep sigh, he relented. "Alright, he can stay, but he's going to earn his keep. I expect him to work as much as anyone else around here."

Leaning forward and embracing her husband, she pecked a kiss on his cheek and said, "You're a good man, Edward Leyer."

Both laughed together when they heard cheers from the children inside the home, who'd been listening intently through an open window.

Chapter 9

In January 1876 on a bitterly cold morning, Helena stood in front of the wood stove fixing breakfast just before first light. All the Leyer children reached out toward the wood stove to warm their fingers and faces. August and Eddy were coated up and stood beside their mother, trying to capture as much heat as possible before heading to the barn to tend the animals.

"Eddy, I'll keep breakfast warm for you and August once you've finished your chores," she said.

Nodding his head and grabbing a bucket of food scraps on the floor beside the stove, he lugged it out the door—August following closely behind him—to the pigpen to feed the hogs. Between the house and the barn, Eddy paused, while August lifted out two buckets of water from the well to pour into the pen, knowing the mud and water in the sty were sure to be frozen.

Not two minutes later, both boys screamed, "Papa! Papa! Come quick!"

Given Edward had just left the house to begin his own morning chores, he heard the boys' shouts and ran through the darkness to find them crying and bewildered, standing beside the pigpen with a lantern.

"Who would do this?" August wailed to his father. "Who?"

Taking the lantern from Eddy, Edward lifted it to find out what was causing his sons' distress.

Lying in contorted mayhem, frozen to the mud, were fourteen pig carcasses, all of which had been beheaded. The lifeless bodies, each a victim of nothing less than senseless murder, knew no mercy, no justice. "These thieves come in the dead of night to destroy me!" Edward cried out as he dropped to the ground on his knees.

First light crept over the eastern horizon as Edward stood and walked from the barnyard to face the rising sun, before yelling, "You want to fight me? Then act like a man and fight me!"

Gathering himself, Edward began storming around the scene in search of any evidence or clues. In the shop just inside the barn, he found a bloody stick and shovel. "Given the number of slashes on the pig's necks," he told the boys, "the shovel must have been used to hack each pig until it bled out. Then, as if death wasn't sufficient, they continued chopping until the heads separated from the bodies."

Turning away from the mass carnage, Eddy nervously asked, "Can we still butcher the meat, Papa?"

"We can't. We don't know how long they've been like this or if they were poisoned. So no, there's too much risk of getting sick."

Later that afternoon, as Edward, Eddy and Haddenbruck dragged the frozen pig carcasses to a burn pile, Old Ben walked up from the nearby woods. He frowned as he stood by in the cold winter air watching, and then raised his arms and shrugged his shoulders.

"Someone killed all our pigs last night," Eddy explained, mouthing the words carefully.

Ben's eyes grew large, and he stomped a foot angrily on the frozen ground.

Haddenbruck suddenly lashed out at the old man, "Why don't you go home, you old fossil?"

Edward didn't hesitate a second, whacking the boy on the side of his head with the back of his hand, knocking him onto the frozen mud next to a headless pig. Rubbing the side of his head, his left ear stinging, Haddenbruck winced, "Ow-w!"

Edward, who stepped forward so he was standing directly over him, yelled, "If *anyone* is going to leave here, it will be you! Ben is our friend, and you'll show him respect, or I'll return you to Fulton Avenue in the blink of an eye!"

Haddenbruck begrudgingly nodded back at Edward, humbly replying, "Yes, sir."

The four of them stood solemnly around the fire as it sputtered and sizzled with the pigs' carcasses burning. For a while, Ben watched the flames burning away over the charred remains, but when he glanced toward the forest with his one good eye, he fiercely uttered, "Frey Coo!" and then spit on the ground.

***

Just two months later, in the third week of March, Edward walked slowly, leading one of his horses to the edge of the woods on the far end of the Leyer's property. But the horse lurched in pain every time her weight shifted to her right front leg.

"Come on, Hilda, just a little more to go, then you can rest."

When he felt she'd reached her limit, he lifted her bridal off her head and tossed it to the side into the tall weeds. Stroking her nose and looking into her eyes, he said in a soulful tone, "Hilda, you're a good ol' girl, and you always gave your most. We'll miss you."

Without removing his eyes from hers, Edward lifted the already-cocked pistol to the side of her head and fired it.

Back at the house and seated at the family table, Mina finally stopped crying and sobbed, "But how, Papa? How did Hilda come up lame? She's been in that pasture for years!"

"I wish I knew. When I finally found her this morning, her leg was broken. She may have stepped in a gopher hole or tripped over a rock."

"This is the fourth horse we've lost in the last year," Herman said. "No one has luck this bad. You add in the slaughtering of our hogs in January, and there's no mistake someone wants us gone."

"And there's only one man I can think of who is this hateful," Edward muttered. "It has to be the work of Cook or one of his mob."

Chapter 10

"I should tell you I've written to Rudolph, my cousin Erich's son," Edward said while watching Herman file down the burs from some newly forged horseshoes. "He came to America a few months ago and is living in Indianapolis. We need help if we're going to make this farm work, and I'm asking Rudolph if he'll stay with us for a while. There's no one else in this neighborhood who I can trust, except Old Ben."

***

On June 4, 1876, Rudolph Leyer walked the long lane to Edward's farm. As he approached the house, the front door flung open in front of him and both Edward and Helena hurried out to greet him, followed closely by several shouting children.

"This is Rudolph," Helena said to the kids gathered around her.

"You look just like your father, when we were young," Edward said, before hugging the young man.

Eddy lifted the bag from Rudolph's shoulder to carry it for him, as Helena said, "Come inside, you must be tired from your journey. I have fresh bread with butter and honey for you."

"I'm so glad to be here. It does my heart good, to hear German spoken again," he replied. "I was beginning to think I was the last person on Earth who knows the language."

After showing him where he would be sleeping, Edward faced the young man, grabbed his shoulders and smiled. "We are family. We should be together. This is what matters."

Later that evening, with Helena's hearty German meal under his belt, Rudolph shared, "After arriving in New York, I traveled, mostly by foot, to Indianapolis. I did some odd jobs, at first, when I could find work, but there are very few people in this country who speak German."

"We've found the language difference to be a huge problem here, too," Edward agreed. "We've found Germans are not liked very well outside of Evansville."

"We're just happy to see you," Helena interrupted, setting down a hot cup of coffee and a fresh muffin in front of Rudolph. "You seem so young to make such a long journey by yourself."

"I'm eighteen. From your letters to my father, I knew if I wanted to make something of my life in this world, America was the place it would happen."

"Your father and I were like brothers, growing up. But I pray I didn't paint too colorful of a picture," Edward chuckled. "There's opportunity in this country for a man who's willing to work hard, but there are also cutthroats and thieves ready to take it all away."

Rudolph, Edward and Helena talked well into the evening about family in Germany and life in America, before succumbing to exhaustion. By the following day, after more discussion over breakfast, Rudolph clearly understood the ongoing feud between the Leyers and the Cooks.

***

"I don't want to go to school anymore," Haddenbrook said after only a few days into the Fall term.

Edward stopped nailing a wood slat while Haddenbrook continued mucking a stall. "You just started school. Give it a chance. You'll catch up to the other children."

"It's not that. The kids are mean to Eddy and August. They call them 'stupid Dutchmen.' Some of the girls pick on Mina, too. They know I live with you, so they call me 'Dutch lover.' I just don't like it there."

Edward held another plank before nailing it in place. "They're just being kids. You should learn to ignore people when they try to hurt you with words."

After a few moments of silence between the two, he told Haddenbrook, "You don't have to go to school if you don't want to, but that doesn't mean you stop learning. I want you to stay with Rudolph from now on. Learn from him, because he has much he can teach you. In return, I want you to teach him English. He'll never succeed in this country if he can't speak the language. Agreed?"

Haddenbrook leaned against his shovel and smiled before answering, "Agreed!"

"Don't worry, I'll talk to Eddy, Mina and August about the way they're being treated in school."

Eventually, the school year settled down for the Leyer children. Nonetheless, early one Saturday morning, Rudolph came rushing into the house from the barn and yelled to Edward, "Come quickly! We have a horse down."

"Which one?" Edward asked, standing up from the table and grabbing his hat.

"Ushie, and she looks pretty darn sick."

Grabbing Herman, they followed Rudolph to the barn. In her stall, Ushie was lying in the straw on her side, not looking up to acknowledge the familiar people who circled about her.

Kneeling beside the recumbent horse, Edward lifted her lips to inspect them closely. "She's frothing," he muttered, then frowned and grumbled something under his breath. "Rudolph, bring some water. Herman, let's see if we can get her up."

After getting a rope around her neck, Herman tried coaxing her to her feet, while Edward lifted her head. Rudolph poured water on her mouth, trying to get her to take some, but she simply maintained her rapid pace of breathing. Suddenly, she kicked her legs wildly as though she wanted to stand, let out a loud whinny, and then collapsed lifeless onto the bed of straw.

Distraught, Edward moaned as he slipped down to the stall floor next to Ushie, with his back against the stable wall, closing his eyes and gently stroking her neck.

"Papa, are you sick, too?" Herman asked.

Edward neither looked up nor answered. Finally, he turned to the boys and whispered, "That's five horses we've lost. Someone in the neighborhood wants us to fail."

"Do you think she was killed?" Herman asked, kneeling to get a better look.

"I think Ushie was poisoned. She was healthy last night, and now she's dead."

Standing up, he said, "Rudolph, dump all the water and replace it with fresh water. Herman, bury her feed. Don't give it to the other horses."

Both boys turned and hurried out of the stable.

A month later, Herman found their plow horse, Henrietta, lying dead in a field, exhibiting the same conditions—indications of poisoning—as Ushie.

After leaving Henrietta's body, Herman returned to the house and told his father what he'd discovered. Furiously stepping outside, Edward found a large stick in the yard, brandished it over his head, and slammed it on the ground. "Cook is a murdering thief!"

As Helena watched the scene from a window—her husband slamming the wooden branch repeatedly against the side of the barn while facing the Cook farm—she gathered her children close to her.

"Rudolph!" Edward shouted, finally tossing the stick to the ground and walking toward the house. "Drag that horse to the fence as close to Cook's front door as possible. Let him have some of the stink of his dirty work!"

Wanting to put the drama behind them, Helena sent Haddenbruck and Mina to the barn to collect eggs from the hen's nests. As they walked across the yard, they saw Rudolph leading a horse that was dragging dead Henrietta through the field by ropes tied to her hind hoofs.

"What are they going to do with her?" Haddenbruck asked.

"Rudolph is taking her to Cook's. Papa says he wants Mr. Cook to smell her for a while."

Haddenbruck stopped and watched intently, until Mina tugged hard on his sleeve. "Hey, Mama wants these eggs today, not tomorrow."

That evening, Edward sat at the table with his head in his arms. Helena stood behind him, rubbing his shoulders to console him. Herman, Rudolph and Eddy were also sitting at the table, while Haddenbruck went about quietly playing a game with August on the floor.

"We have to sell," Edward said without lifting his head. "We lost our crops and animals this year, and don't have enough to get us through the winter. Cook and his damn henchmen have ravaged us."

"Where should we go?" Helena asked, looking up and noticing the children sitting motionless, listening intently.

"I don't know. Louisville, maybe? Back to Evansville?"

"Well, we *do* still have friends in Evansville," Helena answered.

Edward lifted his head and looked at Herman sitting across the table. "What do you think? Maybe we should go to Evansville and look for a shop we could buy. I've had a few offers here from men who want to buy the farm, but none are for what it's worth. I could try to find a buyer who will pay a fair price. With the money we get from the farm, we should be able to open a smithing shop in Evansville."

When Herman simply nodded, his father nodded back and reached across the table, squeezing his son's hand.

The two left the following morning for Evansville to follow up on the few leads Edward had.

After spending two days in Evansville trying to find a suitable shop for smithing, Edward turned to Herman on the journey home and said, "I can't do this alone. Would you be willing to join me in business? We'll call it 'Leyer and Sons.' You and I can start out, but we'll quickly bring Eddy on as an apprentice."

Herman reflected for a moment, then said, "I like the idea."

"Someday, when I'm too old to work, you'll take over and change the name to 'Leyer Brothers.'"

Upon returning to their homestead, Herman asked his father while helping unhitch Trixie from the wagon, "Must we leave, Papa?"

"It's not my wish, son," Edward answered with a saddened tone. Putting his arm around Herman's shoulders, they walked across the yard and he continued, "God wants us to love our neighbors, but we're surrounded by suspicion and hatred. It's no longer safe for us here."

Before opening the front door, he stopped and turned to his son, "We'll be fine as long as we stay together."

Herman nodded, "Yes, Papa."

Once inside the house, Edward told Helena about what they'd done, describing the deal they'd made with an elderly man to purchase a barn, they could turn into a father and son blacksmith shop.

"That sounds good," she replied. "The sooner we leave, the better. I have a terrible feeling about what will become of us if we stay here. I'll miss this farm and what few friends we have, but in truth, there's nothing 'happy' for us here in this valley."

Chapter 11

On Friday, December 1, 1876, Helena walked swiftly from the house to the barn, the sound of a hammer striking steel being a dead giveaway of where to find her husband. Looking past Edward, she noticed Herman and Rudolph focused on fixing a broken spoke from a wagon wheel.

"Good, you're all here," she said with an agitated voice. "Edward, Herman, Rudolph… come to the house."

"We're working," Edward grunted.

Helena had already turned to head back to the house, holding the front of her dress high enough to keep it from dragging through the dirty snow. "I said now!" she yelled.

When the three men entered the house, Helena, who had been sitting at the table with Mina, promptly stood and instructed them all to sit. "Go ahead, Mina. Tell them what you heard at school today."

Managing to compose herself between sobbing gasps, she said, "Some of the children at school told me their fathers say Papa and the Leyer boys killed Mrs. Cook. They're saying she was poisoned. Then the boys started teasing me, saying my father was going to *hang*."

Helena sighed and leaned back against the kitchen counter with her arms folded. Then, turning toward her husband, asked, "Edward, why would they say this about you? Have you or Herman done something to cause this sort of talk?"

"I have *no idea* why they're saying such things."

When she looked over to Herman and Rudolph, both of them shook their heads, as well.

"My fight is with Fred Cook, not his *wife*. I would never harm another man's wife."

After giving Mina a loving hug and wiping her tear-stained face with her apron, Helena sent their daughter into another room and took a chair at the table. "It doesn't matter to these English what anyone did or didn't do. What matters to them is what they *think* you did."

"What can we do to change how people think about us?" Herman blurted out. "Fred Cook runs this district and has done all he can to turn everyone against us!"

Helena pointed a finger in Edward's face and said, "You need to talk to people around the neighborhood to see if we're being accused of a crime. If we are, we need to pack up *now* and move back to Evansville. Once these people decide you're guilty, there will be *no* way to sway them with the truth."

With a sigh and a nod, Edward stood and walked to the window in the kitchen, then stared out at the old barn and fields of tall, brown grass swaying in the icy December wind.

"Okay, I'll go tomorrow to Ebenezer Day and speak with him and his son, William. Ebenezer is a fair and honest man who seems to hold no preconceptions about others."

Early the following morning, Edward sat with Ebenezer and William, near the fire in Ebenezer's living room. "What have you heard about Elizabeth Cook's death?" Edward asked after taking a sip of coffee.

"I'm hearing it was not by God's hand," Ebenezer replied.

"Billy Cook told me she was poisoned," William added. "They think someone put arsenic in the Cook's cistern and she drank of it."

"But who would so such a thing?" Edward asked.

Ebenezer and William paused as they looked to one another for an answer. "Well," William finally replied, "Billy said the poison likely came from the Leyers."

Over the next week, Edward traveled around the district discussing this same matter with some of the other locals, gathering their perspective and picking up pieces of information along the way.

While Edward forged an ax head at his kiln, Henry Flock rode up and proceeded to gather the tools he had left in Edward's care for repair the previous week. "Mr. Flock? I haven't finished the repairs."

Henry turned to Edward and angrily replied, "I don't need no murdering Dutchman working for me. I'll take my business elsewhere!"

When Edward told Helena what had transpired between him and Henry Flock after dinner that night, Helena said, "I tried going to the Cook's this afternoon to bring them some soup, but John Criswell stopped me at the door and said we had already done enough harm. He wouldn't even let me leave the soup for the family."

Edward sighed and said, "We have no choice. Frank Morris's offer for the farm is for much less than it's worth, but it's the only offer I have."

On December 7th, Edward saddled Sandy and paused, standing beside the barn, looking wistfully around at the farm.

Seeing him through the kitchen window, Helena came out of the house, took his hand and said, "Everything will be alright, Edward."

Embracing her tightly, he whispered, "I'm so sorry, my love. I believed we could make the farm work."

"We've been through worse, dear. Remember… Love bears all things."

Releasing her from his arms, he smiled and kissed her before saddling up. "I'll be staying at Weisheimer's," he said, "As soon as I'm finished conducting business with Frank Morris, the farm will be his. Get the children to help you start packing and load everything on the wagon. I'll be back in a day or so to help."

Then he turned Sandy around and rode off the farm.

Helena watched in silence until Edward disappeared from view. A frosty breeze had gathered some powdery snow, which swirled lightly around her boots. "At least the sky is clear today," she said to herself. "God be with you, my love." Then, closing her eyes and lifting her face to the sky, she added, "Please, God, be with my man!"

Once inside the house, Helena warmed her hands over the wood-burning stove in the kitchen, next to the table where her oldest son was sipping a drink. "Your father just left for Evansville. And what I'm going to say, you cannot repeat to anyone, in or out of the family, not even Rudolph!" Moving to the table and sitting down across from him, she continued, "He may be there for a while. He's trying to sell the farm *and* looking for a place for us to live. But for now, my concern is with you."

"Me, Mama?"

"Yes. Your father heard Fred Cook is trying to get both him *and* you charged with murder."

"But *why*? We've done nothing wrong. What evidence do they have against us?"

"These people don't need proof. Rumors are spreading like wildfire and they're pointing their fingers directly at this family. We can't trust anyone in this town, except Old Ben. My fear is they'll try to do you and your father harm. If they come for you, I want you to promise me you'll go to Old Ben's place to hide until I send for you. Will you promise me?"

With a defiant tone, he replied, "With Papa gone, I'm the *eldest*, Mama. I need to stay here to protect you and the children."

Helena studied her son's determined look, then reached across the table and took his hands. "No, Herman. I can take care of myself and the others, but I *can't* protect you from a bloodthirsty horde of Englishmen. Leaning forward, she squeezed his hands even tighter and concluded, "I need you to *promise* me you'll go to Ben's."

"Yes, Mama," he reluctantly replied. "I promise I'll go."

With his reassurance, Helena eased her grip and, smiling with relief, replied, "Good."

Chapter 12

ARREST OF HERMAN LEYER, OF WARRICK COUNTY, ON THE CHARGE OF POISONING THE COOKE FAMILY.

A Band of Masked Men Invade his Premises to Lynch Him.

HIS LITTLE BOY'S HEROIC TRAMP TO SAVE HIS FATHER.

Given December 9th was a bitterly cold and snowy day, Herman and Rudolph brought in an extra supply of wood to keep the wood-burning stove in the kitchen fed and the home warm throughout the long night. Around midnight, Herman was awoken abruptly by his mother shaking his shoulder. "Wake up, Herman! Wake up!"

"Yes, I'll get the wood."

"No! I hear horses. It's time for you to go! Grab your things and run out the back!"

"But…?" Herman rubbed his eyes and yawned.

"Don't argue! You *must* get up. Do as you promised, Herman! Go now, quickly."

Realizing what was happening, he sprung out of bed, got dressed, grabbed his coat and hat, and made his way through the snow toward the barn. When he reached the corner of the building, Herman saw about twenty horses approaching the house at full gallop. Under cover of darkness, he made his way through the paddock, across the pasture and into the tree line at the edge of the woods. Looking back, he saw a horde of shadows spreading out over the farm. Some encircled the house, while others went directly toward the barn and corn crib. Herman dashed forward, sprinting as fast as he could through the woods in the direction of Old Ben's place, without looking back.

The sounds of a fist pounding on the door were followed by a man hollering, "Leyer! Edward Leyer!"

When Helena opened the door, three hostile men pushed past her and began rounding up everyone in the house. Within moments, all eight had been herded out of their beds by the intruders, Helena pulling the terrified children close to her.

With barely a word, they were shoved and rushed out to the stable, barefoot and in just their nightclothes, while the blackened-faced intruders finished ransacking the house for any sign of Edward or Herman.

On their way across the yard, Helena saw men scouring each and every outbuilding with lanterns and torches. But she and the others were hurried to the barn through the biting cold wind.

When they were all finally gathered into a corner of the barn by one of the men, Helena turned her gaze to see Mikey, the family dog, rushing in through an open gate. Immediately, he began barking wildly at the ruffians, baring his teeth, his hackles raised in protective anger.

A moment later, when a piercing blast rang out, Mikey fell dead on the hard dirt floor. One of the men had shot him point-blank in the head, and the frightened children buried their faces into their mother's nightgown, while with both hands she did what she could to cover their eyes from the sight of their beloved dog lying lifeless in a pool of blood.

"Keep looking for Leyer and his son," one of the men shouted at the others, pointing toward the hay loft.

"Billy Cook?" mumbled Rudolph with a puzzled expression, staring at the man nearby who had just spoken. The tall, blackened-faced figure paused, his mouth gaping open as he stared at the young man who'd just identified him. Then with a grunt, he rushed over and punched Rudolph in the face, knocking him to the ground. Aiming a shotgun at his head, he prepared to fire.

Before he pulled the trigger, another man grabbed the gun barrel and yelled, "What are you doing?"

The man with the gun leaned in toward him and whispered, "He knows who I am. He said my *name*!"

"Don't worry. He can't prove nothin'."

One of the men approached Helena and demanded, "Where's your husband and your boy Herman?"

"I don't know. They aren't here."

Albert shifted in her arms and began to whimper, so she pulled him close to her and turned to glare back at the goon.

"What kind of men are you, who would terrorize children?"

Narrowing his eyes, he huffed with a crude snort and stepped past her to continue grilling each of the captives.

One by one, each of them was prodded with the same questions, but the only replies given were blank stares or frightened looks from the younger children and "I don't know" from the older ones.

Eventually, Ed Haddenbruck was pulled aside and questioned by the thug who'd tried to intimidate Helena. Ed glanced over to the wagon, where he saw her huddled with some of the children. "None of us knows where they went. They just snuck out and ran away," he said, looking down at the floor. "And I ain't a part of this family," Ed added, fidgeting with his nightshirt buttons.

"You best get dressed and come with us then," the man replied, grabbing the back of his neck and shoving him in the direction of the barn door. Then, the man turned and sneered at Helena. "We'll be back here again tomorrow night and every night after, 'til we catch both Leyer and his son. Hanging is too good for 'em, so we're gonna' burn 'em alive. That way, they'll know how much Elizabeth suffered 'fore she died."

After the hoodlums rode off with Haddenbruck into the icy darkness, the Leyer children ran back to Mikey's body, still lying on the barn floor. Sniffling, they stroked the soft fur of their dead, loyal companion. August ran into the house, changed out of his nightclothes, and sat down to strap his boots on. Moments later, he was joined by Rudolph and Helena, who was still holding Alfred, followed closely by the other children. As they entered the house, Helena lit the wick of an unbroken oil lantern and looked around at the mass destruction of their home. Dishes were broken, furniture upturned and beds flipped. To ward off the bitter cold in the house, Rudolph restarted the fire with some still smoldering embers. The children were placed on the floor in front of the fire and covered with an abundance of blankets, which soon stopped their shivering and whimpering.

As the room started to warm, Helena sat close to them and softly sang German lullabies, while rocking Albert. One by one, the exhausted youngsters drifted to sleep.

Across the room, she saw August grab a thick jacket and put his hat on. "What are you doing?"

"I need to know where Papa and Herman went. *Please*, Mama. Do you know where they are?"

"You're not going anywhere, young man. Not at this hour of the night."

Ignoring her son's plan, she motioned for Rudolph to sit at the kitchen table and, when he was seated, took his chin in her hand, carefully examining the bluish swelling on his cheek and around his eye where he'd been punched.

"*Mama*," August pleaded, "I have to warn them!"

"You'll never find them," she answered sternly while still focusing on Rudolph's bruise, grabbing one of her rags from the counter, wetting it with cold water and handing it to him. "Here, hold this on your eye. It will help stop the swelling."

Taking the rag, he lightly pressed it to the swollen area.

August circled the table, stood behind Rudolph, and faced his mother in an effort to gain her attention, "I must try, Mama! If Papa and Herman come back here, those men will kill them."

"August, be reasonable. You're fourteen years old! And we don't even have a horse here. Papa took the last one."

"Then I'll run!" August insisted defiantly.

Helena plopped herself in a chair at the table and looked around at the devastation in her kitchen. "Listen to me. I've already warned Herman. He knows to stay away. Papa is in Evansville. That's twenty-two miles from here. So-…"

"Where's he staying?"

Reluctantly, she answered, "At Weisheimer's on Main Street. But you can't-…"

"I *need* to go see him."

"Alright, alright. Do you know the place?"

"Yes, I do. Don't worry, Mama. I'll be back."

For hours, August made his way down country lanes, dodging snow drifts, trudging along at a steadfast pace, through the bitterly cold night.

It was nearly noon when August opened the door to Weisheimer's Hardware Store. Chilled to the bone, he stood just inside the doorway as his eyes adjusted to the darkness of the room. His nose, cheeks and lips were blood red and chapped from a long night of frigid wind.

Finally he asked, "Is my father here?"

Upon hearing his son's voice, Edward stepped out of a back room. "August? How did you get here?"

Running across the wooden floor to his father, he embraced him, then whispered into his ear while motioning to the room from which his father had come, "Can we talk back there?"

Stepping back into the small room, Edward helped August take off his coat and boots, then pulled a chair next to the coal-burning stove for him to sit near it and thaw out. Immediately, August began recanting the previous night's events.

"Did they hurt your mother?" Edward asked.

"She's scared, but they didn't hurt her."

"Eat this," Edward said, handing his son a bowl of warm egg soup.

As August rested on the cot after eating, Edward couldn't get his son's warning out of his mind. *There was a mob who had black on their faces. One of the men shot Mikey. They wanted you and Herman, but Herman got away. The men in our home broke everything. The leader told us they were going to burn you alive when they find you!*

August slept the remainder of the day and that night. The following morning, as father and son ate a light breakfast, August said, "You can't come back to the farm. I heard one of the men say they'll be watching for you."

"I know. I'll stay here. But I need you and the rest of the family to come here as quickly as possible. Cook and his outlaws are out for blood, and they don't care who they have to kill to get it."

"Where should we go?"

"I've already rented the house, just three doors from here. It'll be ready for us when you get back. I don't need a horse while I'm here, so take Sandy back to the farm to pull the wagon. Take only what we need and leave the rest. There's nothing on the farm worth dying for."

"Alright, Papa. I'm ready to leave now."

"Make sure your mother knows I'm safe. Tell her to bring my rifle and pistols. I'm going to buy another pistol today and keep it on me. Come with me, I'll show you the house on our way to the stable."

Once they were standing no more than ten feet from the front door, Edward said, "It's small, but I think it'll do until we find something better. There's a little workroom in the backyard, which I can use to store my tools."

"I'm scared, Papa," August admitted, ignoring his father's comments about the house.

Edward paused before putting his hands on both of his son's shoulders, "I'm scared too. I'm also angry I wasn't there to protect you the other night. Once we're together again, and we find Herman, we can put Fred Cook and his murdering mob behind us."

"But what if they come to Evansville to find us? What will they do if they find you?"

"Don't worry, August. I'll be ready for them this time."

August nodded without a word.

***

August arrived safely at the farm the following afternoon. "Sit, you're chilled to the bone," Helena said, as she set a steamy bowl of hot dumpling soup in front of him.

"I found Papa," he announced, as Rudolph and Eddy joined him and Helena at the table. "He said to tell you he's sold the farm, and we should pack up and go to Evansville as soon as possible. He showed me where our new home is on Main Street."

"What did he say about the mob?" Eddy asked.

"He said he isn't coming back here, because they'll try to kill him. He thinks we'll be safe in Evansville."

Chapter 13

Later that same day, Helena pulled Rudolph aside and said, "Watch over things. Keep a pistol handy. If the mob returns, protect the children." Then, she grabbed a large bag and hung the strap from her shoulder. "I'm going to tell Ben we're leaving."

She slipped through the tree line beside the road to avoid being seen and finally came to the clearing where Old Ben lived.

After surveying the area to ensure no one else was around, Helena approached the doorway to the hermit's lair and called out, "Hello! Hello!"

Hearing his mother's voice, Herman flung the door open, rushed forward and hugged her tightly.

"It's so good to see you," Helena said, taking his hand and leading him to a log behind the cabin.

"August went to Evansville to warn your father about the mob that came to the farm, and I've come to warn *you*. Things being the way they are, Herman, I need you to do as I say without question. Are you ready?"

"Yes, ma'am."

"Good. Now listen and listen carefully. You're not to return to the farm. Your father sold it to Frank Morris. We're moving back to Evansville this week. Rudolph will help me pack your father's blacksmith tools. We're only to take our personal belongings. You're not *ever* to attempt to communicate with us or find us. We'll find *you* when the time is right. I'm sorry I have no horse for you, but I want you to go to Louisville. You're *never* to use the name 'Herman' or 'Leyer' again. Take my father's name. That's the *only* name you will answer to. When you get to Louisville, find work and a place to live. Now here's the most important part. On the first Sunday of every month, at 3:00 in the afternoon, go to Saint Peter's, where we had the christenings. Wait there until 4:00. When we're safe in Evansville, and the danger is behind us, one of us will meet you at Saint Peter's on a first Sunday. Will you do this for me? For our family?"

"Yes, I promise. Can I at least say goodbye to the children?"

Helena's eyes filled with tears as she answered. "No, my dear. I'm not telling them where you are. I won't even tell your father when I see him. Only *I* will know. You have to trust me. This is for the best, and it's the safest way to go forward from here. I promise we'll be together again, but I don't know when that day will come. You can tell Ben you're going home before you leave, but don't tell him one word about our plans."

"I don't think I could have stayed another night with Ben," he confessed with a chuckle. "I love the old man, but I couldn't sleep a wink. I felt like spiders and snakes were crawling on me all night."

His mother laughed. "I guess coming here to hide was a good idea. No one would expect someone to stay here with all the little creepy crawlies everywhere," Helena said, dangling her fingers in the air like a spider.

Herman lifted his fingers and mimicked her, laughing together with her. When she leaned forward, they held each other in a tight, silent embrace, and upon parting, Helena handed him the large bag that contained a bundle wrapped in a woolen blanket.

"Here, I packed you some food, along with what money I can spare. But remember, do *not* try to contact any of us, understand?"

"I understand."

Taking the bag from his mother, he pulled the strap over his shoulder. "Well, Mother, every journey begins with the first step, right?"

Together they stood and walked to the front of Ben's cabin. Pulling him to her, she gave him a final hug. "Stay off the roads until you get closer to Boonville. Ask Ben to come see me. I'll wait here."

Then, she kissed her son on the cheek and said, "Goodbye, and may God protect you... *Charles*. I love you."

"I love you, too, Mama," he choked out. "Please be safe!"

Helena tried to keep her composure as she watched him enter the cabin to wake Ben from his nap. As smoke rose from the wood clapboard chimney, she stared at the gaping holes around the loosely hung door.

Eventually, "Charles" emerged from the ramshackle dwelling, followed by Ben, who wore a heavy coat that, she could see, had been fashioned from two or three other coats. Helena watched as the two men shook hands, after which Charles cautiously walked toward an old logging trail through the woods that would eventually lead him east toward Louisville.

As Old Ben approached her, Helena stood to greet him, seeing his boyish grin through the matted white beard.

"Purdy Lady," he said, but his smile dropped upon seeing the expression on her face change. "Purdy Lady, sad?"

Helena nodded, briefly studying the hermit's cloudy blue eye. She saw both his eyes were trained on her lips, waiting to read her words. Looking skyward, Helena wiped her wet cheeks with her sleeve before telling him, "Ben, Edward has gone to Evansville to sell the farm. We can't stay here any longer. These people destroyed our crops and livestock. Now, they want to destroy us. It isn't safe for us here."

He stammered, "A'war, Purdy Lady, chil'ren?"

Helena sensed the old hermit's sadness, even before a tear fell from the crusted corners of his eyes, and his face melted into a wounded expression.

As Ben repeated himself—"A'war, Purdy Lady, chil'ren, away?"—his words came with an anguished squeal she had never heard before, the sound he would make when he was crying hard.

He turned to run into his home, but circled back to look at her one last time. Helena stepped toward him, silently lifting up a brown paper package and handing it to him.

Sobbing and slightly hiccupping as he held the package, Ben asked, "Brey?"

She nodded, "Yes, bread."

Once again, Ben squealed in anguish and ran in a circle around his home. When he returned, he lifted a leather string he wore around his neck. Hanging from the string was the tail end of what was clearly a very large rattlesnake. The hermit put it over Helena's head and stared briefly at how it hung below her neck. Finally, with the package of bread under his arm, he turned and cried out a last heart-rending squeal, as he ran straight to his door and closed himself in.

Chapter 14

From a safe distance, Fred Cook and his henchmen had been watching the Leyer farm day and night for signs of Edward or Herman. Finally, one of his men approached Cook after a couple of days and reported, "It looks as though the family's packing a wagon with all their household goods."

Later that day, Fred stood with his attorney behind the table facing Judge Hailstone, having hastily assembled the grand jury.

The judge explained, "I'm sorry for the loss of your wife, Mr. Cook, but there is no evidence against Edward Leyer for which I can have him arrested."

"Judge Hailstone," Fred began, as his attorney stood silent. "I have sworn statements from numerous citizens who saw Leyer on the road in front of my farm on the day of the poisoning, and still others who will swear to his nervous behavior since my wife's death."

"That's not sufficient evidence for me to deny a man's freedom."

"Your Honor, Mr. Leyer and his son, Herman, have already fled Greer. My wife was a daughter of the Butcher family, and you know as well as I do what that means to this community. If you let him escape, you're letting a murderer go free."

Judge Hailstone sat silent for a moment before proceeding, "Clear the courtroom. I'll discuss this with the jury."

After standing outside the courtroom for just ten minutes, the bailiff walked out and handed a warrant to Fred Cook, signed by the judge, for the arrest and return of Edward Leyer and Herman Leyer to Greer Township.

"Give this to the sheriff," he said, along with a nod.

***

On the 13th of December, 1876, officers Jacob Miller and Chris Vogt, both of the Evansville police department, were given the very same warrant and began to search for Edward and Herman Leyer.

A little before sunrise, Officer Vogt told his partner, "I found them."

"Where?" Miller asked.

"For several weeks, Leyer has been negotiating with a fellow, Frank Morris, for the sale of his farm." He continued to read from his notes while sitting next to his partner's desk at the police station. "I tracked down Morris, and he told me all of their meetings have taken place in Weischeimer's Hardware on Main Street. I'll bet you a week's salary Leyer and his son are staying in the stock room of that hardware store."

Just before daylight on the morning of the 14th, the manhunt ended at Weischeimer's.

"Edward Leyer?" Officer Miller yelled at the man lying on the cot in the back room. "Wake up! I have a warrant for your arrest!"

Shaking his head from having been awoken from sleep, Edward tried to focus on the two silhouettes standing in the doorway. "I've done nothing wrong," he declared, slowly sitting up on the cot to face them.

Ignoring his protest, Officer Vogt took hold of Edward's arm, pulled him to his feet and cuffed his hands behind his back. "Is Herman Leyer with you?" Vogt asked.

"No, Herman is not here."

Seeing the early morning cold was causing their suspect to shake uncontrollably, Officer Miller grabbed Edward's coat and threw it over his shoulders.

When Leyer questioned them, "Where are you taking me?" the officers ignored him and led him away from the hardware store and down the street toward the courthouse.

Just before 9:00 a.m. that morning, Officers Miller and Vogt brought Edward before the local magistrate, Esquire Samuel Burke, who remanded him to their custody. They put their prisoner in a tiny cell and guarded him all day in the police headquarters. Later that afternoon, Edward was told he was to be transported to Warrick County to stand trial for the murder of Elizabeth Cook.

Upon hearing this news, Edward implored Miller and Vogt, "Please don't send me back to Greer Township. They'll kill me if I return. My young son, August, told me a lynch mob came to my farm, looking for me, with the intent to murder me. So I stayed in Evansville for the sake of my life. They'll make sure I have no trial to allow me to prove I'm innocent."

The officers didn't know what to do, as the warrant upon which he was arrested was returnable before the Justice of Greer Township. Edward held the bars to the cell so tightly his fingers turned white, "You can take me with you to Boonville, but I will be dead before nightfall if I'm sent back to Greer!"

Finally, Peter Maier, Esq., was called in, and after listening to the officer's concerns, wrote a long explanatory letter to Judge Handy of Boonville, detailing the circumstances and the prisoner's fear, and requesting that Leyer be kept in the Boonville jail.

Boonville Sheriff Gurley Taylor accepted the prisoner into his care, but with a word of warning to Mr. Maier, "If sentiments are as fevered as you describe over the fate of the prisoner, let me assure you I will not risk my life, the life of my deputies or even the lives of the other prisoners under my protection, for this Dutchman."

Later that afternoon, Edward was transferred to the Booneville jail, where he shared a crowded cell with six other prisoners.

"Looks like you already have a visitor, Leyer," Sherriff Taylor said, smiling as he opened the shackles on the prisoner's ankle and replaced it with a restraint that connected both of Edward's ankles to a single chain between them, permitting him to walk with a limited stride.

T. D. O. Moore, Esq. of Boonville, a local attorney, was the first to meet with Edward. Sitting at a small dining table next to the kitchen, Moore spoke quietly. "I have been assigned your case," he explained. "But I want to bring in Peter Maier, Esq. from Evansville, if you have no objections. He's a good man, and I believe his familiarity with the citizens and businesses in Evansville will be useful to your defense. The charge against you and your son, Herman, is that of murder in the first degree of one Elizabeth Cook by use of arsenic thrown into a cistern from which she drank. Do you understand?"

Edward nodded silently.

Mr. Moore continued, "From the evidence at hand, I expect there to be some trouble in making the case against you. So far, no druggist has been found who sold you any arsenic. William Weber of Evansville sold you a bill of goods several weeks ago, but it consisted only of ordinary articles and did not include arsenic. It was rumored that druggist C. H. Hut had sold you some of the deadly drug, but he denied it and stated he had not sold any arsenic to *anyone* during that time period. The Evansville police have been very active in searching for testimony of this kind, but have had no success. Without proof of you carrying or purchasing arsenic, the prosecution's case is purely circumstantial."

"Other than what little I used to poison rats in my barn, I've never used arsenic," Edward replied.

"Good, I want you to remember that statement and repeat it to the judge and grand jury when asked. Then, we'll see if we can resolve this case quickly and get you back with your family before Christmas."

Edward smiled faintly and thanked Mr. Moore before being returned to his cell.

Chapter 15

On December 21, 1876, Deputy Campbell unlocked the outer cell door of the timeworn Boonville Jail and stepped back to let Helena pass into the narrow hall with the two adjoining cells. Anxiously, she stood in the holding area, carrying a wicker basket covered with a red towel, while he opened the door to the cell where Edward sat with six other prisoners.

"Edward!" she called out, rushing past the deputy.

"Lena, you came!" Jumping from his cot, he kissed her cheek, held her in a firm embrace and whispered in her ear, "I haven't stopped praying I'd see you today, my love!" Looking into her face, his heart sank upon seeing the dark rings under her eyes.

The other men respectfully retreated to the far side of the 14x18-foot room. One prisoner, John Curry, who was shackled to Edward, could withdraw no further than the three-foot chain between their ankles would allow; but he still sat away with his back to them.

Conversing in German, the two sat close enough to one another to whisper. "I have missed you, my Lena," he sighed, gazing into her eyes and caressing her hand.

"And I love you, my dear, forever and always."

Edward smiled and asked, "The children?"

"They're home, safe. Rudolph is out front with the horse and wagon, but Herman is gone."

"Gone where?"

Helena pulled back far enough to look him in the eyes, so he could see the slight movements of her head back and forth, conveying, *Don't ask.*

Edward acknowledged with an equally slight nod of his head.

"Please, Edward, hold me again," she said, as they embraced in front of the other prisoners. Lowering his arm between them, he felt the cold steel she was passing him from a pocket sewn inside her coat. Carefully he slipped the small pistol down his leg and into his boot.

Then, putting her hands firmly on his cheeks, Helena whispered, "If they come for you, protect yourself. What else do you need?"

"I could use another pistol," he quietly replied, as he pulled back from her.

"I'll see what I can do."

Then, she dropped her eyes to the sleeve of her coat. Following her lead, he saw the tip ends of two of his files. Slowly, he slid his hand inside her sleeve to palm the files before slipping them into his other boot.

Shifting her seated position slightly toward her husband's cellmates, she pulled a package from her basket and said loudly enough—in English—for the prisoners to hear, "Share this with the others."

Edward unwrapped the bundle and began breaking off fist-size pieces of the bread loaf, handing a piece of his wife's gift to the other men. Each man nodded to her politely and replied, "Thank ye, Mrs. Leyer," as they accepted their respective portions.

As Helena turned back to resume the private conversation she'd been having with Edward, he quietly said, "Promise me, dear, no matter what becomes of me, you'll do everything you can to keep the family together. Promise me."

"I do, Edward, I promise. But there's no need. You'll be home with us very soon. The children miss you. *I* miss you. You'll see, life in Evansville will be better than before."

At that moment, Deputy Campbell appeared at the cell bars and cleared his throat before saying, "Excuse me, Miss, it's time to say your goodbyes."

Helena looked up at the man standing in the open cell door and gave him a polite nod. Then, after a final, longing look at each other, she and Edward stood together and embraced once again. "Happy birthday," she said next to his ear.

Tears welled up in the corners of Edward's eyes, and he dropped his head onto her shoulder as he suddenly realized it was December 21st. He had to compose himself for a moment before responding, "Thank you. I'm forever in love with you, my dear."

"And I with you. Take care, and protect yourself. You'll be home as soon as we get all of this cleared up."

With one last kiss, Helena turned and exited the musty cell, giving the deputy a casual nod as she hurried past him. Behind her, she heard the large metal door loudly clank as it shut and relocked.

With a long sigh, Edward crossed the cell and plopped down on the bunk to better position the pistol and files in his boots, so they could remain concealed. Then, after he heard the outer cell door latch, Edward pulled a file out of his boot and began the process of cutting through one of the links of the chain attached around his and his cellmate John's ankles. The other prisoners, seeing what he was up to and appreciating his wife's recent generosity, immediately started covering for him by making noises and talking loudly to overshadow the sound of metal grinding against metal.

One prisoner who shared the cell with Leyer, Hezekiah "Stamp" Wellington, was a handsome man, five-foot-eight, with auburn hair and blue eyes. The offspring of a long lineage of thieves and liars, he'd remained in keeping with his family history and was now serving time for stealing.

"What are your plans when you cut that link?" Stamp asked, moving closer and craning his neck for a better look. "We're still locked up, y'know. You think you can file through those bars?"

Edward paused and looked at the massive cell door. "Most likely I can't break out of here. But if they come for me, I can't move fast if I'm still chained to John."

John Curry snickered to himself when he heard the German's comeback, then leaned over to help hold the chain steady.

"Who?" Stamp asked, his brows furrowed. "Who's coming for you?"

Edward turned toward Stamp and waved the file as he spoke, "I told you the other day. A mob came to my farm to kill me. One man told my boy they were going to set fire under me."

"And you think they'll break into this jail to lynch you?"

"That's exactly what I think," Edward answered, speeding up his filing. "I can't fight my way out of here if I have to drag John around like a bag of potatoes."

Stamp chuckled and nodded in agreement, slumping to the floor to watch his cellmate's handiwork. "That's a good file. You're already making progress."

"I made it myself. To get a file hard enough to cut through steel, you have to add hydrocyanic acid during the smelting process."

Two hours after all the inmates had finished their meager suppers, the faint sound of filing finally stopped. In the dim candlelight, the prisoners of Boonville could see Edward Leyer and John Curry standing far apart, while the German held the end of a broken chain in his hand, out of site from the cell door. A few of the prisoners began to laugh when Stamp patted Edward on the back and said, "Well, bust my buttons and call me a pole cat! You did it, Leyer!"

Chapter 16

BOONVILLE BULL-DOZ-ERS.

Attempt to Lynch Leyer, the Poisoner.

Masked Men Demand the Keys to the Jail from the Sheriff.

Citizens Come to the Sheriff's Rescue and Disperse the Mob.

Three and a half hours later, two solitary guards were making their rounds, checking on the slumbering prisoners, while the sheriff napped at his desk. At the stroke of midnight, both guards heard the sound of galloping hooves breaking the stillness of the night. Stepping up to look out the window of the Boonville sheriff's office, they saw three horses suddenly stop in front of the jail. The older ran to the back to awaken the sheriff, who pulled his hat back from his eyes and asked, "What's goin' on?"

Before the guard could answer, they both heard a man calling out, "Sheriff! Sheriff Taylor!"

When his feet slid off the desk where they had been resting, Sheriff Gurley Taylor's boots slammed down loudly on the worn wooden floorboards. Grabbing his holster, he strapped it on and checked his pistols. *Twelve bullets, twelve shots.*

Then, with a lantern in hand and a deep breath, he opened the door and stepped cautiously onto the front steps, sizing up the situation, while pulling on his coat to fend off the bitter winter wind.

As he held the lantern high, barely able to distinguish the three horsemen before him, he hollered, "Who are you? What do you want?"

"We've come for one of your prisoners!" the blackened-faced rider in the middle yelled back. "Hand Edward Leyer over to us, and we'll leave you in peace!"

"You know I can't do that!" Taylor replied.

Setting the lantern on the porch and pulling back his coat, the sheriff exposed his two pistols and rested his hands on their handles. "You men go home before I lock you up for disturbing the peace."

"Last chance!" the center horseman warned. "One way or the other, we're taking Leyer with us tonight."

Taylor briefly flinched when he heard the sound of a pistol's hammer click.

"Give us the key to his cell, and no one will get hurt!" the horseman on the right yelled.

Taylor didn't turn his head an inch when he heard the door open behind him, his two deputies stepping forward to stand on either side of him, both clicking the hammer back on their Winchester rifles.

"You boys have three seconds to ride out of this town," the sheriff shouted back, "before my deputies shoot two of you off your horses! The other one is *mine*!"

Both deputies raised their rifles and pointed them at the two outside riders. A second later, Sheriff Taylor pulled out his pistols, aimed them squarely at the middle rider, and started his countdown, "Three...Two..."

The horsemen pulled sharply on their reins to turn their steeds around before calling out, "We'll be back, Sheriff! This time it'll be a hundred against three!"

"I'll be here!" Taylor called back, holstering his weapons and watching the three riders disappear into the frigid darkness.

Deputy Campbell walked to the edge of the porch and stood beside the lawman. "Sheriff, when do you think they're coming back?"

"Soon, son... real soon."

With a slight shudder, Taylor pulled his coat tighter around his neck, and looking up, saw snow flurries falling from the black sky floating past the solitary streetlamp not far from the sheriff station's porch.

"James," he finally said to Deputy Campbell, "gather all the keys and go warn my wife to take cover. If you hear them coming, wake this town and get every able-bodied man down here. Tell them to arm themselves."

"Right," answered Deputy Campbell, as he spun around and hurried into the jail.

"Derek," he said to his other deputy, "get the prisoners up. Check the locks and tell them what just happened. Light this place up. I want every lantern burning. Make sure all the guns are loaded and place one next to each and every window."

Derek nodded and strode quickly into the jail. Inside, Derek saw James had already collected the keys.

"Hey, pass me the keys to the outer cell door," he said, "so I can warn the prisoners about what's gonna' happen! Then you'd better hightail it outta' here!"

Moments later, James ran out of the back of the building. Out front on the porch, Sheriff Taylor heard the sound of distant thunder, which slowly grew louder. He stepped back inside to fetch his rifle and then headed back out to the porch. Standing alone on the front step, the sheriff leaned the gun on a post near the door, unbuckled his holster, and laid it over his shoulder. Then, after buttoning his overcoat, he took the holster and buckled the belt around the outside of his coat. *Rifle, loaded... pistols, loaded. Alright, I'm ready.*

Surveying the street, Taylor suddenly realized the thunderous sound was coming from his left *and* his right, approaching from both ends of town... that it was hundreds of hooves pounding the frozen dirt beneath them.

Derek stepped back out on the porch, a loaded rifle in hand, to stand by the sheriff. Taylor holstered his pistols and stood quietly waiting.

"I hear 'em," Derek said.

Taylor pushed snow from the banister before leaning against it. "Hold your fire, Derek. There's too many of them. And besides, James has all the keys. There's nothing they can do."

James had made it as far as the school, when dozens of horses, wagons and riders rode past him in full gallop toward the jail. The largest bell in town hung in front of the school, which he began vigorously ringing in an attempt to awaken the town with its piercing sound.

Deputy Campbell knocked as loud as possible on the front door of Sheriff Taylor's house, while calling out, "Mrs. Taylor! Open up!"

As the door slowly opened, Anita Taylor recognized the deputy. "James? What are you doing here? Is Gurley alright?"

"Mrs. Taylor, the jail is under attack. Your husband sent me to warn you and to tell you to stay in a safe place. I'm going house to house, getting as many armed men as I can find to come to the jail."

"Oh my Lord!" she said, opening the door to invite the deputy to step inside. "What do they want?"

Deputy Campbell held back from going into Taylor's home, saying, "They're trying to lynch one of the prisoners, Mrs. Taylor. I'm sorry to leave you, ma'am, but I need to wake more men. Please, lock this door and open it for no one until this is over."

Once the deputy left, Anita quickly changed into her dress, pulled on a heavy overcoat, grabbed a loaded shotgun, and then went outside. Down the street, she saw dozens of armed Boonville citizens moving quickly toward the jail and she didn't hesitate to join their ranks.

Suddenly, a tug on her coat sleeve broke her stride, and she heard Deputy Campbell saying from behind her, "Mrs. Taylor, the sheriff wants you to stay home! What do you think you're doing?"

"Turn me loose, James. If my husband is in danger, then so is law and order in this town. Now you can come with me, or I will go it alone. Your choice."

He considered her determination for only a moment before responding, "Here, take the keys. The road in front of the jail will be blocked by now. We'll go through the back door."

When the horsemen of the mob rode right up to the jailhouse, the two lawmen looked startled by their sheer numbers. Those hooligans who sat in wagon beds jumped to the street with their rifles on full display. One of the wagons pulled up under a large oak tree directly across from the jail.

"Hand me the rope," one man yelled, as he stood up in the wagon's bed. In seconds, a noose hung from a tree limb, swaying in the night air, ready to tighten around the neck of Edward Leyer.

"Give me the keys!" one masked rider demanded of the sheriff.

"I don't have any keys," Taylor hollered back, his fingers tightening on the handles of his pistols. "There's not going to be any lynching tonight, so you and your men just go back home!"

The man who'd yelled his demand snickered and shook his head, as he dismounted from his horse and walked up the steps, a rifle in hand.

Standing alongside his deputy on the wooden porch, Sheriff Taylor lifted one of his pistols and pointed it at the approaching man's gut.

"Sheriff Taylor," the man said, grinning with a big toothy smile that radiated through the black face paint he and his mob had applied to conceal their identities. "We're here to collect one of your prisoners who murdered an innocent woman. We have no beef with you, or anyone in Boonville, for that matter. But we do have a score to settle with the Dutchman, Leyer."

"And I have a duty to protect him and the rest of these prisoners," Taylor sneered, still pointing the pistol barrel directly at the man's stomach. "Every one of these men will have a fair hearing for any crimes they may or may not have committed."

Without warning, two men standing alongside their horses sprinted up the jailhouse steps carrying sledgehammers. Derek turned to aim his rifle at one of the men, but a third ran forward from the mob and pulled it from his hands, then pushed him backward into the building, the deputy stumbling over the door stoop. The man who'd approached Sheriff Taylor quickly wrapped his hand around the barrel of the sheriff's pistol and shoved it to the side.

A moment later, the sheriff fell to the porch floor with a loud thud when another goon used the butt of his rifle to clout him from behind. Holding the side of his head, the sheriff moaned from the blow.

"Now, Sheriff Taylor," the toothy ruffian smirked, "get yourself up and step inside, and no harm will come to you or your deputy."

Reaching down and picking up the lawman's pistol from the floor, he escorted the wobbly sheriff into the jailhouse, a stream of blood running down the side of the sheriff's cheek.

"See if the jail cell keys are on either one of them," he said to the two men who followed them inside.

After checking the sheriff's and deputy's pockets, one of the mobsters exclaimed, "They ain't got no keys on 'em."

While holding the two lawmen at gunpoint, they tied each of them to chairs.

"You can't do this!" Taylor protested. "You can't take the law into your own hands. Leyer hasn't been tried!"

Pulling a handkerchief from his own pocket, the ringleader stuffed it into the sheriff's mouth, then bent down close to Taylor and whispered, "I say he's guilty. We *all* say he's guilty. And that murdering German is gonna' swing tonight."

Turning around to see his men dawdling and snickering amongst themselves, he snapped, "Now find those keys, you idiots!"

As the goons began ransacking the sheriff's office, violently pulling drawers out and dumping them on the floor, he and the men holding sledgehammers rushed to the back room. With a nod from their apparent boss, the brawny men started hammering the hinges on the outer door leading to the prisoners' cell.

Hearing the commotion and what was being said just beyond the door, all of the prisoners but one shared whispers and hopeful smiles among themselves, sensing their chance for escape fast approaching. But cowering on a bunk in the back of the cell hunched Edward Leyer.

"They're coming for me!" he yelled to the others.

Instead of surrounding him for protection, the men in the cell separated, giving Edward a clear view of the cell door.

Pulling his right leg toward himself, he fumbled in his boot for the pistol, keeping an eye on the cell door. Grasping the weapon's handle, he pulled it out and, holding it with both trembling hands, kept the barrel aimed at the cell door, as he scooted back on his bunk until he was tightly pressing his back up against the wall.

"Don't let them take me!" he screamed at his cellmates.

But they ignored his pleas, given they were too engrossed in the riotous frenzy just beyond the outer cell door.

Edward closed his eyes and prayed, *My God, I have not been a perfect man, and I ask for your forgiveness for my transgressions. Please allow me your mercy. Please help me, dear Lord.*

Seconds later, he heard the outer cell door come crashing down, followed by clamoring men rushing the short hallway leading to the prisoners' cell, an oncoming storm of hollering and cursing.

Upon seeing the number of bloodthirsty brutes surging through the doorway and gathering outside the cell, Edward—recognizing his six bullets were no match against this horde—vaulted from the bunk, grabbed Stamp by his collar and begged him, "Kill me, please! Don't let them take me! Please shoot me!"

Pushing the pistol into Stamp's hand, he backed up to give him a clear shot.

With the other prisoners adding to the fury by cheering the mob on, Stamp, dumbfounded by Edward's request, held the pistol loosely in his hand and then glanced up at the German with a terrified expression.

"What are you waiting for? Shoot me! Shoot me now!"

"I can't!" Stamp yelled back, the gun wobbling weakly in his hand. "I'm a thief, not a murderer!"

Dropping the gun on the floor, he backed away from it.

Edward picked up the pistol and ran toward the wall at the back of the cell. Spinning around, he once again held the gun up and pointed it at the cell door, which was being sledgehammered by two of the masked men.

"Please forgive me, Lord," he whispered, as he pulled the hammer back on the pistol.

At the sound of the second of three hinges breaking loose, a shot rang out above the heads of the vigilantes.

Suddenly, the yelling and hammering stopped, as all eyes turned to the small woman standing outside the fallen door, resting a rifle on her hip.

"You gotta' leave, little lady!" one of the bruisers holding a sledgehammer yelled. "This ain't no place for a woman!"

"I am Anita Taylor, Sheriff Taylor's wife. All of you men are under arrest for assaulting the town sheriff and destroying public property. Lay down your weapons and those sledgehammers, or my next shot won't go over your heads!"

"We have no quarrel with you, Mrs. Taylor," the toothy mob leader replied, pushing his way toward her through the crowded room. "We just want justice."

"Yeah, all we wanted was the key, so we could take the murdering Dutchman out and show him some American justice," added a short, plump man who was inexplicably waving his hands in the air.

"You want the key?" she laughed, pulling her husband's keys from her pocket and holding them high. "Which of you are stupid enough to assault the sheriff's wife to take them from me?"

As she stared down the crowd of ruffians, Mrs. Taylor dropped the keys into her cleavage, allowing them to fall into her corset. Smiling wryly, she readjusted the rifle on her hip and stood firm.

Angered by her smug challenge, one of the burly men with a sledgehammer raised it in the air and demanded, "Give me the keys, woman!"

"Back away!" warned the black-faced ringleader, stepping between the sheriff's wife and the man. "Now, if you don't mind, Mrs. Taylor, the keys, please. And don't think I'll hesitate to retrieve them."

Moving in closer to her, he studied her face, while flashing a sly smile and holding out his hand.

Without budging, she smiled back and aimed the shotgun squarely at his chest. Seemingly out of nowhere, Deputy Campbell rushed up beside her, brandishing two pistols in front of him. Pointing them directly at the ringleader's heart, he demanded, "You and your men lower your weapons, or by God, my first bullet will be yours!"

Slowly, the leader stood down, and with a nod of his head, the others in the room lowered their guns. As both the deputy and Mrs. Taylor motioned with their guns to the doorway, the mob members slowly retreated to the street, mumbling amongst themselves as they exited the jail.

The prisoners stood motionless and silent at the bars of the cell, watching the men leave and their hopes for escape vanish. Edward collapsed on his bunk at the back of the jail cell, dropping his pistol on the blanket.

Outside the jail, the armed citizens of Boonville had encircled those of the mob who remained after over half of their numbers had already fled. Two well-spoken, literate men, William Swint of *The Enquirer*, and John Nester, the town auditor, stood at the top of the jailhouse steps.

Mr. Nester raised his hands to quiet the crowd before shouting, "This past July, this country celebrated one hundred years as a sovereign nation. We believe in justice for *all*. You men before me, who hide behind masked faces, are trying to set us back two hundred years, to a time when every argument had only one side, and punishment was decided by the majority!"

Suddenly, a single shot fired into the air from the center of the mob, and a man yelled back, "Murder is murder! Give us the prisoner and we'll show you what real justice looks like!"

Mr. Swint stepped next to Mr. Nester to respond, "The law is not built on 'an eye for an eye.' Every man deserves his day in court, and *the court* will decide guilt or innocence. *The court* will decide a man's fate. Each and every one of you have taken an oath to this nation to uphold her laws." Pointing at the noose, still hanging from the tree across the street, he continued, "If anyone hangs tonight, then every one of you will be arrested, charged and tried for murder. I hope you brought a hundred more ropes, because we're gonna' need em'!"

Eventually, the two men's resolute insistence persuaded the mob to get on their horses and into their wagons and leave town.

The following morning, still aching from his head injury, Sheriff Taylor kissed his wife goodbye and left on the 9 o'clock train for Evansville, where he was to transport the following named prisoners for safekeeping—delivering them into the custody of Sheriff Wunderlich of Vanderburgh County—until the court convened: Edward Leyer, Robert Bonner, Tom Lennert, Samuel Baker, John Curry, and Bub Vandever. They were hurried out of Boonville, the train making a through run to circumvent the notion that some of the mob would make an attempt to board the train, in hopes of retrieving Edward Leyer and lynching him themselves.

As he sat in the dusty boxcar of the train, shackled with other prisoners, Edward closed his eyes and began to reminisce. *How long has it been since I've known the warmth and love of my family, the smiles and laughter we shared? How I yearn to be sitting next to a cozy fire while Helena reads stories to the children. I miss the farm, the fresh smell of golden hay, the sweet perfume of the honeysuckle that bloomed on the pasture fence, and the twittering of the barn swallows as they circled and frolicked overhead on a warm summer evening. I remember the day I stood in my field, leaning against the scythe after a long day of cutting wheat, watching the setting sun.*

Suddenly, the train jarred to a stop in front of the Evansville, Indiana station, rudely rousing Edward from his thoughts. *My God*, he prayed. *What's to become of me?*

Part 2

The Trial

My life and liberty are on trial. These English don't understand my ways. I struggle to master their language. I am an outcast, spurned by everyone except my wife and children, who I love dearly. Everything I have worked for is going to lawyers who must prove that I deserve to live.

- Edward Leyer

Chapter 17

THE HUSBAND'S TESTIMONY.

First Day of the Warrick County Poisoning Case.

Cook on the Stand—The Family Physician's Testimony—Foreshadowing the Line of Defense.

Two competing newspapers, *The Evansville Courier and Press*, and *The Evansville Daily Journal*, followed the Leyer case with much intrigue, each edition conveying the day's court proceedings, followed by another.

The case of the State of Indiana against Edward Leyer and Herman Leyer of Warrick County was called for trial in the criminal court on Tuesday, March 20, 1877, and all parties announced themselves ready. Leyer was charged with poisoning a cistern in the yard of Frederick Cook of Greer Township, near Boonville, from the effects of which Mrs. Elizabeth Cook died. The indictment, returned by the Grand Jury of Warrick County, charged him with murder in the first degree. The defendant entered a plea of *not guilty*. Promptly, at the judge's behest, the bailiffs began to impanel a jury, but this required time and labor, and it was not until about one hundred men had been called that a jury of twelve men was found from the outer townships who had read no newspaper accounts of it and formed no opinion of the case. Accordingly, the case was adjourned till the next morning at nine o'clock, at which time the trial would commence.

***

Compared to most cases in Vanderburgh County, there was an imposing array of counsel on either side. The State was represented by prosecuting attorney James Hodson and Messrs. E. R. Hatfield and Curran DeBruler, while the defendant's counsel was Judge Isaac Moore of Boonville, Gen. James Shackelford, Mr. John C. Richardson, and Col. Victor Bisch, all of Evansville.

After three hours of verbally challenging the morals and ethics of prospective jurors and the rejection of thirty persons, a successful panel was obtained. At 5 o'clock, the jury members were sworn in by Clerk Welborn "to well and truly try the cause."

There hadn't been a case of murder in the first degree in Vanderburgh County, Indiana since 1871, that being the trial and execution of Ben Sawyer. In addition to the usual form of questions propounded to jurors at the hearing before their acceptance, each was also asked whether or not, *if* the State was successful in their case of murder in the first degree, the juror had any objection to inflicting the death penalty. To this, there were several prompt responses on the part of jurors who were opposed to the death penalty.

When the jury was eventually sworn in, Judge Hargrave spoke directly to the panel: "Gentlemen, the indictment charges Edward Leyer and his son, Herman Leyer, with the crime of poisoning, but Herman eluded the officers after his father's arrest and has not been seen or heard of since. Owing to the importance of this case, and for your protection, you will not be allowed to separate and, at the adjournment of court each day, you will be placed under the charge of a bailiff."

Then the court announced it was ready to proceed with the case of *The State of Indiana vs. Edward Leyer and Herman Leyer.*

On Wednesday, March 21st, 1877, testimony began. Among the spectators was the entire faculty of the Evansville Medical College, demonstrating their keen interest, as Dr. Frederick W. Achilles, professor of chemistry, made the analysis of the poison. Every seat in the court room was occupied and the walls were blanketed with bystanders. In fact, per *The Evansville Courier and Press*, it was reported the attendance was so large in the afternoon that when court opened, the prisoner and his counsel could scarcely elbow through the crowd in the aisles.

On this first day, the counsel on both sides was present in full, and Leyer, the accused, sat quietly with his lawyers.

Judge Hargrave called the court to order and gave a special appeal to the jurors: "Gentlemen, this case will demand your undivided attention, and so I implore you to look past the counsel for the defense to focus on the evidence. You will be witness to the best litigators this state has to offer on both sides, but I wish to single out one man for his past accomplishments. Gen. James Shackelford's contribution to the war effort is well documented, and we are grateful for his service to our country. But in this case, and in my courtroom, you will see him not as a war hero, but as a respected attorney representing a man whose life and liberty are at stake."

Gen. Shackelford partially rose to address the judge, "Thank you, Your Honor."

Turning to Mr. Hatfield, the judge set the trial in motion. "You may proceed, counsel."

The opening statement for the prosecution was made by E. R. Hatfield, Esq., who, in addition to other statements, explained, "Gentlemen, it is my job to present to you, in clear and concise terms, the circumstances of this case. Before you sits a man who has committed such a heinous, despicable, loathsome crime that I can scarcely consider him a man at all. Over the course of this trial, I intend to prove that Edward Leyer had made continuous threats against his neighbor, Frederick Cook, while laboring under a fixed idea that Cook had wronged him. These threats of revenge were carried out in the poisoning of his wife and children during his absence."

Frederick Cook, a farmer aged 30 years old, with a red mustache and imperial, was the first witness called for the State. According to reports, Cook's answers were given in low tones, and his manner was composed and firm. Given Hatfield's line of questioning went into great detail, the prosecutor kept him on the stand for roughly four hours, starting at 11 A.M. and finishing at 4 P.M., with an hour's recess at noon.

In the course of his cross-examination, Cook was asked by Gen. Shackelford whether he, in conspiracy with other citizens of Warrick County, in disguise and armed with deadly weapons, made an attempt on the life of Edward Leyer, while the latter was confined in the Boonville Jail.

Prosecutor Hatfield immediately spoke up, "Objection, Your Honor. The alleged Boonville mob has no relevance to this trial. If the Defense wishes to hunt down and bring to justice men who may or may not have sought vengeance in Boonville, then he should open a new case. Even if the witness were one of the mob, the perpetration of one criminal act would not affect the reputation of the witness for veracity."

Judge Hargrave turned his attention to the Defense, at which point Gen. Shackelford rebutted, "Your Honor, if any witness in this trial was involved in an attempted lynching of my client, I believe the jury has the right to consider that witness's testimony hostile in the least, and at most, vengeful. The question was asked to develop the fact that Cook had threatened to kill Leyer after the alleged poisoning, law or no law."

Judge Hargrave pondered both men's arguments for a few moments before banging his gavel and saying, "I'm going to overrule the objection and allow the question. However, no witness during the course of this trial will be required to answer any question that would in any way tend to criminate him."

The judge then instructed Mr. Cook to answer the question, or not, as he pleased.

Looking over to the prosecutor, who was already making eye contact and shaking his head, indicating he should refrain, Cook then answered, "I decline to answer it."

The ensuing questions were as follows:

Gen. Shackelford –

"Have you not entered into a conspiracy or confederation with other persons in Warrick County, Indiana, to take the life of the prisoner, Edward Leyer; and in conformity with said conspiracy, did you not on or about December 9th, go to his house in said county, in company with such persons, all in disguise?"

Cook –

"I decline to answer."

Gen. Shackelford –

"In pursuance of said conspiracy and confederation to take the life of said Edward Leyer, did you not on or about the 21st day of December 1876, go to the county jail at Boonville, Indiana, where said defendant was confined, in company with other persons in disguise, and attempt to break down the jail doors, to take said Leyer out for the purpose of hanging him?"

Cook –

"I shall not answer it."

Gen. Shackelford –

"Were you not present as one of the mob, both at the house of Leyer on or about the 9th of December, 1876, and at Boonville about the 21st of December, 1876, who had gone to each of said places, for the purpose of hanging or killing the prisoner, Edward Leyer; and did you not go each time in the night; and were not said mob, including yourself, disguised, by having your faces blackened, and otherwise; and were you, and those associated with you, armed with pistols, guns, clubs and other weapons?"

Cook –

"I shan't answer that question."

Upon the asking of each of these questions by Gen. Shackelford, along with his incriminating tone, a considerable stir was caused in the courtroom. The witness, however, maintained a formal tone of exactness, and his answers were given decidedly and curtly.

Following Fred Cook's testimony, Dr. Charles J. Keegan was called to the stand, at which time he gave testimony to the condition of Mrs. Cook during her final hours, as well as his discovery of arsenic in the cistern, the effects of which he believed had sickened both her and the Cook's children.

Chapter 18

IS HE A BORGIA ?

Two men stood by a door upon which the name "E. R. Hatfield, Esq." was painted on the opaque glass. As Mr. Hatfield returned to his office following the first day of testimony, he was formally greeted by one of the men. "Mr. Hatfield, sir?"

"I haven't the time or the energy, gentlemen. Come back some other day."

"Mr. Hatfield, sir, my name is J. D. Carmody."

"And I'm T. W. Venemann," the second man added.

"As I said, gentlemen, I've had a long day and wish only to retire to my home and family."

"It's concerning the prisoner, Edward Leyer," Carmody declared.

Hatfield stood for a moment, contemplating the men's intentions. Finally, he unlocked the door to his office and said, "Come through."

After entering the office, Hatfield settled behind his cluttered desk, stacks of books and papers in twisted, chaotic piles spread across its substantial length and breadth. As he sat down, the attorney added a handful of new folders from the day's hearing to one of the mounds.

Instructing the men to pull up two chairs to the opposite side of the desk, they did so and sat at a level from which they could barely see Mr. Hatfield over the numerous case files.

"Mr. Venemann and I," Carmody began, "were on a coroner's jury here in Evansville in 1867, when strong suspicions rested on Edward Leyer."

Hatfield sat higher in his chair, craning his neck to better view his guests. "Go on."

"Yes, sir. Well, I read in the paper that a trial commenced this morning and the defendant is Edward Leyer. We thought you ought to know Mr. Leyer does not hold a favorable reputation in this town, at least with those of us who had crossed his path some years before. You see, sir, back in 1865, a young bachelor named Christian Mauck was keeping a file shop in Lamasco, across from Setchell's stable next to Leyer's residence, and they became acquainted. Mauck was a man aged 38 who was alone in the world, with no relatives nearer than Germany. However, he was a Christian and a church member, a steady, industrious and exemplary man in his manner of life. And being a regular attendant at church, he told a number of acquaintances he had saved some $600 or $700, which he had secreted at home, and had made a will bequeathing it all to his relatives in Germany."

Taking even greater notice of what the man before him was saying, Hatfield leaned forward in his chair, folded his arms tightly across his chest and nodded.

"The fact is, sir, Leyer persuaded this man to join him in a partnership, and they began working together. Time passed, and Mauck eventually went to Leyer's to board and took up his residence there. After a while, he told the superintendent of his Sunday school he believed Leyer was trying to poison him, given he was prone to vomiting every time he ate food brought to him by Mr. Leyer. Mauck was soothed and persuaded against this by some of the parishioners, there being no idea such a crime would be attempted in our late civilization. But according to his pastor, his uneasiness never disappeared, and at last, he took ill. The sickness lasted for several days and grew more severe, and he died suddenly one night in horrible pain. When the friends went to view the body the next day, they laid him out in a respectable suit of clothes and prepared him for the grave. He was buried early the next morning."

"If I may add something, sir," Venemann said. "As soon as Mauck was underground, rumors of his concealed savings spread, and his close friends began searching the house for the money and his will. They found neither, and suspicion took form as to the manner of his death and the disappearance of his savings. A complaint was made to the coroner on the grounds that Leyer must have caused his death, appropriated the money and destroyed the will. After the body had been buried a week, it was exhumed, and the corpse was discovered in a *common shirt and drawers*. The dead man had been robbed of his grave clothes! The grave and coffin gave no evidence of having been tampered with, so the robbery of the corpse's clothes *must* have been perpetrated before it was buried."

"Was a search made of Mr. Leyer's home for the burial clothes?" Hatfield asked.

"None that was mentioned to us on the jury," Venemann said, before continuing. "Dr. H. W. Cloud made a chemical analysis of the stomach and found in it a trace, a shadow of something, which he was inclined to think was poison. But as a conscientious chemist, Dr. Cloud told the jury he was not entirely satisfied with the result. He explained to us the spot approached nearer the resemblance of arsenic than anything else. In the absence of *indisputable* proof, however, the jury found Mauck came to his death by means unknown to them, and the body was reinterred. The suspicion was allowed to die out. There was no direct interest in Mauck, no intimate friends to prosecute the investigation, and the mystery was not cleared. That suspicion, however, remained with Edward Leyer."

"Are there others who would corroborate your story?" Hatfield asked.

"Oh, yes, sir, besides which, what I've described to you is of public record," Carmody said. He added, "Leyer promptly took over the file shop. And since then, I heard of another tale involving Edward Leyer. Several years after Mauck's death, Leyer's file shop was moved to another neighborhood in Lamasco, on the block where Kappler & Salmon's planning mill burned in 1871. While living there, a young shoemaker boarded with him, and the boy stated to several persons he had saved several hundred dollars, which he kept at home. Unfortunately, I can't recall his name.

"One night, the planning mill, Leyer's house and several other buildings were destroyed by fire. It was mysterious and nobody could ever discover the cause of the fire. The next day, a number of boys digging around the ruins discovered the charred remains of a body. Leyer said it was the body of his dog. It was so mutilated that it was necessary to have the coroner thoroughly examine it. Well, it was finally identified as the body of the young shoemaker. Leyer had not mentioned this fellow's disappearance, but acquaintances then remembered the boy had not been seen for several days before the fire. There was *again* suspicion the boy had been foully dealt with. The burning of the house swept away all claims for the money he had saved, as it was, of course, burned with the rest of the contents, if it indeed had existed at all."

"I'm afraid, gentlemen," Hatfield explained, "this all falls under *hearsay* if no hard evidence can be provided."

"But there's more, sir," Venemann said. "After all these occurrences, Leyer became keeper of the County Pestilence House some six or seven years ago. He and his wife cared for the sick and dying. While he occupied the position, the ugliest and most repulsive rumors about his manner of conducting it ran rampant. It was reported that patients sent there with fine clothes and valuables were received, but rather quickly died, and Leyer fell heir to what was left. If true, Mr. Hatfield, this man would be the most despicable vermin to ever walk the earth."

"Was Leyer ever held accountable for confiscation of these personal belongings?"

"Not to my knowledge," Venemann said, "But surely these accusations can't all be coincidences. And now, to read that an unfortunate soul has fallen victim to a crime that mimics the death of Mauck, and that Edward Leyer once again stands accused is what brought us to your doorstep. Somehow, this man invites suspicion, but dodges judgment at every turn."

"It was curious to us," Carmody concluded, "that Leyer, who had before that time been regarded as an impoverished man, subsequently seemed to have a fair amount of money and purchased a farm in Warrick County. So I was *not* surprised to read a mob had set out to lynch him. Truth be told, a similar incident occurred in our fair city, which served to drive him from our town."

Hatfield stood from behind his desk and studied the men once more. "Gentlemen, I want to thank you for sharing this with me. All too often, this sort of information is brought to light after a trial's conclusion. By bringing such matters to me now, I have a new appreciation for the man and his alleged crimes. I want to assure you I will do everything in my power to see justice is finally served and Edward Leyer never again darkens our streets or terrorizes our citizens. I can't say his past is admissible evidence, but you have convinced me he does not deserve the benefit of the doubt in these proceedings."

Hatfield sat behind his desk and shuffled some papers before pausing. Then, after folding his arms and leaning back in his chair, he concluded, "I believe Leyer to be a Borgia."

"A Borgia?" Carmody asked. "Begging your pardon, sir?"

Hatfield cleared his throat, "A number of years ago when I was studying cases of poisonings, I came across an article where a man who poisoned friends for monetary gain was compared to a 'Borgia.' The article went on to explain; Borgia is the family name of a scandalous Italian family that lived in the 1400s. They used arsenic to poison friends and neighbors to gain wealth. A *Borgia*, gentlemen."

Chapter 19

THE LAY OF LEYER.

Second Day of the Warrick County Poisoning Case.

On Thursday, March 22, 1877, the Evansville criminal court was crowded again, as testimony in Edward Leyer's trial continued and news about the trial spread like wildfire throughout the town.

The following is an abstract of the day's evidence:

Dr. Thomas Smith testified he'd attended Mrs. Cook during her last illness and believed her symptoms were consistent with those induced by an irritant poison.

Elisha Madden testified Edward Leyer had told him Fred Cook had poisoned his horses and, in response, he'd drug the colt close to Cook's home, so, he reported Leyer had said, "the scoundrel could get the stink of it."

D. W. Thompson, Tabitha Thompson, Luther Stateler, William Keifer, Susan Keifer, Robert Butcher and Eliza Butcher all testified they had been at Fred Cook's during his wife's illness and had become sick after drinking water from their cistern.

Edward Haddenbruck, who for more than a year had lived with the prisoner's family, was next introduced and testified at great length. During his nearly two hours of testimony, Haddenbruck described Leyer's plot to procure arsenic through his son, Herman, and also explained his own willingness to leave with the men whose faces were blackened, on the night the mob came to the Leyer farm.

Julia Haywood testified she'd witnessed Edward and Herman Leyer walking on the lane near Cook's farm on the 19th of November, the date of the suspected poisoning.

Harrison G. Christmas testified he had seen some white marks on the curbing and puncheon (wooden frame) of the cistern, while visiting Mrs. Cook during her illness. These same white marks were later tested by Dr. Keegan and determined to be arsenic.

John J. Criswell, William Thene, Henry Flock and Henry Sanders testified to their knowledge of and exposure to the ongoing feud between Edward Leyer and Fred Cook. In addition, the witnesses, upon cross-examination, stated the symptoms of arsenical poisoning had been described to them by Fred Cook, and each one in giving their testimony was very accurate and consistent in detail in describing the symptoms of those who had drunk the water.

The proceedings were then closed for the day, with the court charging the jury to maintain an impartial frame of mind, as they were adjourned until 9 o'clock the next morning.

Chapter 20

How the Deed Was Done.

ONE DAY OF EXCITING TESTIMONY IN THE LEYER CASE.

Two Fellow-Prisoners Relate an Alleged Confession of Leyer While Confined in the Boonville Jail—That He Put the Poison in the Well — Increasing Interest in the Case.

On Friday, March 23rd, the crowd in the courtroom was so great at times, there was no access to or egress from the room. A local reporter observed the bar was filled with lawyers, doctors and ministers. And yet, though the delivery of the day's testimony at times caused some sensation, usually the proceedings were quiet, broken only by short episodes between the opposing counsel and the court.

Samuel Feagley, William West, Henry Cruise, Charles B. Thiel and Joseph H. Flack testified to their conversations with Edward Leyer concerning the killing of his hogs and poisoning of his horses. All men claimed to have heard Leyer threaten to have his revenge on Fred Cook.

John Pilkington, Ebenezer Day, Joseph Cook, Richard Gaffney, Mark Benton and Simon Flack affirmed they were present when Mrs. Cook's body was exhumed. All identified the body.

Next on the stand were William T. Vandever and Hezekiah "Stamp" Wellington, who were in the Boonville jail during Edward Leyer's incarceration. Both men maintained he had confessed to poisoning Fred Cook's cistern.

Under oath, Vandever stated, "Leyer and I were sitting up one night. All the rest were in bed. I was sitting on a table when he brought up his chair. He told me Fred Cook had poisoned his horses and thrown down his fences, and that his son, Herman Leyer, got five cents' worth of arsenic at three different places, plus they had some at home, and that he and Herman slipped out one night between 1 and 2 o'clock and pitched the arsenic into Cook's cistern. Leyer said he wasn't strong enough to fight Fred Cook, so this was the only way he could get his revenge. He also stated if Cook had ever come into his yard, he would have shot him. Leyer also said that was not the first person he'd ever poisoned."

Upon taking the stand, Wellington made a similar statement: "Edward Leyer told me he bought fifteen cents' worth of the poison in Evansville at three different places and had ten cents' worth left of that, which he had at home to give his horse for distemper. He said he did it because Cook did him dirt, poisoned his horses and threw down his fencing, and added he put the poison in their cistern at night, but didn't say exactly at what hour. I remember him telling me he put it in and expected to poison the *whole* family."

Sheriff Gurley Taylor, of Boonville, testified he had received a letter, purportedly written by the co-defendant, Herman Leyer, confessing to poisoning the Cook's cistern and exonerating his family, including his father, Edward Leyer. The prosecutor handed the letter to the bailiff, in order that it be entered as evidence.

Sarah Lacefield, the servant hired by Fred Cook after he'd come back and found his wife sick, gave her statement as to the effects of the cistern water; that is, it made her sick upon drinking from it.

Ben McCool established a link in the boy Ed Haddenbruck's testimony by corroborating that he had told Edward Leyer of Mrs. Cook's death the next day, and Leyer said he had not heard of her illness. McCool said Leyer strongly emphasized to him he was "*a friend to his friends and an enemy to his enemies.*"

Frank Morris testified to his purchase of the Leyer farm in December of 1876 for $1,950.

Joseph Welt was called to the stand, sworn in and declared, "I thought Leyer's farm was worth from $2000 to $2400," which the prosecutor pointed out underscored Edward Leyer's desperation to sell the farm and leave Warrick County, following Mrs. Cook's death.

William P. Hedges followed Mr. Welt in his testimony, stating he thought the farm was worth $2400, adding he, too, was at Fred Cook's home on the Sunday when Mrs. Cook drank water from the cistern and became sick.

At day's end, the jury was committed to the bailiff until 9 o'clock the following morning.

Chapter 21

LEYER AND THE LAWYERS.

Fourth Day of the Warrick County Poisoning Case.

Testimony of the Chemist Dr. Achilles—Searching for Arsenic.

Was Cook's Wife Poisoned?

To the majority of people in attendance, given this particular trial centered around a poisoning death, Saturday, March 24th was a significant day. The testimony of Dr. F. W. Achilles, Professor of Chemistry at Evansville Medical College, occupied both much of the day and the attention of the jury, as well as those present in the gallery. According to a local reporter, Dr. Achilles enjoyed a high reputation as a skilled chemist, and his expert testimony was deemed valuable by his colleagues and the court. Per *The Evansville Journal*, Dr. Achilles, had analyzed the various substances he'd received for the purpose of ascertaining their possible relation to the death of Mrs. Cook, and showed up on the 24th prepared to testify as to his findings.

Dr. F. W. Achilles injected significant scientific findings into the proceedings, laying out the steps he'd taken and details about the analysis he'd performed regarding the water, mud and bark taken from the cistern, as well as the body tissues taken from the deceased.

"As a chemist," he said, "I'm satisfied there was arsenic in the water and mud from the bottom of the cistern, which Fred Cook brought to me to be analyzed, and also in the piece of bark given me by Dr. Keegan. I next analyzed one half of the viscera and half of the portion of the liver I took from the exhumed body. I applied the sulphuretted hydrogen test first. That test found no arsenic. I then applied Marsh's test. From those results, I would say there was no arsenic in the stomach."

Throughout Dr. Achilles' lengthy responses and presentation of various tests and subsequent results, the defendant appeared impassive and unmoved. He occasionally leaned over to whisper to his attorney, but his eyes were usually fixed upon the chemist testifying.

The prosecuting witness, Fred Cook, was always present and also seemed to narrowly watch Dr. Achilles's testimony.

The examination of Dr. Achilles began at ten minutes past 10 in the morning and was closed at half-past 4 in the afternoon.

When called to testify following Dr. Achilles, Mrs. Mary Lippert, a nearby neighbor of the defendant, relayed to the court and jury, "Edward Leyer came to our house to return a saddle after Mrs. Cook died. He asked if we had been over to the Cook's. I said we would get troubled from her death. He asked why, and I replied somebody had poisoned the cistern. He said that was too bad, then added nobody would do that. I told him anyone who would poison a woman and her children ought to be hung up by the feet. He looked pale and was sweating in the face. I saw a drop of sweat fall to the floor. He then left."

Henry Lippert followed the testimony of his wife by saying, "I was at Leyer's house at harvest time in August. We cut wheat in July and August. I borrowed some arsenic from him to kill rats with."

The case was adjourned till Monday morning, with the jury being ushered out to their quarters by the bailiffs.

Chapter 22

THE OTHER SIDE.

What the Defense Have to say for Leyer the Accused Poisoner.

Fourth Day of the Warrick County Poisoning Case.—Testimony as to the Boonville Mob.

The murder trial of Edward Leyer continued on Monday, March 26th, and began promptly at 9:00 A.M. Four doctors, Dr. William S. Pollard, Dr. W. B. Rose, Dr. George P. Cosby and Dr. E. C. Linthicum, all testified for the prosecution in the forenoon. In substance, their testimonies stated that, given the symptoms exhibited by Mrs. Cook during her illness, they would suspect arsenical poisoning as the cause of death.

After a recalled testimony from Fred Cook, the prosecution rested, and the court adjourned at 11:45 A.M. until 2 P.M. At that time, the court reconvened, with the usual large crowd in the chamber.

The afternoon session was marked by the opening of the defense.

One of the defendant's attorneys, Judge Isaac Moore of Boonville, made the opening statement for the defense. "Gentlemen of the jury, we of the defense intend to show Edward Leyer's situation in Greer Township, where he was a comparative stranger and friendless. He was entirely surrounded by the

Butcher family, that of Elizabeth Cook, who were interrelated with every family in the township and were wealthy and influential. The mere suspicion that Leyer had poisoned Mrs. Cook was sufficient to arouse intense feelings against the accused. And this accusation took the form of a deep desire and intention to take Leyer's life in revenge for her untimely death. First, it developed into an attempt by mob violence, then at the examining trial by prejudiced evidence. Again, mob violence at the jail, and now this effort has intensified in this trial. Evidence lacking at the preliminary examination has been suddenly discovered and put forward by men who refuse to swear they have not committed themselves to taking Leyer's life.

"To explain the situation in clear, the Cooks draw their water not from a modern, deep well fed by fresh underground streams, but their water source is an antiquated *cistern*, which is a shallow hole in the ground. The sides of the cistern are of stone, through which tree roots readily grow. The bottom of the cistern is comprised of mud and pebbles. Mr. Cook has readily admitted to keeping live fish in the water, from which the family drank. In short, the cistern is little more than a pond, the likes of which horses and cattle would otherwise drink. If you plan to partake from a cistern, it is commonly known it needs to be drained and cleaned periodically, or else you risk the growth of bacteria, unfit for human consumption.

"The prosecution has proven arsenic was found in the cistern, but they have not established any connection between Edward Leyer and the poison. Most concerning is that, by their own medical professional's testimony, the prosecution has established arsenic was *not* detected in the deceased. Arsenic is a naturally occurring mineral. Again, I say this, gentlemen… arsenic is *naturally occurring* and can be found in both plants and earth. Therefore, it is not surprising that traces of arsenic would be detected in the stagnant water of a cistern.

"The only positive testimony on the point was that of the two convicts brought from Jeffersonville, who stated in their evidence Edward Leyer had confessed the crime to them while in jail at Boonville. This evidence cannot be credited, as we are prepared to impeach the testimony of the two men, both of whom are convicted criminals willing to perjure themselves for reasons we can only imagine.

"What you are about to witness is the defense, in this case, discrediting all of the State's testimony. The innocence of the defendant, Edward Leyer, is certain and absolute. We have no fear of the verdict."

Testimony for the defense was then introduced, an abstract of such is as follows:

William P. Hudson and George Roberts were both guards at the Boonville jail during the attempted lynching of Edward Leyer by a vigilante mob. Both offered similar testimony as to the events of the night, given they were both present when a mob of approximately 100 men rode up to the jail where Leyer was being held prisoner, with the expressed intent to hang him.

Rudolph Leyer, a young German who testified through an interpreter, stated he was also the prisoner's cousin and had lived with the defendant's family since June 4th, 1876. He began his testimony by stating he'd helped Edward by working on the farm, and then directly contradicted the story told by Ed Haddenbruck in every particular.

At the conclusion of Rudolph Leyer's testimony, the court adjourned until the next morning at nine o'clock.

Chapter 23

WAS IT POISON?

That is the Question the Jurors in the Leyer Case are Expected to Answer.

Fifth Day's Proceedings—More of the Mob—Medical Testimony of Value to the Prisoner.

Per a report in *The Evansville Journal*, on the second day of the defense, Tuesday, March 27th, the testimony introduced by the medical community served to give hope to the defendant, Edward Leyer, although the prosecution didn't decrease in intensity any of its determination, and still clung to the prospect of proving the indictment. The most defined line of the defense, the article stated, was the attempt to prove, by medical testimony that Mrs. Cook did not die of poison. If she had, the poison would, necessarily, have been found in the tissues of her body, as analyzed by Dr. Achilles. His testimony was to the effect he *did* find in the stomach a shadow of a trace of arsenic, but that it was not a sufficient amount to satisfy him. Given the inconclusive test results, the chemist could not, in clear conscience, testify that the cause of Mrs. Cook's death was arsenic.

The medical testimony, in general, was that if the patient had taken arsenic for the number of days declared, then arsenic should have been found in the tissues. Only one physician testified that, in his opinion, it might be possible to consume arsenic without detecting its presence in the stomach. All concurred, however, the violent and horrific nature of Mrs. Cook's death, taken in consideration with those of others under the same influence, indicate, beyond a doubt, the death was caused by some sort of poison.

The testimony of Leyer's cousin, Rudolph, and the Leyer children, contradicted that of every witness for the prosecution.

That is, Mina Leyer, Eddy Leyer, Jr., and August Leyer gave similar testimonies to the events on the day of the suspected poisoning, which aligned with Rudolph's version *and* contradicted that of Edward Haddenbruck.

Five doctors, Dr. M. J. Bray, Dr. Daniel Morgan, Dr. A. M. Owen, Dr. J. F. Hillyard, and Dr. John Laval, all practicing medical professionals in the community, testified that if a person died from the effects of arsenical poisoning over the span of several days, arsenic would most definitely be detectable in the soft tissues of the victim's internal organs.

Dr. John Laval, Sr. a local druggist, stated during his testimony, "I know the defendant's wife and son, Herman, and sold them a memorandum of drugs. However, I sold them no arsenic."

Court adjourned till the next morning at nine o'clock.

***

After Edward Leyer was returned to his cell, Sheriff Wunderlich happened upon Col. Bisch as he was entering the jail. "Colonel, a moment, sir?"

"Sheriff," Col. Bisch replied as he stopped on the jail's front steps. "What's on your mind?"

"I know my position requires complete impartiality regarding the guilt or innocence of the prisoners in my charge, and I strive to maintain that frame of mind. But I wish to convey a unique observation regarding the prisoner Edward Leyer, if I may."

"Certainly, Sheriff, go on."

"Throughout the last 15 years, I have observed that a prisoner's behavior in jail is far more telling of his conscience than his behavior in court. They often let their guard down in the presence of other prisoners who may share a similar situation. One thing that is always true is a prisoner's wife knows his heart better than any judge or jury. I have seen wives visit their husbands for no purpose but to beat them senseless for their crimes. Other wives may not visit their husbands, even once. But never, in all my years, have I seen a wife and children as devoted and loving as Mrs. Leyer and their children have been upon their visits. His children have no fear of him, as evidenced by how they climb onto his lap and hug his neck. Their sincerity has not been, in my view, an act to gain sympathy during the trial. Since Leyer was brought here from Boonville, his wife and children have visited with him at least once a day. She brings his meals, clean clothes and any other personal items he's permitted to have. In fact, Mrs. Leyer is so regular in her visits, she's just as much a fixture around here as any of my deputies. I also understand from Sheriff Taylor she did the same in the Boonville jail. I don't know how the jury will decide the prisoner's fate, but I can state with absolute confidence Mrs. Leyer feels certain of his innocence. And believe me, it's much more difficult for a man to fool his wife than a juror."

Chapter 24

THE CASE CLOSED.

The Closing Evidence in the Warrick County Poisoning Case.

The Prisoner's Testimony—More Medical Experts on the Stand.

LEYER'S CHARACTER.

On Wednesday, March 28th, the trial of Edward Leyer, charged with poisoning the wife of Fred Cook of Warrick County, was resumed at 9:00 a.m. in the local jurisdiction's criminal courtroom. The gallery was crowded as usual, and according to a reporter for *The Evansville Journal*, all present seemed enrapt by the proceedings.

The following is a synopsis of the testimony taken, per *The Evansville Journal's* report on the trial:

Four more doctors were called to offer their opinions, which were similar to those from the previous day. Dr. W. S. Ross, Dr. J. W. Irwin, Dr. J. W. Compton and Dr. M. Muhlhausen all shared their testimony that arsenic would have been detected in Mrs. Cook's body by Dr. Achilles' tests, had she died from the effects of the poison.

Edward Leyer was then called to the stand, and when he took his seat, there was a hush of expectation, so much so that one could hear a pin drop from anywhere in the room. The prisoner scanned the whole of the room, his gaze passing from face to face, given all eyes were fixed upon him.

As Leyer gave his testimony, which was expectedly favorable to his innocence, he seemed composed and somber, even though he spoke English with difficulty. Holding a tone and manner congruent with sincerity, he denied all accusations, including the testimony of the two prisoners, Vandever and Wellington, who claimed to have received Leyer's confession during their shared time in the Boonville jail.

Fred Lauenstein, the proprietor of the German newspaper, *Demokrat*, was called to testify as to the attempt from Edward Leyer to sell his farm six months prior to Mrs. Cook's death.

"This is a file of a portion of the newspaper from May 2nd, 1876. The defendant advertised his farm for sale in the paper on that date. He paid for the advertisement to be inserted for three months and told me the reason for his wanting to sell was a desire to change his business."

When the defense announced they were through, the prosecution proceeded to introduce testimony aimed at impeaching the character of Edward Leyer.

Joseph Cook, Robert Butcher, George Brammer, David Miller, Christ Kanzler, Fred Brinkmeyer and Fred Lechner—each being either a neighbor of or somehow associated with Edward Leyer, through doing common business with him—all testified that Leyer's reputation for honesty "is poor," citing examples from their own experience with him.

Court adjourned until the next morning at nine o'clock.

***

After the day's proceedings, Helena and the Leyer children were allowed to visit Edward in his cell. "Give it to your father," Helena said to Mina, who was holding a wicker basket with a towel covering the contents.

Mina lifted the towel and handed a fresh roll to each of the three prisoners who shared the cell with Edward.

"Thank-ye, Miss," each man said upon receiving their gift, enchanted by the young girl's generosity.

"Here, Papa," she said, handing her father the basket with the remaining rolls.

"I have to get the children home for dinner, now," Helena told Edward. Standing up, she embraced him, while rubbing her hand up and down his back. "It won't be long now. You'll be home soon."

As the prisoners sat on cots in their cell devouring their rolls, they heard loud talking from the hallway. A moment later, a large black woman appeared outside their cell, clutching a bible against her chest with both hands, staring starkly at the inmates through the thick bars.

"Look alive, men," barked the guard who'd led her through the corridor. "You have a woman on the floor."

One of the prisoners who shared the cell with Edward laughed crudely and asked, "What'd she do to get thrown in here with the likes of us?"

"Public nuisance. We bring her in several times a year. Today, she walked into a saloon and smashed one whiskey bottle after another, while yelling bible verses at the patrons."

Standing outside Leyer's cell, she noticed the men enjoying the rolls, given to them by Mina, and began speaking loudly, "Lord God, see these sinners! They are partaking in the body of Jesus!" Then theatrically throwing her hands in the air and looking up to the heavens, she concluded, "Bless them, O Lord, bless these sinners!"

With that, she quieted and rested her dangling hands through the bars of Edward's cell, smiling strangely at him with a wildness in her eyes.

Stepping toward her, the guard said, "Okay, Margaret. Show's over. Let's get you to your cell."

Leyer looked at the remaining rolls in the basket and then back to the woman. "A moment, please," he called to the guard. Then, standing up slowly and shuffling his feet, he brought a roll to the cell bars and held it out to the woman, "Bread?" he offered with a slight smile.

Furrowing her brow, she glanced at the roll in his hand and then back at Edward's face, while the guard watched curiously. Cocking her head, she slowly took the roll from his hand and held it up to her nose, breathing in the freshly baked scent. A smile appeared on her face as she looked at Leyer and sang out, "Thank you, Brother. So in everything, do unto others what you would have them do unto you."

Edward stepped back a bit, surprised by her thunderous gratitude, but nonetheless gave the woman a slight nod.

The amused guard approached the pair and said, "Alright, Margaret, move along."

While being led to her lockup, three cells down from Edward's, she continued to shout, "For this sums up the Law and the Prophets! Lord, give me, Margaret Powell, your daughter in Jesus, your grace as I partake of this holy bread."

Taking a small nibble of the roll, she slowly moved her head from side to side with a look of heartfelt satisfaction upon her countenance.

Part 3

Circumstantial Evidence

They know I had no arsenic. They know the woman died with no poison in her body. Yet the prosecution is determined to prove me guilty of poisoning her with arsenic. I'm afraid.

- Edward Leyer

Chapter 25

The Leyer Case.

ELOQUENT ARGUMENTS OF COUNSEL.

Speeches of Messrs. Curran A. DeBruler and Victor Bisch.

When the criminal court opened the next morning, the room, both inside and out of the bar, was filled with an eager audience who came to hear the closing speeches of counsel – even the doorways and open windows of the room were packed with listeners. Court convened at half past 8 o'clock on Thursday, March 29th, with the prisoner, Edward Leyer, being promptly brought in, accompanied by his wife and children.

After calling court in session, Judge Hargrave outlined the proceedings. "Mr. Curran DeBruler will make the opening speech for the State and will be followed by Col. Victor Bisch for the prisoner. Gen. Shackelford will make the next speech for the defense, and Mr. Hatfield will close the case with a final argument for the State."

In his unsurprisingly lengthy summary, DeBruler's argument for the State occupied the entire morning till 11:50 in an almost uninterrupted monologue, marked by its eloquence and logic, mingled with both accusation and condolence:

"I wish to begin by congratulating the jury on the approaching close of their long confinement, and know the facts you have listened to must have convinced you, without the shadow of a doubt, of the defendant's guilt. When the lawyers have finished their arguments, the moment of supreme responsibility for each of you will have arrived, for you must then determine whether the defendant has evolved the shadow of a doubt. Doubt must be such as the testimony creates.

"I have no objection to the law which gives the defense the benefit of doubt, nor to a fair administration of justice. I simply desire that justice should be done. The jury has nothing to do with the consequences of a verdict. Their justice must be like God's justice, which invariably visits on the violator of His laws the penalty for the violation. Men should be taught they can no more evade man's justice than they can the justice of The Almighty.

"If we have reached that state when we can countenance such crimes as that of which the defendant is accused, we should also reach a state when juries will say, 'Just as sure as you commit such crimes, you shall meet the law's penalty.' The prosecution is here to plead for justice: for a desolated home, a murdered wife, for orphaned children deprived of her love and care, for a ruined husband whose life is made waste; and it is confidently hoped this appeal will be heard. The safety of all depends upon affixing the death penalty to murder, and the penalty is not as great as the crime."

DeBruler proposed to review the testimony in the case, and reason with the jury to show it led to the defendant's guilt. Before doing so, however, he offered to discuss a feature introduced by the defense intended to break the force of circumstances against Edward Leyer. "From all indications, the defense intends to depend upon the fact that there was a mob determined to lynch the prisoner; but the jury had nothing to do with that. We can review the actions of the mob until the cows come home, but I ask you, are you trying the mob? It was but a makeweight to divert the minds of the jury from the case – from the question of whether Leyer is guilty or not. Whether there was a mob or not does not illustrate any feature of the case being tried. The defense attempted to say those who would engage in such a mob would come into court and swear falsely.

"I will not attempt to apologize for the mob. On the contrary, I recognize the maintenance of society depends upon the maintenance of the law. The principle of the mob is wrong – always is wrong – but in times of great excitement, some of the best men have been carried away by it. Nevertheless, it does not thereby follow that because men may unite with a mob when their ire is aroused, they will come into court and commit deliberate perjury after all passion has subsided. Such an assumption is at war with common sense. The men who composed that mob were the best in that community, and to say they would deliberately commit perjury is absurd."

Mr. DeBruler painted a most descriptive picture of the home he concluded was ruined by Leyer, as well as the scene Fred Cook came upon when he returned from the hunt, finding his wife suffering the agonies produced by what was deemed to be poison. The experienced attorney also depicted in explicit detail the emotions the scene elicited—per witness testimony—and the effects it had upon those who either saw or heard about what had happened; and at this point he included those friends and associates of Fred Cook who formed the mob.

"Those people were not accustomed to think much about jurisprudence. But, seeing the devastation wrought by the prisoner, Edward Leyer, their wrath was triggered, indeed. And yes, it depends on every man to demonstrate not only the mob is wrong, for that is obvious, but that there is no necessity for it; for the mob rises from the idea that through some trick of the law, criminals escape justice.

"The defense said the State hoped to convict by the testimony of men who had banded together to take the defendant's life. It is not so, however. I would be willing to strike out the testimony of all who were engaged in that mob, and still, the evidence will prove Leyer's guilt. Of course, you should not expect to establish guilt by direct and positive testimony. Crimes like Leyer's are not committed in open daylight. The accused crept in the silent watches of the night when he thought there were none to see him, and with stealthy tread approached the depository of the poison with which he hoped to accomplish his awful crime."

Mr. DeBruler briefly mentioned Leyer's confession as testified by the Boonville prisoners, referring to it as merely a strand of steel that, when woven with other strands of evidence, forms an unbreakable chain.

"Those who heard the expert evidence must conclude Elizabeth Cook sleeps in her grave from drinking the water of the cistern. If he applies to this testimony the same tests as to other matters, he can lead to no other conclusion. It is of no avail to say men can be mistaken. All the testimony requires is to lead to a conclusion of guilt without a *reasonable* doubt, not without a *shadow* of a doubt."

He proceeded to read the indictment brought against Edward and Herman Leyer. "If you, the jury, should find that Mrs. Cook died by poison from drinking water from a cistern and that Leyer poisoned it, the guilt is established. As time went on, the other family members were stricken with symptoms like those the mother died of. The doctors know of no disease that will produce them. As the hours passed and more poison was taken up, nearly every person visiting the place was affected, according to the amount of poisoned water taken."

At this point, Mr. DeBruler's oration was interrupted by a singular voice from the street outside, "Hang the murderer!" This lone voice incited a chant on the road that spread into the court, "Hang him! Hang him!"

Judge Hargrave repeatedly banged his gavel and called for order, until the crowd was silent. "One more outburst like that, and I will clear this courtroom! There will be no lynching in my court. This man is on trial for his life and deserves a fair hearing and protection under the law."

Then, addressing the jury, he said, "I apologize to the jury for this interruption. You will disregard the sentiments of the crowd and give your complete attention to the council and evidence before you."

Turning once again to the courtroom and those on the outside, he declared, "Another interruption like this and I will declare a mistrial!" followed by a final hammering of his gavel. "My apologies to you, as well, Counsel. Please proceed."

Mr. DeBruler continued, "Mr. Cook's home became a pest house to the whole neighborhood. The symptoms were the same, all more or less indicated in those who were about the house and used the cistern's water. Can there be a doubt it was poisoned? Dr. Keegan seeing all stricken alike, concluded there was something wrong. What was it? He investigated the cistern, and there, upon one of the puncheons inside it, was the tell-tale spot with the arsenic, where Leyer, in his conscience-stricken nervousness and haste, had dropped it. Here, on this spot, lies the evidence of guilt that would not be obliterated, where Dr. Keegan, taking his knife, cut the bark from the puncheon, with the powder on it, made an examination and ascertained it to be arsenic.

"The defense put forth a supposition that someone may have tampered with the water or the mud taken from the cistern, or the fish taken from the poisoned water and consumed, while Mrs. Cook lay breathing her final breaths; but this would not apply to the bark Dr. Keegan had kept safe from all contamination. You will remember Dr. Keegan observed first-hand as Dr. Achilles applied the tests of his wonderful science to it and developed arsenic. The theory is that Mr. Cook poisoned the cistern himself or didn't take proper care of the water and the mud. But what is the *fair* presumption? No such assumption can stand when the bark is brought forward, for Dr. Achilles shows the presence of arsenic in it by a conclusion as accurate as a mathematical calculation.

"The picture given by the witness Statelier, of everyone vomiting at once, all their symptoms and the presence of arsenic, correspond to show conclusively that Leyer did as his confession stated: he put poison in the cistern to avenge himself against Cook, who he said had ruined him.

"You, gentlemen of the jury, were selected from different walks of life because you were only required to apply your common sense to the case, and to do so, you cannot avoid the conclusion that the cistern was poisoned, that Elizabeth Cook died from drinking water from it, and that Leyer put the poison there. The constant absorption of poison by the water strengthened it day by day, and everyone who drank the water became affected in the same way, presenting the same symptoms she developed.

"I have never seen the attempt to break the force of absolute facts succeed by quoting the jargon of books or by the theories of men who have studied a little, but have had no practical experience. Here are the facts: that the only source of water for this family was poisoned; that Mrs. Cook was poisoned; that the thirst begotten by the poison only led her to take more of the poisoned water, and day after day, the thirst growing and the cause increasing, her agony increased; and that not knowing what caused the thirst, she only drank more and more of the poison.

"Dr. Keegan did not pretend to be a very learned man, but his experience of twenty years and his common sense told him it was arsenical poison, and his evidence is not opinion; it is knowledge. All the professors who could conjure up theories cannot shake the fact of this seasoned man's experience.

"According to all the experts, the symptoms were of arsenical poisoning, and no other cause will produce all of them; no epidemic is known to them; no one else is stricken down. The defense argues that Dr. Achilles, who, three days after Mrs. Cook's death, examined a small portion of the remains submitted to analysis, and did not discover enough arsenic to enable him to swear positively as to its presence. Based upon this, they tried to make a break of it.

"Another doctor was introduced who said that after thirty days' death, arsenic should be discovered in the soft parts of the body. What is the opinion worth? It must be known what it is based upon. I hold the physician's profession in high esteem, but is a physician a chemist? Generally, he is not, and the question is not one for a physician, but for a chemist. One of the medical witnesses had never examined a case of arsenical poisoning and had never analyzed a stomach. Another thought he had a case of poisoning once, but the patient got well, and therefore no thorough examination could be made.

"These physicians, never having seen a stomach analyzed, got their information from books, and the same books said there were cases of poisoning where the stomach failed to disclose the presence of poison. Books are full of conflicting cases, and yet a defense has been sought here to be established on their theories. Dr. Muhlhausen said in a case of poisoning, the stomach after death would show the presence of poison. He got his information from books, yet one of the books he quoted showed a case where no poison was found. Dr. Bray doesn't believe half there is in books, yet the books are brought here as a foundation to build a defense."

Detecting a lull in the litigator's arguments, Judge Hargrave hit his gavel on the bench and said, "Let's take a 15 minute recess."

Recess

Following the recess, DeBruler then read aloud from T.R. Beck's *Elements of Medical Jurisprudence*, page 598, regarding a family in Scotland who ate poisoned porridge. One member took a hearty breakfast from it, another just a little, and the others as usual. The first died after seven days, but the others recovered. The stomach of the deceased showed equivocal signs, but none of the salt or milk used to make the porridge was analyzed. Still, a part of the stomach and duodenum was examined, and no trace of poison was found; yet a brother-in-law of the family subsequently confessed he had put arsenic in the salt that went into the porridge.

"Here is a parallel case to this," DeBruler gloated. "The one who partook most of the poison died, yet no poison was found in his stomach or duodenum. So the books show mixed results; and when physicians say they expect to find poison, they merely mean it will *probably* be found.

"In A.S. Taylor's *Principles and Practice of Medical Jurisprudence*, he says on page 155, 'If the person has lived fifteen or sixteen days, no trace of the poison may be found.' It also says it has been incorrectly impressed on the public mind that poison must be found in the stomach after death. According to Taylor, the amount found is no indication of the amount taken, because natural processes eliminate more or less. The terrible vomiting and purging prove that much or most of it is carried away, and, on the contrary, we have only the testimony of men who have gathered their only knowledge from books. Taylor, on page 156, says it has been sought for and not found in a short time after death, where all evidence pointed to it.

"How can anyone who has never looked within a stomach without firsthand knowledge, say how one dies of poison? This same book says the longer a person survives, the less likely poison will be found in the remains. And on page 307 of T.G. Wormley's book, *Micro-Chemistry of Poisons*, he states, when arsenic is taken, it is rapidly absorbed and, after a time, eliminated and thrown off in about fifteen days. He adds that, independent of this, the poison may be rapidly removed by vomiting and purging. In one case, which he cites as an example, the patient died eight days after taking poison, but none was found, although the man took more than two ounces. In another case, where death occurred a few days after taking arsenic, again none was found. The liver usually takes up much of it, he says, but it may be absent there and present elsewhere. In other words, gentlemen, *sometimes you find it, and sometimes you don't.*

"In this case, we have all the symptoms, all the circumstances and all the evidence of poisoning by arsenic. First, the defense put a hypothetical case to Dr. Bray, but left out an important part of the case, and Dr. Bray couldn't tell if poisoning would be evident. Then, the prosecution put forward the same case, but with all its details, symptoms and circumstances, and Dr. Bray said it was a case of arsenical poisoning.

"So, with many persons being stricken alike and no known causes producing all the symptoms, Dr. Bray concluded Mrs. Cook's cause of death was poisoning by arsenic. He did not say so because he is a doctor, but because he is a man of sense, of experience and of observation. After this answer, the defense wanted no more hypotheses. They could only make the most of it when Dr. Achilles said there was a faint trace of arsenic in the stomach and would not swear positively. This faint trace, this shadow, is a shadow of doom to Leyer, he who is accused of murder."

At this point, DeBruler turned to face Edward, staring at him silently with an accusatory look for a long few moments.

After then looking over to the jury, he continued, "Turning back to Beck's *Elements of Medical Jurisprudence*, on page 593, questions whether we are justified in concluding arsenical poisoning has occurred from symptoms alone. Beck thinks such a conclusion justifiable and quotes the distinguished Scottish toxicologist Dr. Robert Christianson, who advanced the same opinion.

"The prosecutor then reasoned from the Scottish case, where there was no evidence but the symptoms, but the symptoms brought the accused Scottish murderer to his demise. The physicians all say no disease produces all these symptoms at once. One physician who testified in the case thought there was such a disease, but could not name it.

"Back to the text by Wormley, on page 241, he says the symptoms are subject to great variation; yet Dr. Keegan found all the symptoms described. Those who saw Mrs. Cook, and their opinions are worth more than all others, know more than what the books tell them.

"Does it weigh against Dr. Keegan that he was mistaken and thought Mrs. Cook was better the day before she died? In *Wharton and Stille's Medical Jurisprudence*, Francis Wharton, on page 417, says authenticated instances exist in which there have been intermissions in the symptoms. Some physicians, who never read this, argued it could not be; that a woman who was poisoned would be better one day and worse the next, yet the books tell them all they know.

"This same book, on the same page, gives the case of the girl Davidson, where the vomiting was less on the fourth day, disappeared on the sixth, and returned on the seventh with redoubled force, and she took no more poison in the intervening time. The case of McDay, by the same author, showed two days of intermission. Dr. Christianson says a short intermission or a total remission is no evidence that symptoms will not return with increased violence.

"How does the defense hope to break Dr. Keegan down? They say his treatment was incorrect. He does not pretend to be a man of books. He thinks after the poison is absorbed, the antidote is ineffective. The doctors think he's wrong, but his theory may be as good as theirs; and even if he's mistaken in his theory, he's shown to have been right in his treatment of the case. The poison had done its work, Leyer's poison had gone to its destination, and he could not remedy it.

"Here, beyond question, to the exclusion of all doubt, was the proof that the cistern was poisoned. Men, women and children had been poisoned by drinking the water. The woman was ill and dying of arsenical poisoning. A doctor with twenty years' experience says she died of it. The arsenic is found on the bark of the puncheon, and all the contrary evidence from the physicians with no chemical experience is that they expect to find arsenic in the stomach or liver."

DeBruler walked slowly and solemnly toward the jury box and then stopped, facing them squarely.

"An awful crime has been committed. Who committed it? Who, of all those living there, had a purpose or reason to injure Cook? Not one man, but Leyer. Where's his enemy? Who could conceive this crime to kill the wife and children of his enemy? None but Leyer, who said to virtually everyone he met that Cook had injured him, and he would have revenge. The only one who possessed this vengeful spirit was Edward Leyer."

Pointing at the defendant, DeBruler raised his voice and declared, "*Here* is a man with a fixed idea that Cook had injured him, and he spoke to many of nothing else. However, he would not fight Cook, but would instead have a secret revenge, if he could. Gentlemen, Edward Leyer is not a man of honor who would challenge an enemy to a fight in a court of law. No, this man has the spirit of an assassin. And though Leyer now has denied this, in doing so, he is disputing eight other men *to whom he made the threats*.

"Indeed, he accused Mr. Cook of poisoning his horses, and Henry Lippert has previously testified to hearing the defendant say he would have revenge, if it took him ten years. He had this revenge more callously than had he shot him dead. He disputes those who accuse him of vengeful threats, yet Edward Leyer has been compelled to admit on the stand he thought Cook had injured him.

"You'll recall Chas D. Thiel testified Leyer said he could slay several of them, and they wouldn't know how it was done. He would have revenge, was too old to fight, but would get even. Here was a man with the fixed idea Cook had done him harm and murdered his animals. It has been sufficiently demonstrated in witness testimony; Edward Leyer was possessed by this idea of revenge and talked of it continually."

Recess

Stepping over toward the defendant, all the while looking in his direction, DeBruler went on. "It was said his confession in jail was absurd and incredible, but was it not just as incredible he should make these repeated threats? Yet they are proved by men who lived at a distance, were not in the mob, and were disinterested. He talked of his purpose to seemingly everyone. This was a purpose that possessed and controlled him to make Fred Cook suffer like his horses, which he said Cook had poisoned. But Leyer made a mistake, and the innocent, defenseless woman suffered what was intended for the man.

"We've heard from witness testimony Fred Cook had an interview with Edward Leyer about the latter's dogs annoying his sow, and Leyer was subsequently violent and abusive toward Cook. And although Leyer's boys contradicted Cook, *they* were contradicted by another, who said they were not present at the altercation in which the accused threatened to make Cook suffer. Indeed, Leyer's malice against Cook is shown by his hauling the carcass of a dead colt close to Cook's house, in order that the smell of it should annoy him. This Leyer also denied, but others, disinterested witnesses, contradicted his denials.

"The boy, Haddenbruck, lived under the same roof with Leyer and was treated as a member of the family. Their relationship was close. He was known to call Edward Leyer 'Father.' Yet the boy witnessed a plot within the Leyer household to poison an innocent family and could not be a part of such a devious crime. Although Leyer's family contradicted Haddenbruck, *they* were discredited by others. Haddenbruck pointed to the malice of Leyer against Cook as manifested by his throwing down Cook's fences, exposing his growing corn, and his hauling the dead colt as close as possible to Cook's home, so Cook might be annoyed by the stench.

"From Haddenbruck's own words under oath, Herman Leyer had been sent to the barn for poison by his father, who gave him a sample to ascertain if it was poison and, if so, to get some like it. Of course, Leyer contradicted this, but why wouldn't he? Leyer's contradiction of Haddenbruck is destroyed by his confession in the jail, where he told Wellington and Vandever he had poison in the house and bought more in Evansville."

When Gen. Shackelford began to light his pipe, several of the jurymen turned to watch.

"We've heard Rudolph Leyer testify," DeBruler continued, "that Billy Cook and Emory Lee were in the mob; that he recognized Cook as the one who struck him. Yet it has been successfully contradicted as to both Cook's and Lee's participation in the mob, who were shown to have been elsewhere."

Mr. DeBruler then quoted from recent testimony to show Leyer had been making inquiries to learn who was at home at the Cook's about the time the poison would begin to work. These inquiries DeBruler attributed to Leyer's desire to know if the poison had affected, in any way, his alleged enemy or his family.

"Here, there may have been a hesitant moment for Leyer, that he was actuated by a fear it might kill the innocent wife and children, that even his conscience might have some qualms."

DeBruler then lowered his voice and raised his hands as he began to animate Leyer's predicament. "Imagine if you will, gentlemen, word spreads of Mrs. Cook's illness. Friends were coming from all parts to visit her. Then, the rumor goes abroad—

reaching Leyer's little girl—that the Leyer or his boys had poisoned Mrs. Cook. Now we have a clear understanding of the fear engulfing the panic-stricken murderer, forcing him to fabricate a tapestry of lies and deceit."

DeBruler then loudly clapped his hands together, causing several of the jurors to flinch, and raised his voice. "Edward Leyer's attempt to conceal his crime was bungling and betrayed him. He talked continually of it, couldn't sleep, and when told, by Mrs. Mary Lippert, there was a suspicion the cistern had been poisoned, great drops of sweat burst out upon his face, though the day was cold.

"The defense wishes to discredit those who had participated in the mob. As I have explained, there is no room for lawless vigilance in a nation of laws. But because a man's indignation was excited by the commission of such a heinous crime, and he obeyed a natural impulse, though indefensible, that is no reason why he should not be believed. If such a rule of credibility was established, people had better burn up the courthouse; for anarchy would rule over the common sense of otherwise law-abiding men.

"The very nature of perpetrating the horrible crime of murder will cause the steadiest hand to shake. This very natural agitation caused Leyer to spill some of the poison on the puncheon, where it was found by Dr. Keegan, who ascertained that the matter was arsenic. The burden of guilt for his crime drove him to confess to any willing ear. The corroboration of the confessions heard independently by Wellington and Vandever would be impossible to fabricate."

DeBruler conjured an incredulous look on his face and rhetorically asked, "How can we escape the conclusion of Leyer's guilt? It wouldn't do to say he was guilty because Mrs. Cook died of arsenical poisoning. It wouldn't do to say he was guilty because the cistern was poisoned, if that was all there was in the case. It wouldn't do to say he was guilty because he said he would have his revenge on Cook, if no other evidence was available. It wouldn't do to say he was guilty of any one of these pieces of evidence. But when they all concur, and when Leyer is said to have bought the poison and confessed his crime to a fellow prisoner, all these things correspond and form a continuous chain. The conclusion cannot be avoided."

Retrieving a letter from the prosecutor's table, DeBruler held it up to face the jury. "The defense wants you to believe this confession letter was written by the hand of Herman Leyer. Yet, the accused admits his son cannot write in English. This letter was forged to throw doubt into the jury's mind. The only confession that holds water is that of the prisoner himself to his fellow inmates.

"You, the jury, must not commit to judge him with prejudice or pity. The murderer's guilt prompted him to do the most absurd things, and his acts can be accounted for by the operations of a mind warped by guilt. Consider the absurdity of the English philologist turned murderer, Eugene Aram. During his trial, his guilt was brought to light, and the case formed one of the most remarkable in the annals of crime. *Murderers were continually laying the very traps that betrayed them, their guilt clouded their minds, and their most cunningly devised plans often produced the strangest proofs against them.*

"Why did Leyer attempt to break out of jail? Why did he want those files to cut off his irons? He says it was to get out of the Boonville jail and come here to the Evansville jail for security. But we've heard testimony from Mr. Wellington that Leyer told him it was to escape and lie in a swamp below Henderson till the excitement should subside, at which point he and Herman were to go to Mexico, where he had, for some while, intended to go."

At this point, DeBruler stepped into the center of the space between the jury and the judge, and declared, "If you fail to convict, it is not because there is a defect in human testimony, and not because Leyer's guilt is not established, but because of your belief in a senseless jargon drawn from the books to create doubt where none exists.

"It's to no one's amazement the testimony of Leyer and his children contradict that of every other witness. And why shouldn't it? With Haddenbruck out of the picture, the Leyer's had weeks to concoct and rehearse their defense before the father's arrest. Why else would Herman Leyer flee, other than to escape the wrath of justice?"

Having addressed these last matters in thorough detail, DeBruler strode toward the jury box and, with both hands on the railing, began presenting his closing argument. "Gentlemen, by your verdict, you will be saying whether courthouses were built, courts instituted and laws enacted in vain, or whether life should be secure and mobs rebuked by a full, fair and impartial administration of the law, showing no necessity for their rising."

Chapter 26

THE LAY OF THE LAWYERS.

Arguments in the Warrick County Poisoning Case.

The afternoon session was called to order by Judge Hargrave at two o'clock, "We will now hear final arguments from the defense. Col. Bisch, are you ready?"

At that moment, Bisch was engaged in a hushed tone conversation with his client.

Judge Hargrave hammered his gavel before asking louder, "Col. Bisch?"

Bisch broke off his conversation with Leyer and swiftly stood, "My apologies, Your Honor. Yes, sir, I'm ready."

After patting Edward on the shoulder, he approached the jury box.

"I feel deeply the responsibility resting upon the defense in this case. I experience a feeling of sadness that, when human life is at stake, the counsel for the prosecution should not consider themselves ministers of justice, instead of ministers of vengeance. I regret the prosecution has resorted to the lower expedients, calculated to win the applause of the people of Greer Township, Warrick County, at least those who have fought to take the defendant's life. To crack jokes on such an occasion is as if one should enter a church at the moment of the transfiguration and make sport of the solemnities. It is this spirit, probably, which has kept the official prosecutor away from the court during the last few days. He has evidently abandoned the case to the attorneys nominally for the State, but really of Fred Cook and his conspirators. This case is the first time I have appeared in defense of human life, and I feel the full weight and solemnity of it. I praise Mr. DeBruler for his articulate opening arguments and his skill in fixating on particulates of testimony to advance his goal of unjustly incriminating an innocent man.

"The assassin who in the street drives his dagger into the heart of his victim is an angel of mercy compared with one who could commit the crime of which the defendant stands accused. When one is presented to the Grand Jury for such a crime, his defense is not heard, but the State, to compensate him for this, provides that he shall be held innocent until his guilt is established beyond a doubt. In this case, the prosecution would, on the contrary, have the State prosecute in a spirit of vindictiveness. They came as the mob came, and would have the State take the defendant by the throat, aided by the clear brains and nimble fingers of able and shrewd counsel."

Col. Bisch briefly paused his arguments, walking slowly and deliberately toward the prosecutor's table.

When he was directly facing the opposing attorney, Col. Bisch continued speaking, "I see with what skill and eloquence Mr. DeBruler has presented the case, omitting those things which tended to show Leyer's innocence. They had purported to show Herman Leyer had prepared to run away, afraid of the consequences of his guilt, but had abandoned that plan. I appreciate what Mr. DeBruler said about supreme responsibilities and will follow him in some of his quotations where he omitted sentences that would overthrow his theories. I sympathize with the poor little ones who were left motherless by Mrs. Cook's sad death, for which they sought to fix the guilt upon Leyer. With a hatred for his German neighbor with whom he had some words, Fred Cook thought over this case, brooded over it, and added to it till nothing could satisfy him but Leyer's conviction. It is easy enough, given such intention, to fan indignation to a flame, and the result we have here before us is clear.

"Three things have to be established to show Leyer's guilt. First, Mrs. Cook's death, which all have admitted; second, that she died of arsenical poisoning; third, that Edward Leyer poisoned the cistern from which she drank. In the prosecution of these, the defense has made out its case. But, where science has taught that if certain things occur, the effects are to be seen, where the results can be ascertained with mathematical certainty, these results must be shown, or the case is not made out.

"The prosecution resorted to science when it suited their purpose, but they scoffed at science as uncertain when it did not. They said certain physicians derived their learning from books and that books prove and disprove alike, yet they resort to these books when it suits their purpose. It would be just and reasonable in a case where a man has been killed by small shot pellets that the finding of a single ball disproved the killing. It is not the quantity of poison found. It is necessary that the evidence of its presence should be clear, distinct, conclusive and satisfactory – this, per Taylor's *Principles and Practice of Medical Jurisprudence*, noted on page 155.

"It was not sufficient that a quantity of water be taken in a bottle by an irresponsible party, carried in his pocket and taken to a chemist for analysis. The analysis should be systematically made. In his analysis of the viscera, Dr. Achilles had been careful, conscientious and systematic, but no such system was observed in the water analysis."

Stepping a few paces back to the table behind him, he picked up a book and began to read from it, even introducing it by saying: "In Wormley's *Micro-chemistry of Poisons*, on page 160,-..." but then stopped himself just prior to quoting the book and instead briefly summarized it, before going on to point out the relevance: "He proceeds to demonstrate how the poison's analysis should be made, in order to show that the result is unreliable *if every care is not observed.* And you'll recall, Gentlemen, Dr. Achilles had conscientiously observed these conditions in making his analysis of the internal viscera of Mrs. Cook, and he could *not* show she died from arsenical poisoning. And if this is not shown, the prosecution falls to the ground.

"During the pre-trial hearing, friends and neighbors of Mr. Cook testified to the Grand Jury, describing various symptoms and ailments following their visit to the Cook's home. But while testifying in this trial, every one of these rural, uneducated farmers, along with their wives, produced nearly identical medical diagnoses of their conditions. I find it absurd they could learn all these intricate matters in Greer Township, Warrick County."

Recess

Stepping away from the defense table and over to the bar, Col. Bisch stood facing Helena and her children, who were all seated in the front row behind Edward. However, he spoke to the jury while his attention remained on Edward's family, drawing the jury's attention to them, as well.

"The prosecution appealed for the bereaved children of the deceased. I sympathize with them; I truly do. But there is another case where there are six children and a poor woman, a poor Dutchwoman, who has seen this case tear at the very fabric of her family. Should *she* and her children be sacrificed because Mrs. Cook has lost her life?

"Circumstances are not safe evidence on which to take a man's life. Some of the most notable cases had indicated by circumstances that seemed indubitable the guilt of accused parties; yet, years after they had been sacrificed, their innocence had been established. Here, too, it is sought to prove Leyer declared his intention to be revenged. I sincerely doubt whether this man knew the meaning of the word *revenge*. He is illiterate and has not mastered the English language. It was probably that when he spoke the word, he imagined he had a sweet morsel of English, which he used on every occasion when he probably meant *redress*."

Col. Bisch stopped for a moment—watching Albert squirm in his seat to lean against his mother's arm—before turning his attention back to the jury.

"The prosecution scouted the reliability of the knowledge gained from the books, but the wisdom of the books was merely the compilation of the results of the experience of the most learned men in the profession. They wanted to reject the evidence of science and have this case tried on common sense, but they wanted science when it could be used to promote the prosecution. I present to you, in all earnestness, that although poison had been rendered inert by antidotes, it would still be found by chemical analysis. I ask the jury whether you would take the prosecution's arguments *against* the authority of eighteen medical practitioners of long experience who had been subjected to searching examinations. The structure of the prosecution is based upon sand, and will fall to the earth from whence it came.

"So once again the prosecution asked that the jury reject experience, reject science, and take their theories, as they had done time and again… upon which they constructed their story of Edward Leyer creeping to the cistern at midnight to poison a man with whom he'd admittedly had more than a few unpleasant words. Still, the fact remains that Leyer, finding himself living in a neighborhood where he was disliked, tried to sell his farm and leave it. He had offered his place for sale for years, but immediately after the death of Mrs. Cook, a purchaser being found, the suspicion was immediately fastened upon him that he had poisoned her. As soon as it was known he had sold his farm, Fred Cook's dislike of Leyer became suspicion, and from a breath, the suspicion became a storm. But before the suspicion of Mrs. Cook's death should be allowed to fasten itself upon Edward Leyer and cause his conviction, Mr. Cook should have resorted to all the means provided by science to discover whether his wife had died from poison. Is this not what sound reason and the law would demand of us?"

The crowded court room became a sea of muttering voices, causing Judge Hargrave to slam his gavel to regain control.

Col. Bisch took advantage of the interruption to take a drink of water, and then continued. "Young Haddenbruck, when looked at with objective eyes, could be seen as a viper whom Leyer had endeavored to rescue from the life of a criminal, and yet who turned upon his benefactor when the latter corrected him for his dishonesty. In contrast, remember the testimony of Rudolph, who was one of the most outspoken and clear of all the witnesses, consistent in fact and testimony. Many trivial circumstances were taken up to show the defendant's guilt. Leyer takes a walk on Sunday morning down the lane toward his own field, and the prosecution twists this simple chore into an act prompted by remorse and conscience. It would be just as reasonable to say a jury member was taking a walk in his own garden and a crime had been committed a quarter of a mile further on; the walk would be taken as evidence of guilt. When the canvas is unrolled, showing what the prosecution's witnesses would swear to, it was apparent the hand of Fred Cook had painted the storyline for all to follow. Men who, at the preliminary trial, testified to a little bellyache came here and were able to give accurate and scientific descriptions of the minutest symptoms. It was apparent and obvious Fred Cook had coached the witnesses.

"The spectacle of Ed Haddenbruck leaving Leyer's at midnight with a band of would-be assassins and going with them to Joe Cook's, where without any previous acquaintance, he was accepted and given a home, was too absurd. I acquit the gentlemen of the prosecution of any hand in setting up the evidence, because I know them too well; but they had managed the prosecution with such material as Fred Cook had brought them. We have seen many of those witnesses who denied being among the murderers have sworn falsely. It's too sweeping for belief for *all* to have denied it, so three of them declined to answer. I believe Rudolph had testified truthfully that Billy Cook was with the mob, notwithstanding his mother and sister testified he was home at the time. And even if Rudolph was wrong, it did not discredit him, for he identified Billy by the sound of his voice and his threats of murder."

Reviewing the symptoms of those affected by the poisoning, Col. Bisch went on to remind the jury that, per witness testimony, the family had partaken of fish and that one of the witnesses said he got well when he vomited up the fish.

Elaborating further, he said, "No one could tell whether the fish was sound or unsound. Yet here was a probable cause for the illness. If the testimony of Haddenbruck were true as to Leyer sending to Evansville to procure poison like the sample found in the colt, the prosecution, if they believed it, would have searched the city to learn where it was bought. And lest we forget, Haddenbruck, who became a refugee from home in order to avoid going to the House of Correction, took advantage of the prejudice against Leyer to ingratiate himself into Fred Cook's good graces, telling him the story he wanted to hear. It has been testified what the messengers had brought from town, and no such matter was among them.

"Those who say Edward Leyer had gone around talking about revenge, who said he had talked of Fred Cook all the time and talked too much, had taken but fragments of his conversation. If we take fragmentary sentences, months apart, and put them together, every man in the house could be slandered and tried for a crime, indeed for *any* crime, with as much evidence as these conversations show. Mr. Creswell testifies to a conversation, of which he remembers only a sentence of Leyer's, that *If Cook didn't move the road, he would move Cook, by God*. What business did Creswell have injecting himself into a boundary dispute between Cook and Leyer? This man was a busybody who had first suggested Cook's road encroached on Leyer's property. Leyer's son contradicted Creswell's testimony about this, and he displayed great officiousness in volunteering testimony to Cook.

Mr. Christmas had testified to seeing something like whitefish in the cistern, but at the preliminary trial, he never mentioned it. Regarding the hauling of the colt to a point near Cook's, the evidence showed Leyer not only had nothing to do with placing it there, but had said it was too near the road and should be removed.

"We are asked to believe two criminals, who must be impeached. Stamp Wellington was the son of a criminal, the grandson of a thief, and if he ever became a father, would surely transmit his criminal characteristics further. Vandever, if he is not in the penitentiary, ought to be, and these witnesses were led to testify to Leyer's *confession* by promises of immunity."

Recess

Turning in the direction of the jury, Col. Bisch disputed the accuracy of Sheriff Taylor's memory as to when Dyer procured the files and pistol.

"Mr. DeBruler had said Leyer confessed when he expected to escape, but it was apparent the files and pistol were *not* in his possession till nearly a week after the probable date of the confession. Were the witnesses ever better than these two, there would be a reasonable doubt about the truth of this pretended confession. Was this confession likely for a cunning murderer to make to two utter strangers, as were Wellington and Vandever?

"The procuring of a pistol was a very natural thing for Edward Leyer to do when Sheriff Taylor said he would run no risk for him when they'd found out a mob was coming to take the defendant from the jail. It has been ascertained Leyer's wife brought him the pistol and the files. I ask you, who among us, being chained and his life threatened, would not wish for someone to provide him with such resources for self-preservation and endeavor to escape? And upon sober reflection, sirs, self-defense could not be made to serve as a link in the chain of evidence against Edward Leyer; instead, there was *only* in it evidence he did not intend to be immolated by an inflamed mob, simply to gratify the revenge of Fred Cook."

While standing in front of the defense table, Col. Bisch accepted a note from Mr. Richardson. After reading it, he returned it to his co-attorney.

"I will remind each of you," Bisch went on, "the defense is not required to *prove* the accused's innocence. The absence of *proof* that Mrs. Cook died of arsenical poison was of itself sufficient to acquit the defendant. The presence of arsenic in the cistern a month after Mrs. Cook died was no *proof* she died of that kind of poison, when there was no evidence of its presence in her viscera. I will not accuse Mr. Cook of putting the arsenic there, but I will say he did *not* take the necessary precautions when taking the mud and water to be analyzed. Several important questions remain and cast doubt upon the accusations of murder made by the prosecution. *Why* was the husband of the deceased allowed to collect the evidence for the prosecution? *Why* did they not take some of the discharges of the deceased and some of the shavings from the floor, which could reveal the presence of the most infinitesimal quantities of the poison? *Why* were no discharges collected of those who claim to have been sickened from the water?

"The case of Mrs. Geldreich of Perry County illustrates the danger of convicting upon circumstantial evidence. She was murdered and her husband was arrested for the murder. His boots matched those lifted from the tracks made by the murderer, some of her money was found in his possession, and the jury was on the point of finding him guilty when that reasonable doubt interposed, and he was acquitted. However, years passed, and a man named Joseph Sohu, on his deathbed, confessed he and one Richard Dannhauser had perpetrated the murder. It further transpired that Sohu was one of the coroner's jury who committed Goldreich for the murder. Here is a lesson for jurors, which should cause *every* juror in this case to shudder.

"Gentlemen, I appeal to your common sense, your most basic intuition. Do not let the prosecution convince you an innocent man should lose his liberty *and* his six children should be deprived of his protection and care, when not a *shred* of verifiable evidence has been produced against him. Ask yourself, if you proceed as the prosecution would have you, will you be able to sleep in the years ahead, knowing you had reasonable doubt in the guilt of Edward Leyer?"

***

Following that day's court session, as evening was approaching, in the dim light of his cell, with his eyes closed and head hanging so low that his thin, bony chin rested on his chest, Edward began to pray: "Our Father, who art in Heaven, hallowed be thy name, thy Kingdom come, thy Will be done, on Earth as it is-…".

He stopped abruptly when he heard a female voice yelling from several cells over, "And when you pray, do *not* keep on babbling like pagans, for they may think they will be heard because of their sinful words. Brother, what is that gibberish you are praying over there?"

He recognized the voice as that of Margaret Powell calling out.

"I pray the Lord's Prayer… in German,"

After what seemed like a long silence, Edward heard sobbing coming from Margaret's cell, but suddenly she began to shout, "Oh Lord, forgive me, your daughter and faithful servant! I have sinned, I have offended my brother as he prayed to you, Lord Jesus! Please forgive me… for I know if we confess our sins, He is faithful and just to forgive us and to cleanse us from all unrighteousness!"

Margaret's yelling then turned in his direction, her voice cracking. "German, forgive me as God has forgiven me!"

Looking back through the bars, he cleared his throat and spoke sufficiently loud toward her, "I forgive you."

Immediately, Margaret hollered, "Hallelujah, my German brother! My Savior's forgiveness and your forgiveness have redeemed me! God bids you now carry on with your prayer!"

Margaret then broke into a loud rendition of "Amazing Grace."

Edward returned to his cot and lay down, listening to the woman sing, her voice strong and rich with soul, and he found comfort in the words she sang. Then, mercifully, he fell asleep.

Chapter 27

> **THE LEYER CASE.**
>
> CONTINUATION OF THE ARGUMENTS—POWERFUL EFFORTS OF GENERAL SHACKELFORD AND E. R. HATFIELD, ESQ.

By the evening prior to Friday, March 30th, word had spread that Gen. Shackelford would present his closing arguments in the morning session; hence, the crowd at the criminal court was even greater than the previous day. All available seats were taken, the aisles filled with people standing, and groups of people stood outside at every approachable window, gazing inside for a glimpse of the proceedings or leaning their ears to hear even a morsel of Shackelford's line of reasoning.

After banging his gavel to silence the murmuring crowd, the judge asked, "Are you prepared to deliver your closing arguments, Gen. Shackelford?"

"I am, Your Honor."

He walked slowly to one of the open windows and gazed at the overflow of citizens who clambered to hear this war hero's final speech. Then turning to address individual members of the jury, he began:

"Mr. Good, as a student of the law and a juror in this most unusual case, you will soon be called upon to sort the conflicting testimony between prosecution witnesses and those of the defense. So much hinges on the testimony of convicts who were willing to swear to the defendant's confession. No one but these felons claims to have heard Edward Leyer confess to a crime he didn't commit. Mr. Wallace and Mr. Johnson, you are both farmers, members of the hard-working backbone of this country. Imagine how you would react if you woke to discover your crops and livestock destroyed, day after day, until you were left destitute. The defendant took the high road, sold his farm at a loss, and endeavored to start his life anew in this city, only to discover a bounty on his head, instigated by the very neighbor who had destroyed his livelihood. Mr. McFadden, you are a merchant. You know your customers and the goods they purchase. How insulting it would be to have accusations lodged against you purporting that you don't remember selling a large quantity of poison to a man, or his wife, both of whom you've known for years.

"There's a storm of excitement and prejudice that has for months been gathering against this unfortunate defendant. I am not a believer in the fates, but in the justice of the ever-living God. But in this case, it seems as if the defendant is foredoomed by a band who have federated together to commit upon him the very crime of which he stands accused. Twice had they gone forth in the night to wreck upon him their vengeance. Never did they go in the light of day, but in the dead of night, and this, too, upon mere suspicion of a crime which they themselves sought to commit. Failing to find the defendant when they surrounded his house, they took the ingrate Haddenbruck to become an instrument of their fabrication against the truth. Failing to find him thus, they established a recruiting station. When they had gathered in sufficient numbers, they made an attack upon the Boonville jail, where Edward Leyer was confined, and he was told the Sheriff would run no risks on account of him. His first intimation of their presence was the sound of the sledgehammer and crowbar, every blow of which was to Leyer as a death knoll.

"The bells of the town were rung, and not until the mob was outnumbered did its members desist. We are told they were a civil lot. Aye, as civil as ever scuttled a ship or cut a throat, as civil as any savages that ever piled the fuel around their victim and danced around him while the forked-tongued flames licked his roasting body. We are told there were but three of this mob upon the witness stand, but who believed it? The hesitation of witnesses when asked if they were in the mob, their non-committal answers, and their manners showed there were more, and they inspired the prosecution with the spirit which actuated the mob. The jury are strangers to the prisoner and have been selected because they are believed to be men of sense, men of integrity, and men of impartiality. The defense will not appeal to their passions, their prejudices or their vengeance, but will appeal to their judgment, their sense of justice, their regard for law, and no other appeal to them. You are the guardians of the pure stream of justice and shall see that its waters are not sullied by impure means, but will flow free and undefiled as heaven intended.

"You are not to jump to conclusions. Denunciations are not to be taken for arguments. I believe the jury is made of such material as will not mistake their duties. Not only the defendant, but the jury, too, has been unfairly dealt with, and I will demonstrate it.

"The counsel for the State said they wanted justice administered like God's justice. Then why not deal fairly with the jury? When Justice descended from Heaven, Mercy, it is said, came in the same chariot, and were it not for this, neither the counsel nor the jury could have been here.

"The prosecutors tell us they are here to plead for a ruined home, for orphaned children, and for a broken husband. Aye, it was literally true they came here for Fred Cook, and money was in one scale and blood in the other. I appeal to their prejudices, for there is no word of a ruined home or orphaned children in the indictment, and thank God, twelve men and the court sit between the defendant and the revenge of the mob.

"They say there is no mob spirit now, that the mob has quieted down, but it's not true; for the mob spirit has already intimated to the public the defendant must not be acquitted. The best men of Warrick, they say, were in that mob. If so, God save Warrick County when her best men band together to take a man's life on a mere suspicion begotten of prejudice."

Shackelford stopped talking when a man standing in the back shouted, "You would have done the same, had it been your wife!"

After glancing at the judge, who made no effort to chastise the interruption, Gen. Shackelford continued, "The prosecution tells us the medical witnesses are ignoramuses, the books are all jargon; and yet they find in all the books a single instance in their favor, which they then mangled, in order to show a man who died sixteen days after taking arsenic tested negative for it after death.

"When I was in law school, the late Judge DeBruler, father of the eloquent young gentleman who spoke yesterday, had once appealed to the court to set aside a verdict of a man convicted in a case like this. The judge related at that time a case he had, years earlier, prosecuted, where the defendant was convicted of murder, and the doubt he had always had of his guilt had been a source of deep regret to him. The late Judge DeBruler often said the chain of evidence to convict a defendant must be complete, like a chain holding a ship to her moorings, capable of withstanding all blasts. If one link was defective, weak or missing, the rest of the chain was useless, however strong every other link.

"The State made an appeal to convict the prisoner, that the mob spirit might be vindicated. They say you may burn up your courthouses and throw away your laws if you do not convict him. In cases like this, it has been held that appeals such as these were good grounds for a new trial. They were in the nature of threats of mob rule, in case of failure to convict, and constituted an improper influence which ought not to be permitted to reach a jury.

"I read to you from one of the books the prosecution used to show how unfairly you, the jury, have been treated. In a case so solemn as this, the prosecution should be fair and quote fairly.

"Taylor's *Principles and Practice of Medical Jurisprudence* is filled with evidence that disproves the prosecution's case. In reading from page 155, the prosecution omitted essential matters found on page 154 which upset all their theories. Two cases from these pages show that arsenic was detected in the stomach, the liver, the rectum, the duodenum and other internal organs within *three* hours after taking the poison. The distinguished author goes on to show that in examining the viscera for poison, the liver ought to be preserved *because the poison is always found in the liver*. No one with any respect for the common sense of a jury would base a prosecution on so small a quantity of arsenic as less than the hundredth part of a grain. Furthermore, chemical analysis for arsenic can be fooled by the eating of muscles, sausage and cheese, which produce all of the symptoms of irritant poisoning."

Recess

Turning to face the 12 decision-makers, Gen. Shackelford said, "So I ask the jury, have you been fairly treated by the prosecution in their having made these omissions? It was easy to denounce any man as an assassin, to cry, *'Close your courthouses and burn your books,'* but it was easier still to convict by partial quotations and cunning omissions.

"But the prosecution said nothing, never mentioned that sickness contracted by the consumption of a *number* of spoiled food items could present such symptoms as have previously been described in detail; yet here it is in their own book that the fish, the cheese, the pork, the bacon, all produced trichinosis, a disease that can present symptoms quite like those described by the prosecution's medical experts!

"Even Dr. Achilles, their own witness, had admitted no living man could tell what had produced Mrs. Cook's sickness, but he would *suspect* poison, which was the most he could say. And even after the prosecution had put their distorted view of the case to him, Dr. Achilles could give no stronger evidence for poisoning.

"From Simon Greenleaf's *Treatise on the Law of Evidence*, we learn a distinction is to be drawn between civil and criminal cases, and the guilt of a prisoner accused of a crime must be fully and wholly proved. The reason for establishing this principle that has always been the rule of law is to consider it safer to err in acquittal than in convicting. The principle descended from the Mosaic Law. It is a principle derived from the divine law and will be found in the mode prescribed by the Mosaic Law for the trial and punishment of idolatry. In one year, forty-four judges had been hung by King Alfred for false judgments, as in the case of Freeman, who had judged a man to death when the jury doubted their verdict. It is not enough that the evidence goes to show guilt. The guilt must be proved *beyond all reasonable doubt*, to the exclusion of a reasonable supposition of innocence."

Setting down the Greenleaf text, Shackelford picked up another book from his table, *An Essay on the Principles of Circumstantial Evidence*, and started once again to read aloud. "On pages 40 and 48, the author, William Wills, articulates that circumstantial evidence never was and never can be as good as positive evidence. In this case, I am quoting, a man of high character and credibility prosecuted two men to whose identity he swore, for robbery, and subsequently two others, on being convicted of another crime, confessed they were the robbers. Furthermore, the processes of belief and inference were involved in circumstantial evidence, all of which are subject to the errors of the medium through which they were conveyed to the jury – the human mind. Judges have been forced to warn juries against the danger of taking circumstantial evidence from the tendency of the mind, as Greenleaf says, to take pleasure in adapting circumstances to such other and, if need be, to strain them a little to make them meet, to serve the purpose."

Setting the textbook down, he swung himself slowly around to look first at the judge and then toward the jury. "Now, in *this* trial of Edward Leyer, the prosecution started with the story of the ingrate, Haddenbruck, according to which Leyer must have bought two ounces of arsenic from Weber, when Weber said he never sold him a particle of arsenic. There are other drug stores in town, but they have scoured the town and failed to find where *any* was purchased, *let alone* purchased by the accused. The prosecution has changed front on that and now went on the story the arsenic had been bought five cents worth in one place and the same in another and another. They had also changed front on the symptoms. Not one of the witnesses in the preliminary trial had talked about burning throat, or red or swollen eyes, in describing their symptoms, but now they know all about it."

Here, Gen. Shackelford stared at the prosecutors' table and scoffed, "*Why did they not testify to these in Boonville?* Oh! They say they were not asked the questions. Witnesses sworn to tell the whole truth, omit these *subtleties* if they knew them then? It was suspicious, to say the least, they didn't think of them.

"The evidence showed Mrs. Cook came home on Sunday evening and was immediately taken ill. All the bread, all the coffee and all the cooking was made with the water from that cistern, and no one was affected but Mrs. Cook until Wednesday. On Wednesday, they had fish and pork, and they were all taken ill on that night. Little Dolly and Fred Cook were taken, and Cook vomited up the fish. Cook had been on a hunt and was taken sick when he returned. Dr. Keegan asked if he had been on a spree, in jest, of course. That would be a cause of red eyes and swollen face, too. Cook said he had taken but one drink of whiskey. If he took a drink at all, he probably took more than one; it was in the nature of things he should if he drank at all while on a hunt. All know how that was. It was extraordinary if the poisoning of the cistern caused Mrs. Cook's illness and death, that no one but she died when all drank the water alike, and even Fred Cook took no medicine till Saturday."

Shackelford paused to fill a cup with water from a crock held against a wall, and then drank of it.

"The witness who told of the great drops of sweat on Leyer's face said nothing of the alleged fact on the preliminary examination and admitted she did not think of it till Cook asked her about it. Not her alone, but other witnesses gave different testimony between the preliminary and the trial *after* talking to

Cook in the interim. In *every* circumstance, the witness admitted to remembering the new evidence *after* Fred Cook had reminded them. This newly realized testimony *clearly* shows Cook was coaching the witnesses in general.

"Mr. DeBruler had spoken of the hypothetical case put by the defense. That hypothetical case showed that if, in a case of supposed death from poisoning, where no poison was found in the viscera, the physician would be inclined to change his mind. But, says Mr. DeBruler, 'Didn't we find it in the water? Didn't we find it in the mud?' What mud and what water? Cook says he didn't clean out the cistern for weeks after the death. Even the bark, this *damned spot,* was carried in a physician's pocket for four months. Dr. Achilles, the conscientious chemist that he is, says he did not test his hydrochloric acid, his sulfuric acid or the other materials he used in the analysis to ascertain their purity, but took them from his predecessor as pure. The books showed arsenic often existed in those acids as an impurity and said the analyst should never accept re-agents as pure on this account. From this authority, we must conclude the water, the mud and the bark had *not* been preserved with the care prescribed by the best authorities, and even the analyst had omitted the necessary precautions to test the purities of his materials, did not attempt to grow the crystals, and did not have a glass of the necessary magnifying power to enable him to see the small crystals. These crystals are so small that the least of them weighs but one-billionth part of a grain; yet if it is present in even so small a quantity, its presence can be ascertained. Therefore, Dr. Achilles ought not to attempt an analysis without a glass of at least seventy-five diameters' magnifying, and one made without it is *not* reliable.

"Why did Cook take Dr. Achilles from Evansville to exhume the body? Why did he call on Dr. Keegan to assist? Why were the neighbors called to the grave, and why was the body examined? Because it was *expected* that if Mrs. Cook died of poison, the poison would be found in the body. The medical witnesses said if the woman died of poison, the poison ought to be found. The prosecution thought Dr. Keegan knew more than everybody, because he had practiced for twenty years. Dr. Bray had practiced forty-odd, and Dr. Keegan didn't pretend to be a chemist."

Recess

At this point, Gen. Shackelford stepped behind his table and began thumbing through a small stack of papers, selected two pages and began reviewing aloud the testimony of the physicians. "Thirteen witnesses, expert physicians, testified that when a person has taken as much poison for as long a time as Mrs. Cook is presumed to have done, and the jury is sought to be made believe she took it, the poison ought to be found after death. All of the symptoms of poisoning testified to here were forgotten at Boonville. One of the persons affected ate fish, and when he vomited up the fish, he recovered. Another had a little cramping, according to his evidence at Boonville, but when he came here, he described all the necessary symptoms to make out arsenical poisoning. One witness tells that Mrs. Cook's and the children's faces and eyes were swollen and likely to burst on Tuesday, yet the jury will remember that not a single child was sick on Tuesday at all.

"We must question the integrity of the ingrate, Haddenbruck, whose testimony would forsake his adoptive father in the hour of his adversity. True, Leyer was not the father, but Haddenbruck called him 'Father.' And yet, when the twelve *negroes*, as Haddenbruck calls them, came at midnight to mob Leyer's house, this boy goes with these strange men and takes refuge with Cook. Why did he go there? *Because the prosecution wanted him.* If they could get men to come in here and swear so accurately to symptoms, they could also get Haddenbruck to come here and testify to the story of Leyer having the arsenic and buying more. In doing this, the prosecution has proved too much. Lies can never be constructed so nicely that truth cannot penetrate them. This lie was too clumsy. If Leyer had arsenic in his house, why did he buy more? If he bought it in several five-cent quantities, how did it get into one package, as Haddenbruck testified, taken from Herman's breeches pocket when he got home?

"The prosecution had attempted to prove that some witnesses were not in the mob, yet we must consider the improbability of Cook's brother remaining at home when he himself went to mob Leyer. How insulting is it to this court and the intelligence of the jury to believe only a handful of men made up a mob of two hundred!

"*Sixth v. Munroe* shows us the merits of confessions are very unreliable as testimony. From *Wills on Circumstantial Evidence*, we find cases where several innocent parties were brought to trial—and at least one of them hung—where in one case in Vermont, the person alleged to have been murdered returned to his home, and in another, after the execution of the accused party, two men confessed they were the perpetrators of the crime for which *he* suffered.

"Who are the witnesses that testify against Leyer, who pretend to have heard his confession?"

As the volume of his voice rose and it took on an excoriating tone, Gen. Shackelford declared, "The prosecution would have you believe the criminals, Wellington and Vandever, who were in the Boonville jail with Leyer, hadn't the means or intelligence to concoct a fabrication of evidence. Yet they had the newspapers in jail with all the supposition and suspicion from which to frame it to suit; and if no other motive could be found for these fellows to originate this story, the impulse of a bad heart was sufficient. But there *was* a further motive – the hope of their own freedom. Leave out these lies, *and what is there of this case?*

"Leyer's manner on the stand was completely truthful and consistent. He admitted on the stand he believed Cook had poisoned his horses and would have sued him if he could have proved it. He admitted on the stand he wanted Cook to suffer the stench of his own horse's carcass. And he admitted on the stand he had cross words with Cook.

"Yet we find great inconsistencies of the prosecution's evidence. For example, Christmas says Leyer threatened vengeance upon Cook, and yet subsequent to this, Leyer is found working for Cook and doing friendly offices for him.

"The prosecution would have it believed the witnesses, except Wellington, Haddenbruck, Vandever and the mob, were not to be believed. The prosecution would have *no* case if there were no other witnesses than these. Haddenbruck swears when Morris was at Leyer's, Herman Leyer was hidden in the garret. Morris swears he went into the garret and found Herman was not there. They rely on the fact Herman bought the arsenic, but the jailbirds say Leyer said he bought it. If Leyer bought it, why should Herman take it out of his pocket? Why did Herman buy more if they already had arsenic in the house?

"Mr. DeBruler says if there was no other evidence than that of these thieves, you ought not to convict. But he sought to break jail, and why should he if he was not guilty? Again, reading from the law text of William Wills, we find a person, however innocent, might try flight, considering his own safety. Was that all? If they were told the mob, which has surrounded their houses and dragged their little children out of bed, was coming to the jail *and* overheard the sheriff say he would take no chances to resist them, would *they* not try flight? Taylor says the jail was insecure. *Oh!* But the idea he would break out of one jail to get into another? Leyer says he had written to his counsel to get him out of that, for he feared for his life. Again we read from Wills and see it is a question of moral courage to stand trial where public opinion was excited against the defendant to the extent of an epidemic. But *they* say, *he was running away!*

"It is shown Edward Leyer had, for two years, tried to sell his farm, had advertised it, and when it was sold, had removed his tools to Evansville, and was here opening a shop when the mob was at his house.

"The entirety of this case is based on circumstantial evidence, which requires a higher level of proof than one based on real evidence. On page 394 of the Twenty-Ninth Volume of the Indiana Reports, the state Supreme Court declares circumstantial evidence should be such to establish guilt beyond all doubt, and the facts proved must be susceptible of no reasonable explanation.

"The position of the prosecution is the books are all jargon and the medical witnesses all fools, except Keegan. Rudolph Leyer says he was at home on the day when Haddenbruck says Herman went to Evansville, and added Leyer never told Herman to bring 'that stuff,' that he was there, and that Haddenbruck was with them when Herman came back with the wagon and helped to take the bundles out of the wagon. *No such package* as Haddenbruck had described was brought. Mr. DeBruler says Mina Leyer disclosed the Leyer boys were suspected, but it was testified she was sick *in bed* when she was said to have heard this at school."

Stepping right up in front of the jurors and eyeing them directly, Gen. Shackelford solemnly said, "The jury has the power to take the defendant's life, but I am confident they will not take it on such testimony."

Suddenly, Gen. Shackelford was overcome by an attack of pain in his chest that caused him to release a deep, rattling cough, as he swiftly sat down. Upon regaining his composure, he declared, "I am physically very weak, but I trust my weakness will not be permitted to aid you in taking the life of the prisoner, for you are strong in your sense of justice."

From his chair seated behind the defense table, he continued, "I am reminded of a speech from Daniel O'Connell, a defense attorney who I hold in the highest esteem. In his oratory, he presented an account of the case of the brothers Freeman, whom he defended for murder, and picturing the agony of their mother on seeing them carried off to the place of execution for a crime of which they were innocent."

Rising to his feet, he approached the jury and leaned on the banister before them in such a way as to address each man personally. "Before you jump to a conclusion, to consider whether there is a complete chain of evidence against Leyer, I pray to God we may enlighten you to decide the case *not* on prejudice, *not* on passion, but on your sense of justice, on the merits of the evidence, and on the highest considerations of law."

Chapter 28

E. R. HATFIELD, ESQ.

In the afternoon session, the judge next invited Mr. E. R. Hatfield to present the final argument for the prosecution:

"This has been a remarkable case," Mr. Hatfield said after standing to address the court, "and of all the gentlemen who have attended the trial, no matter what their calling, none have ever seen such a case. Mr. DeBruler had said this was a crime belonging to the effete civilization of the East. But it seemed as if we had reached that point when the crimes of the Eastern civilizations were growing upon us and this boldness which had characterized the crime of the West was now giving place to the subtleties of the East.

"It seems my conduct in the case has not met the approval of the counsel for the defendant. In my conduct of cases, I have not been accustomed to consulting the defense to see in what manner they desired my side to be conducted. No doubt they were dissatisfied with it, but I will, in my turn, criticize, and they might find they have not conducted their case with all the etiquettes, either."

Taking up the Geldreich case referred to by Col. Bisch, he said, "I was the Circuit's prosecuting attorney at that time, and no man was ever tried for the murder. The coroner's jury could present no man for trial, because they had no evidence on which to base such a prosecution. Col. Bisch thought to heighten the effect of the case by saying Sohu was one of the coroner's jury, but the jury being in Spencer County, and Sohu a resident of Perry, he could not have been a member of it. Geldreich had a preliminary examination and, after three hours, was dismissed, and no one was ever tried for the murder. The story of Sohu's confession had no foundation, but given the priest at his funeral remarked he had been a very bad man, and as the Geldreich murder was the worst case ever known there, people attributed it to him.

"As to the case mentioned by Gen. Shackelford, where Judge DeBruler appealed for a man accused of murder, there was no doubt of his guilt, but as to the degree of punishment on account of the defendant's youth. Gen. Shackelford prosecuted him with great vigor, and when the arguments were over and the verdict set aside, Judge DeBruler pleaded guilty for his client.

"Gen. Shackelford has also mistaken the other case referred to by Judge DeBruler. There was no doubt the man had committed the murder, but there was a doubt of his sanity, and that was what had troubled Judge DeBruler, and not a question or qualm of the guilt of the condemned man.

"As to the assertion Gurley Taylor would take no side with regard to Edward Leyer, that was but the expression of opinion by Taylor's servant girl, without Taylor's knowledge, and even she was not brought here to testify to it. This was a clever technique to appeal to the sympathies of the jury, because there are a few Germans on it. I praise the law-abiding people of this city and the gentlemen of the jury, and take exception with the manner of the defense in conducting their case. The flamboyant exploits of Gen. Shackelford are tricks of the trade designed to flatter the vanity of jurymen. It is an insult to all of you that he appealed to individual members of the jury by name, as if their recognition by Gen. Shackelford was a compliment they would appreciate."

Stepping toward the jury and standing closely before them, Mr. Hatfield closed his eyes and recited the following: *Upon what meat has our great Caesar fed that he should grow so great that the mention of your name alone is an honor and a compliment?*

Opening his eyes, the prosecutor declared, "Ever since Cain bore the primal curse, the murderer was invested with all hateful attributes in all descriptions of him. Such are the attributes ascribed to Leyer in his approach to the cistern to fill it with death for Cook and his family, and this is stigmatized by the defense as an atrocity, as a professional tactic, as if the defense had resorted to none.

"The prosecution brought six or eight of the best residents of Greer Township to the trial and, by them, had shown Leyer's character for honesty was bad, and if the defense could have found a man in Evansville to say it was good, Gen. Shackelford would have had him. When a man has sunk to such depth that after half a century of life, he cannot get any other man to testify to his integrity, he is just the man who is capable of doing anything.

"Leyer had told Elisha Madden he hauled the colt near Cook's and the smell of it might annoy him. If we could search through the world's record of crime, there would be none found so deep that Edward Leyer could not have committed it. This man could bring no character before this jury, because no man could be found who could swear the defendant's character was good, although he had lived long enough in this community for it to be known."

Mr. Hatfield held his arm out as he pointed toward the prisoner, never wavering until he knew every eye from the jury box was on him. Slowly, he lowered his arm before continuing.

"The defense tried to make it appear the prosecution considers the doctors all fools, but this was not correct. The defense put a hypothetical case to Dr. Bray, and when he answered contrary to their purpose, they did not put it again. Based on arguments drawn from Dr. Bray's testimony, Dr. Keegan was validated as to what extraneous symptoms indicated. They not only put no more hypothetical cases to the physicians, but prevented the prosecution from going into it when Dr. Owen was being examined on technical grounds. It was admitted by the books and the physicians there were cases of arsenical poisoning where no poison was found in the body after death. The defense read from Wormley, where Dr. Muhlhausen said he could find no case where poison was not found in the body. He had borrowed the book from Dr. Muhlhausen, and not ten pages from the doctor's marks, where he evidently stopped, was found the paragraph saying the poison would be eliminated in about fifteen days.

"The case of Mrs. Cook showed, after the cause of her illness was discovered, she took no more of the arsenic-laced water and had lived long enough to allow it all to be eliminated, especially as she took the poison in solution, in which shape it passes more rapidly."

The case where a man took two ounces of the same poison and died in eight hours, without leaving any trace of it in the stomach, was again quoted from the same author. And then the jury was asked, 'Are you surprised none of it was found in Mrs. Cook's body?'

"Still, another case from Wormley shows there is no certainty in what part of the body the arsenic can be found, if found at all. In cases far more marked than this of Mrs. Cook's, the analyst had failed to find any trace of the poison, but Dr. Achilles had found a shadow of a trace, but that shadow was certain. When about one-third of the symptoms were presented by the defense, the doctors could not say they were sure indications of poison; but when all of them were presented, arsenic was indicated by all.

"When the symptoms detailed by Dr. Keegan are read, the authorities cited are in complete agreement that nothing else but poison ever produces all of them together. Gen. Shackelford said shellfish can produce some of them, as can sausage and cheese produce some; but none of those could leave the arsenic on the puncheon of the cistern."

Just then, Mr. Hatfield paused and leaned across the prosecutor's table for Mr. DeBruler to whisper to him.

"It is of complete improbability," Mr. Hatfield said upon resuming, "of Mr. Harrison Christmas testifying falsely. And if he were not a credible witness, Judge Moore, of the defense, would have made the most of it; but there was no word of disputing his veracity on oath. If juries are to reject a man's evidence merely because counsel earnestly asserted its falsity, they might as well burn their books.

"Christmas saw the poison on the cistern on Sunday, and sometime on Sunday evening, Mrs. Cook drank water taken from the cistern and was at once taken sick.

"It was not true the prosecution advanced the theory Herman Leyer had put the arsenic there on Sunday morning. Such was not the case. Herman Leyer walked toward Cook's on Sunday to ascertain if the poison had done its work. A man who does such a deed does not do it in the light of day. The defense got this idea from the way one of the children swore. They thought this was the theory of the prosecution. The children had been trained to swear accordingly—not by counsel—but they had been trained to swear to overcome it, and hence the child's testimony neither Herman nor Edward Leyer even looked toward Cook's house, much less crossed the fence.

"Others had seen that white spot on the puncheon before, but suspected nothing till Dr. Keegan made such an analysis as he was able; and finding the white matter was arsenic, he was enabled to prescribe the remedy with more certainty, and, except with Mrs. Cook, the treatment was successful.

"One cause for Mrs. Cook's drinking so much more of the poisoned water was she was nursing a young child and needed more drink. Every one of those who drank water from the cistern, except one, was made sick. William Keifer, who ate nothing there, but drank water, was made sick. Another ate dinner, but drank nothing and was not made sick; another, who stayed there overnight with Cook's family, found his children vomited and were swollen in the face and eyes. Ulysses Keifer was the only one who escaped, and he drank only one small draught. It looked like trifling with time to argue these symptoms were caused by anything else than the poison in that water. The evidence was too palpable."

Recess

From the prosecutor's table, Mr. Hatfield picked up the piece of bark, which had previously been introduced as evidence, and showed it to the jurymen as he slowly walked in front of them.

"Dr. Keegan's testimony shows he preserved the bark sample with great care and Dr. Achilles had made the analysis. Dr. Achilles did apply tests to his re-agents, according to his testimony, to ascertain whether or not there was arsenic in the acid or the zinc; and then testing the liquid from the cistern, found the arsenic, and further, there was more in the mud than in the water. This, he said, was natural, as arsenic, being a metal, is heavier than water, and much of it sank.

"The analysis of the fish showed about the same amount of arsenic as the water, which was natural, as the fish took it from the water. All these things prove conclusively Mrs. Cook died from arsenic poisoning and it was caused by her drinking water from that cistern.

"It then becomes important to know who put the arsenic in the cistern. The defense does not attempt to charge it upon anybody; there is no evidence of a motive for anyone but Edward Leyer to put it there. Cook was on good terms with all his neighbors except the Leyers. He saw the dead colt hauled up within thirty yards of his door and did nothing about it. Leyer caused that mean act to be done for Cook's annoyance, as it appears per Haddenbruck's testimony, corroborated by Elisha Madden and

Fred Cook. The defense presents Haddenbruck as an ingrate who cannot be believed, but others corroborate him. The cause for that act is Leyer believed he had an enemy who was injuring him, and on whom he intended to be revenged.

"Leyer's own threats that he could sit in his own house and slay a good many of them without their knowing how it was done was strong evidence. Chas Thiel testified to this, and Thiel was not of the mob. They say Thiel lies. Yes, everybody who testifies against Leyer lies, according to the defense. Crisswell's testimony shows threatening language and an angry spirit by Leyer against Cook. What did this threat that he could slay so many of them mean? It meant poison in the cistern.

"And there is the testimony of Sanders, Leyer's German friend. Col. Bisch said Leyer could not understand English, but Sanders spoke German, and they probably spoke that language together. To him, Leyer spoke of revenge. Leyer was always talking about Cook, his injuries, and his revenge – *always bad talk*. Not just to Sanders; to everybody, he talked of *revenge, poisoned stock, Fred Cook*. It overcame his judgment, and he talked of it continually. This obsession comes from too many witnesses to admit doubt. It throws great light on the fact of his talking about it in jail. The defense insists it is unreasonable, but you cannot judge a criminal by comparing them with honest men. *Unnatural crimes breed unnatural troubles*, says Shakespeare, whom Gen. Shackelford quotes. The same author says, *Infected minds discharge their secrets to their infected pillows*.

"I can follow Gen. Shackelford to the Bible and quote from David that *He has made a pit and dug it, and is fallen into the pit which he made*, and *His mischief shall come down on his own head*, and other quotations equally apt to account for Leyer's bad judgment in betraying his own crime. From Webster on the murder of Capt. White describing the murderer's cunning and showing the guilty soul cannot keep its own secret and is not true to itself, *There is no escape from confession but suicide, and suicide is confession*. Well, might Webster say the human heart was not made for the dwelling place of such a secret, and the Almighty Maker of us all has ordained murder will out the murderer?"

Here, Mr. Hatfield paused and strode across the room, satisfied with the jury's understanding of his biblical references and interpretations. He resumed when the men stopped nodding and looking at one another.

"It's imperative to the defense that Haddenbruck should be broken down to be shown he had stolen something. No one but Edward Leyer testified to this. Young Haddenbruck had undergone a severe ordeal on the stand and, at last, broke down and cried, but did not vary. The worst thing I can say against him is he had been under Leyer's control for nearly a year. If he regarded the defendant as a father, there was no motive for him to lie against him. The motive would be to do the contrary; but if he *did* lie, why did the defense *not* accuse him of contradicting himself in their seven hours of speeches, although he'd been under cross-examination for an hour and a half? Haddenbruck was corroborated by McCool as to the latter, telling Leyer that Mrs. Cook was dead on the 30th of November, and McCool had not heard Haddenbruck testify.

"The pretense that Leyer did not know Mrs. Cook was dead was absurd, and what did the denial mean? When the prisoner told this lie, he did it for a reason, and this reason is found in his statement that his little girl then, for the first time, told him she had heard on Tuesday people saying the Leyer boys had poisoned the cistern. This claim was another lie, and it pointed to Edward Leyer's guilt. He pretended to be ignorant of Mrs. Cook's illness, when McCool had already told him about it on Tuesday. The defendant wanted to appear ignorant of Mrs. Cook's illness.

"Haddenbruck testified Herman Leyer approached the Cook's on Sunday morning. Had he wanted to lie about it, Haddenbruck would have said more. He simply says Leyer asked him if they were at home, and Herman said he couldn't see anybody. Rudolph's testimony about the children hollering out, because the ground walnuts were so good, was absurd and, to its purpose, attributed to a desire to show Haddenbruck, being in the smokehouse, could not have heard what he testified to.

"Remember the postal card that had been shown in evidence to demonstrate Leyer's farm had been for sale? The date on the card, November 29th, proves they had been endeavoring, with renewed anxiety, to sell the farm while Mrs. Cook was lying ill. It has been shown Herman Leyer was concealed in the garret, and Haddenbruck was told Herman had been accused of putting poison in Cook's cistern. This shows Leyer lied when he pretended not to know Mrs. Cook was sick. The fact that Frank Morris did not see Herman in the garret was no evidence, because they all knew Morris was coming and could easily prepare for him by getting Herman out of the way. Gen. Shackelford gave his client little credit for shrewdness, if he thought he could not provide for this.

"The testimony of the Leyer children that their father never mentioned Fred Cook and rebuked them for saying Cook poisoned his horses was all absurd, for had not Leyer told it to everybody and talked of it continually? It was done to break down Haddenbruck. The codefendant, Herman Leyer, was hidden, and the children were instructed to say he was in the Ohio River bottom shucking corn. There was no fear of a mob then; it was fear of a constable. According to his father, Herman's disappearance was uncontrollable, but it throws light on the talk in jail and the letter received by Gurley Taylor. It is true, and it's because it's true, that the various parts of this testimony fit so closely together. Truth is always consistent with itself, but falsehood never."

Mr. Hatfield paused his monologue and walked toward the open window, allowing the jury to witness the spectators in the courtroom gesturing as though in agreement with his last statement.

"Leyer's statement that he brought Herman to Evansville before Frank Morris came out was simply to discredit Haddenbruck. He says he did not sell his farm for fear of a mob. Still, the testimony of Kruck shows Leyer had, before the poisoning, demanded $2,500 to $3,000 for the farm alone. After the poisoning, he sold it for $1,950, including all his personal property, except his blacksmith's tools and household goods. This sale was at a time when farmers had their bread and their meat prepared for the year, when, without any fear of a mob or something else, no one would think of coming to Evansville to open a shop, when business was dull and half the shops here were closed. So he figured up the value of the property at $4,200 and then sold it for $1,950. It was not to come to Evansville, but rather was to follow Herman, to become a fugitive from justice. I believe Edward Leyer made such a sacrifice, *not* from fear of a mob. No, it was from fear of the law and the penalty of his crime."

At 5:30 p.m., Mr. Hatfield saw he could not finish his argument, and Judge Hargrave perceiving that if he did, the instructions could not be given to the jury, court was adjourned to the following morning at 9 o'clock.

***

On Saturday morning, March 31st, in the presence of an audience that filled the room, Mr. E. R. Hatfield resumed his argument on behalf of the State in the case of Edward Leyer.

"Before I continue discussion of the evidence for the prosecution, I'd like to take a moment to bring attention to some of the arguments of the counsel for the defense. Col. Bisch had said if this trial had taken place in France or Germany, the court would have stopped proceedings long ago. I agree this is probable. The court would have stopped proceedings there and taken the prisoner to the guillotine.

"The counsel for the defense quoted several cases they had read about in newspapers, but I would quote from my own experience as to the manner of defendants about to be tried. One case in Rockport was quoted where the defendant appeared to have become insane. He had every appearance of being insane, and physicians pronounced him so. He was discharged, taken in a state of insanity to the Kentucky shore, at which point he leaped on the bank and resumed his sanity the moment he struck the shore.

"The case of Jan D. Parker at Cannolton was cited to show a defendant could simulate illness successfully. Parker grew worse from day to day. Paralysis set in, and Dr. Bemis one night said he must die. A watchman placed over him went to sleep, and when he awoke, Parker was not only gone, but had stolen his keeper's watch. Col. Bisch, in his own innocence, took Leyer's manners as evidence he was not guilty. Col. Bisch and Gen. Shackelford had testified quite extensively, stating many things no witness had sworn to, but cases like this were not tried on the statements of counsel.

"Col. Bisch has admired the testimony of Leyer's children and, in fact, was surprised at it. There was nothing in it to be surprised at, however, for it is most natural that children should do all in their power to save their father. It's natural, but they testified they had never talked with anyone about what they were to testify to, except Gen. Shackelford, not even to their mother. The improbability of this, and their remarkable memories enabled them to repeat word-for-word conversations heard a year before this trial. When dissected, Rudolph's testimony contrasted with the statements of other witnesses, who showed the falsity of his statements about the burying of the colt.

"Could it be expected a man charged, as Leyer has been, would testify the truth, when to do so would send him to his death? Allowing defendants to testify on their own behalf is regarded as a great innovation when introduced into the practice in 1861, but it generally works its own cure. During my experience as official prosecutor, I have never known a guilty man to take the stand without betraying his guilt in some way.

"The defense has tried to stigmatize the prosecution as a private prosecution in the interest of Fred Cook. Is it not natural for a man whose wife had been murdered, as Mrs. Cook was, to make efforts to bring her murderer to justice? Col. Bisch spoke of the absence of the prosecutor and attributed it to disgust. My understanding is the prosecutor is sick and, out of an abundance of caution, chose not to attend recent sessions here and run the risk of infecting the members of this court.

"There was a case in which someone stole a watch from Gen. Shackelford, and that gentleman had prosecuted while the prosecutor sat quietly by, having but little to say. Had it been his wife's life instead of a watch that was taken, I believe the General would not have waited for a mob; but he would have taken the murderer's life before night fell.

"There is no proof Cook had used any improper means to influence witnesses, but had simply asked them what they knew of the case. They wanted the prosecution to show where Leyer had bought arsenic. If they would bring Herman out of hiding, who was said to have bought some arsenic, we would make the rounds with him to see if he could be recognized. Edward Leyer was too well-known to attempt it, so he sent his son.

"The defense has charged that the mob spirit invaded the courthouse, but it's not true. There have never been more than two or three Warrick County men in the courthouse at once during this trial. No testimony was introduced to show the Sheriff of Warrick had been enticed to remove Leyer from the Boonville jail.

"Leyer's testimony showed there was an effort to make it appear his family was affected like the Cook family, and Leyer, despite the efforts of his counsel, tried to testify to the appearance of like symptoms. By Lippert, it was proved they had arsenic in the house during the wheat harvest. This corroborated Vandever, who said Leyer confessed he had some in the house and bought more. It was shown he was dealing in poisons."

"Your Honor!" Gen. Shackelford shouted. "I must object! There has been no motion by either side to imply the defendant was dealing in poisons."

"Sustained," the judge replied, as he slammed his gavel. Then, turning to the prosecutor, he said sternly, "Mr. Hatfield, you will refrain from injecting your opinion. The jury will disregard the prosecutor's last statement. Fifteen minute recess."

Recess

Mr. Hatfield switched topics, and speaking of Mrs. Lippert's prior testimony, pointed out, "Leyer said to her it was impossible anybody would poison the cistern. When she said anyone who would do it ought to be hung, Leyer's paleness and excessive perspiration, according to her, showed a consciousness of guilt. The fear of the consequences, the knowledge the facts would be inquired into produced great agitation.

"For argument's sake, I will accept the defense's date of Herman's disappearance. Their statement *it was about the time the defendant was arrested*, however, was not true; rather, Sheriff Taylor says it was some time after his father was in jail at Boonville that the letter from him dated at Evansville was received at Boonville, and directed to the Sheriff. This proved that Herman, whom his father admitted had written it, knew of his father's arrest before leaving Evansville. This letter corroborates the statement of Wellington and Vandever that Leyer said the letter was only a blind, designed to shift the blame from Edward Leyer. How could they know Herman was 22 years old, if Leyer had not told them?"

Bisch stood to explain, "Your Honor, the letter referred to by Mr. Hatfield clearly identifies the age of Herman Leyer as 22 years old."

Mr. Hatfield continued after Col. Bisch sat down, "The fact that Taylor, Wellington and Vandever were far apart, heard nothing of each other's testimony, and yet swear to a like state of facts is evidence of the truth of all. They do not and cannot dispute or impeach Taylor, and they have not attempted to impeach the integrity of Vandever, whom they would have impeached if they could. He had lived all his life within twenty or twenty-five miles of Boonville, where Judge Moore of the defense lives. There is no indictment against him. The only thing shown is he was accused, but never indicted. Had Vandever been given immunity, there would be some evidence of it, and in the absence of any evidence against his honesty, it must be accepted as good.

"Vandever states while Leyer believed he would soon escape from an insecure jail, he had confessed he knew Herman had not drowned himself. There he repeats his grievance against Fred Cook, which Vandever could not have known, if Leyer had not told it. There Leyer shared aloud how he and Herman had slipped out at midnight and poisoned Cook's cistern. It agreed with his threats to Charles Thiel, and a number of witnesses corroborate Vandever in several particulars.

"To Vandever, Leyer tells how Herman bought the poison, and in this, Lippert corroborates him. Vandever's details show the truth of Leyer's jailhouse confession, because a number of others corroborate every part and detail; hence, it must be accepted as true. The correspondence of the testimony of various witnesses, when taken up and fitted together, corroborates each other and strengthens the chain of evidence."

Mr. Hatfield walked to the banister behind the prosecutor's table and pointed to Fred Cook, who sat three rows back. Raising his voice in a dramatic tone, he declared, "Gen. Shackelford tells us justice and mercy came to this earth together. Would to God a particle of that mercy had fallen upon Edward Leyer. Would to God a ray of that mercy have penetrated his heart to cause him to think of that innocent mother and the innocent children as he crept to the cistern to imperil the lives of the Cook family? No justice or mercy made him think of them then. The light of justice and mercy had gone out forever within him, and he is in no condition to ask for mercy at the hands of the jury. Gentlemen, the defendant is in no position to hope for the mercy he denied others."

After pausing for a few long moments, he walked slowly back to the jury before calmly continuing, "Let's remember Edward Leyer told Wellington this was not the first person he had poisoned, and if he got out of this scrape, there would be more to follow. Nay, his revenge was not satisfied, because the poison had not reached Fred Cook.

"The purpose of the confession letter from Herman Leyer was to secure the release of his father from the Boonville jail. So when Edward Leyer found it did not have that effect, he endeavored to make it appear Herman could not write English and the letter was a forgery; but by other witnesses' testimony, it appeared Herman *could* write English four years ago. The letter was evidently that of a German writing in broken English and bore other evidence of genuineness.

"The statute regarding the crime is clear, the malice and deliberation of the intent, the connection of the defendant with the act, and the completion of the crime by the death of Mrs. Cook; all these together form an unbreakable chain. Given the completeness of the train of evidence, I appeal to the jury to do justice and visit upon the criminal the penalty his crime deserves.

"I admit to the correctness of the law as quoted by the defense, but I insist we have proved the prisoner's guilt completely, fully and to the exclusion of a doubt.

"The cases read by Gen. Shackelford about the unreliability of confessions were correct, but were not parallel cases. The confession of Leyer was not made while he was in fear of death, but while in expectation of escape. He was not under the influence of liquor, and the prosecution did not depend upon one circumstance, but many, by which the chain of evidence was woven link by link, till it was strong and complete, connecting the defendant with the means, the motive and the intent to commit the crime, with a chain so strong it cannot be broken."

Staring silently and solemnly at the jury, scanning each one's face, Mr. Hatfield turned to the judge and said, "Your Honor, the State rests."

Chapter 29

The Last Day's Proceedings — Arguments and Judicial Charge in the Most Remarkable Criminal Case in Our County Annals.

After a brief recess, Judge Hargrave prepared to read aloud to the jury their instructions, which included input from what the counsel on both sides had submitted, as well as some other matters pertaining to criminal law.

"Gentlemen," Judge Hargrave began, addressing the jury directly, "the testimony and arguments are complete. I wish to commend you on your steadfast attentiveness to this case and your unwavering commitment to your judicial duty. After I present you with these final instructions, you will retire to the jury room, whereupon you will deliberate upon the testimony and arguments of this trial. Please listen as I read your instructions.

"1. Gentlemen of the jury, the defendant, Edward Leyer, stands indicted, together with his co-defendant, Herman Leyer, for murder in the first degree, in the alleged felonious, malicious and premeditated killing of Elizabeth Cook on the 19th day of November 1876, in the County of Warrick, State of Indiana, by putting a deadly poison, commonly called arsenic, into the water contained in a cistern, of which, it is alleged, the deceased drank and otherwise partook; that by means of the poison so contained in the water of the cistern she died. There are three counts in the indictment, variously changing the facts necessary to constitute the alleged offense, any one of which, if established by the evidence, would sustain a conviction.

"2. The statute of Indiana defining murder and prescribing a suitable penalty is as follows: 'If any person of sound mind shall purposely and with premeditated malice, or in the perpetration, or attempt to perpetrate, rape, arson, robbery or burglary, or by administering poison, or causing the same to be done, kill any human being, he shall be deemed guilty of murder in the first degree, and upon conviction thereof, shall suffer death.'

"Section 4 of the same act is as follows: 'Any person convicted of treason, or murder in the first degree, may, instead of being sentenced to death, at the discretion of the jury, be imprisoned in the State prison throughout the remainder of his or her life.'

"3. To have made out the case as charged in the indictment, the State must have proven to your satisfaction, beyond a reasonable doubt, that at some time heretofore, in the County of Warrick, State of Indiana, the defendant, either alone or in the company of his co-defendant, mingled arsenious acid, commonly called arsenic, with the water of a cistern, by means of which such water became poisoned to such an extent that when taken, at the times and in the quantities in which it was used by the deceased, it became destructive of human life, and actually caused her death on the 19th day of November 1876, or on some other day previous to the finding of the indictment."

Stopping briefly and lowering the pages from which he was reading, the judge looked at the jury and emphatically said, "In murder, *there is no statute of limitation*; that is, if a man is accused of murder, he may be prosecuted therefore at any time during his life."

He then lifted the pages and once again began reading from them: "4. In every case of murder, it is necessary to prove the facts of the *corpus delicti*, or the dead body, when possible. This crime has been conclusively proven by witnesses who were present at the death and who have related the particulars of the last illness and testified to all the circumstances under which they saw the remains of the deceased.

"The fact of death having been proven, the next inquiry is: *How was the death caused?*

"In the present case, the inquiry has been prosecuted under two heads: first, the general symptoms of the disease of which Elizabeth Cook died, as testified to by her family physician and briefly by a consulting physician and others who saw the patient in her last illness; and secondly, employing a chemical analysis of the waters and mud of the cistern alleged to have been poisoned, as well as the body of a small fish contained in the cistern; and also by the analysis of a substance found on a part of the curbing of the cistern; also, of a chemical analysis of the stomach, duodenum and a part of the liver of the deceased.

"You will doubtless consider it your duty to recall, as fully as possible, the testimony of Dr. Keegan, detailing a history of the case as it passed under his observation from the time he began to treat it until the death, together with the remedies he gave and the effects of those remedies. What were the symptoms of the case as testified in by the doctor and others who were in attendance on the patient? What did those symptoms indicate was the cause of the death? Was it, or was it not, a case of death from arsenical poison? If you believe beyond a reasonable doubt, from the history and symptoms of the case, as testified to by Dr. Keegan and the witnesses who saw the patient in her last illness, that she died of poisoning by arsenic, then you might so find the fact upon the history and symptoms of Mrs. Cook's last illness alone. But you will doubtless conclude additional light would be thrown upon your inquiries by the chemical analysis made by Dr. Achilles, to whose admirable account of his experiments we all listened with much interest. You would then further inquire whether the tests he applied established the presence of arsenic in poisonous quantities in the water of the cistern.

"You have heard a full description of the nature and extent of the experiments performed by Dr. Achilles, and it is for you, in the exercise of an enlightened judgment, basing your conclusions upon the testimony of Dr. Achilles and the other experts and the views of medical and chemical authors in these matters, to determine whether the tests were made with sufficient care to prevent the use in the experiments of impure chemicals or of arsenic, accidentally or designedly placed in the substances treated by the chemist. And I will here say that, under the laws of evidence, a *reasonable doubt*, upon this point, as well as upon all others, is such a doubt as arises upon the evidence; and if, from all the evidence taken together, your minds rest satisfactorily upon the conclusion that arsenic was contained, in poisonous quantities, in the water of the cistern, and detected by chemical analysis and that it was drunk by the deceased; then your belief would not be much affected by the fact that impurities may exist in the air we breathe, or that arsenic may be found in various earths and metals and impure drugs and chemicals.

"5. If you have a reasonable doubt that the deceased died from the effects of arsenical poison and you give the defendant the benefit of that doubt, then acquit him. But if you find that the deceased died of poison by arsenic, then your second inquiry would be: *Was it administered by the defendant as charged in the indictment?*

"6. The defendant pleads 'Not Guilty' to the indictment, and the State must therefore prove him guilty to your satisfaction, beyond a reasonable doubt, by competent legal evidence, or the prosecution will fail. This evidence must be either *direct* or *circumstantial*. Direct testimony is the testimony of an eyewitness, and perhaps this would never be obtained in cases of alleged murder by poisoning, unless by confessions of the defendant.

"On the trial of Dr. Webster, Chief Justice Shaw said: 'The distinction, then, between direct and circumstantial evidence is where a witness can be called to testify to the precise fact that is the subject of the issue in a trial; which is, in a case of homicide, the party accused *did* cause the death of the deceased. Whatever may be the kind or force of evidence, this is the fact to be proved. But suppose no person was present on the occasion of the death, and of course, no one can be called to testify to it. Is it wholly unsusceptible of legal proof? Experience has shown *circumstantial evidence* may be offered in such a case; that is, a body of facts may be proved to be so conclusive a character as to warrant a firm belief of the fact, quite as strong and certain as that in which discreet men are accustomed to act in relation to their most important concerns.'"

Juror number four, looking pale, raised his hand and said, "Many pardons, Your Honor, I'm in urgent need of a recess."

Recess

When court reconvened following the recess, Judge Hargrave paused while the bailiff lit a lantern on his bench.

"Thank you, bailiff," he nodded and continued with the jury's charges. "7. In the present case, gentlemen, the State seeks to prove, by several circumstances, that the defendant, Edward Leyer, was guilty of poisoning Mrs. Cook. First, that there was an old grudge upon the part of the defendant toward Fred Cook, husband of Elizabeth Cook, arising out of supposed injuries inflicted by him in poisoning a number of his horses, in letting down his fences, allowing his livestock to destroy the defendant's crops, and perhaps being involved in destroying his pigs.

"Secondly, the State offered evidence tending to show the defendant, on several occasions, made threats he would injure Cook and he could do so in a way no one would be able to find out.

"Thirdly, the defendant had as much as 2½ ounces of arsenic in his possession, which, on a particular occasion, he procured from Evansville; and in this connection, evidence has been offered to tend to prove the defendant had arsenic in his possession in the summer prior to the alleged poisoning of the deceased, as well as evidence indicating he lent some to a neighbor to poison rats; also evidence tending to show declarations on the part of the defendant he was familiar with certain secret means of injury. The State has also offered proof of a specific white powder being found on a part of the curbing of the Cook family's cistern; and, lastly, the chemical analysis heretofore alluded to has been offered in evidence to prove the water, mud, etc., taken from the cistern contained arsenic.

"Evidence has also been offered to prove other members of the family and other persons, not members of the family, to a considerable number, who drank of the water were taken sick with the same symptoms as those from which the deceased suffered in her last sickness. Further evidence was offered to prove the defendant, together with another prisoner in the jail of Warrick County, had filed in two the iron shackles by which they were confined, with the intention of escaping from jail; also evidence was brought forward showing the defendant had procured a number of small files, which had been conveyed into the prison to him and were used in filing the shackles; and also evidence indicating the defendant had in his possession a Derringer pistol, as well as evidence he procured his wife to convey to him in jail a revolver, which he gave to the prisoner Bonner, who, it is alleged, was an accomplice in the plan to escape from jail.

"It has also been shown the defendant sold out his farm and personal property for cash, at a price claimed to be considerably under its true value, soon after the death of Elizabeth Cook. Also, the State has made efforts to show malice on the defendant's part, pointing out a certain colt of the defendant, which had died from poison, as the defendant claimed, was hauled to and left not far from and in front of the house of Fred Cook. Finally, the State offers evidence to show the defendant procured this to be done for the purpose of annoying his neighbor, Mr. Fred Cook.

"In addition to this *circumstantial* evidence is the *direct testimony*, offered by the State, of the alleged *confessions* of the defendant, expressing he did put the arsenic in Cook's cistern, together with his son Herman. This confession is said to have been made to two fellow prisoners in jail at Boonville.

"I will add direct evidence has been offered showing a letter of the defendants' son and co-defendant, in which he confesses he had put arsenic into the cistern, and this letter was read to the defendant while in jail by the Sheriff of Warrick County.

"There has also been evidence offered indicating the defendant stated to a fellow prisoner that said letter had been written by his son pursuant to a previously arranged plan between himself and his son.

"On the other hand, members of the jury, the defendant *denies* all threats on his part against Fred Cook; *denies* he ever had any arsenic; and produces witnesses, members of his own family, to *contradict* in detail every statement of the boy Haddenbruck, who was, at the time of the alleged poisoning, an accepted member of the Leyer family. The defendant's family also *contradict* the testimony of McCool, that when he, McCool, told the defendant of the death of Mrs. Cook, that he, the defendant, immediately left the room and told his wife. In addition, the defendant *contradicts* the testimony of Lippert, that he got arsenic from the defendant to poison rats; and also Edward Leyer inferentially *contradicts* the statement of the two young women, who testified that on the Sunday before Mrs. Cook was taken sick, they saw the defendant and his son Herman walking together near Cook's house. Also, the defendant himself, being sworn, *denies* the alleged confession in jail at Boonville, *denies* he put the arsenic in the cistern of Fred Cook, *denies* he ever made threats against Cook, and claims he sold his farm for as much as he could expect to get for it, considering his circumstances. He claims he was justified in arming himself and Bonner, as well as in attempting to escape from jail due to the fact he had been notified of the intended attack upon the jail and the plan to mob him."

The mere mention of the mob set off a chattering commotion within the courtroom and among the listening public standing near the open windows. Judge Hargrave hammered his gavel twice to silence the disruption, and within moments resumed his instructions to the jury.

"8. This general view of the testimony on both sides leads me, gentlemen, to instruct you on your duty in weighing the evidence. You are the judges of the law and the evidence, and in weighing evidence, you are governed by certain well-established rules.

"Where there is a conflict of testimony, you first endeavor to reconcile it, so that it may all stand together, if possible; if you cannot reconcile it, then you determine which witness you will believe and which you will disbelieve. You judge the credibility of a witness by his intelligence, his means of knowing the matters about which he testifies, and his freedom from bias or interest in any form of self-serving pursuit, as well as his freedom from prejudice, either in favor of or against the party about whom he is testifying.

"9. As to the testimony of a witness who has been impeached, either by a conviction of an infamous crime or by proof that his character for truth and veracity is not good in the neighborhood where he lives, you may either believe or disbelieve such a witness; although you will, of course, scrutinize such testimony closely before you accept it as true.

"10. Under Indiana statute, a defendant may take the witness stand to testify on his own behalf. His testimony is to be received on the same footing as any other witness, except that the jury may inquire whether the circumstances of peril in which he finds himself and his interest in the trial have caused him to depart from the truth.

"11. I will now instruct you briefly regarding the *malice* and *premeditation* notions, which are characteristic of murder under Indiana statutes. *'Murder in the first degree is the killing of any human being with premeditated malice, either expressed or implied by law.'*

"Of this description, the *malice prepense* or a malicious act planned in advance, premeditated, is the chief characteristic, the grand criterion by which murder is to be distinguished from any other species of homicide. It should be observed, however, when the law makes use of the term *malice aforethought,* meaning 'malice previously thought of,' as descriptive of the crime of murder, it is not to be understood merely in the sense of a principle malevolence to particulars, but as meaning the fact has been attended with such circumstances as are the common symptoms of a wicked, depraved and malignant spirit; a heart regardless of social duty, and deliberately bent on mayhem. And in general, any formed design of doing mayhem may be called malice. Malice is either expressed or implied by law. *Expressed* malice is when one person kills another with a sedate, deliberate mind and formed design; such formed design is evidenced by external circumstances, discovering the inward intention; as lying in wait, antecedent menaces, former grudges and concerted schemes to do the party some harm. And malice is *implied* by law from any deliberate, cruel act committed by any person against another, however sudden.

"So if a man willfully poisons another in such a deliberate act, the law presumes malice, though no particular enmity can be proved. And when one is killed on the consequence of such a willful act as shows the person by whom it is committed to be an enemy to all mankind, the law will infer a general malice from such depraved inclination to mayhem.

"Therefore, if you should find the defendant guilty, as charged in the indictment, of poisoning a neighbor's cistern, out of which a whole family must drink water, and a considerable part of the whole neighborhood did actually drink, then by common consent, he would be such an enemy of all mankind as would clearly render him guilty, as charged, of murder in the first degree.

"If poison is put or placed for the purpose of destroying the life of one person, and it is taken by another, not the person for whom it was intended, and the latter person dies of the effects of the poison, then it would be murder in the person placing the poison, the same as if it had been taken by the person for whom it was intended, and he had died therefrom.

"12. A reasonable doubt is such a doubt as would cause a reasonable and prudent man to hesitate to act in a case where his own most important interests are concerned and where he was acting voluntarily."

"13. If, after carefully considering the evidence, you find the defendant guilty as charged, you say so by your verdict, and assess as the penalty, *that he should suffer death or imprisonment for life*."

"14. If you find the defendant *not guilty, you say so by your verdict*."

"Gentlemen, this most important case is now with you, and you will *make true deliverance between the State and the prisoner at the bar*."

"So say I, W. P. Hargrave, Judge."

***

The jury retired with the case at 11 o'clock Saturday morning, and court took a recess to await the verdict. The lawyers all departed, but the crowd of spectators lounged in the room and waited patiently until night.

A reporter for the *Courier* noted he'd polled the lingering crowd and the prevailing opinion was: "Leyer is guilty, but the jury will disagree."

After dark, only a small crowd of interested persons continued to hold vigil for the verdict, and three bailiffs guarded the jury room.

Edward Leyer was taken back to his cell, and his wife and children were allowed to accompany him. The same reporter noted their collective sense of anxiety could better be imagined than described.

"What happens now?" Helena asked, sitting on a cot across the cell from Edward's cot, watching him eat dinner. He had been moved to a private cell, as was common for prisoners coming to the end of a hearing in which a sentence of death was possible.

"We wait for the jury. It's almost over."

"I couldn't understand much of what the attorneys said, Edward. Is it possible the jury will find you guilty?"

Lowering the spoon from which he had been eating soup, and managing a faint smile, he looked across the cell to his wife, then to his children sitting next to him on either side. "I don't see how that could be. A woman died with no poison in her system. There are no witnesses to a crime. Criminals tell lies about a confession. Witnesses change their testimony. How could I be held accountable for a crime I didn't commit?"

Letting out a deep breath, she replied, "Tonight, maybe tomorrow, you will walk us home, and our children will rejoice that this nightmare is finally over."

***

As they did so often, Gen. Shackelford and Col. Bisch met in Shackelford's office following a long day in court. Shackelford poured his favorite brandy into two glasses. The general handed his colleague a drink before sitting in his wing-tipped chair. Col. Bisch took his usual spot on the cushion of the couch closest to the seated general.

"We knew it would be difficult from the beginning," Bisch said.

"Aye, Judge Hargrave all but told the jurors the outcome before they had a chance to litigate the proceedings."

"Indeed. He ignored every argument we put forth. His instructions included no mention of a poison victim with no poison in her body, a mob with a conviction to murder a suspect, a dead woman's husband who coaches the witness' testimony, the criminal record of the state's witnesses who, in all likelihood, fabricated a confession story, or a suspected poisoner who never bought poison."

"Aye, and in all my years, I have never known a judge who allowed character witnesses brought forth by the prosecutor, but refused the defense equal opportunity to establish the defendant's veracity."

"That poor Dutchman. Given the judge's instructions to the jury, it would seem they have no choice but to convict. *But who knows?* Now is the time we wait to see if they'll spare his life."

Chapter 30

THE SHADOW OF DOOM.

IT FALLS OVER EDWARD LEYER, CONVICTED OF THE MURDER OF ELIZABETH COOK.

SENTENCED TO THE PENITENTIARY FOR HIS NATURAL LIFE.

That evening, an anxious crowd lingered on the opposite side of the street, watching through the courthouse window the shadowy figures of the twelve men comprising the jury, as they gestured at one another, flitted about the room or paced the floor. Finally, at nearly ten o'clock, their discussions appeared milder, at least to those looking on from a sidewalk view.

At half past ten, the jury's foreman was seen bending over the table, apparently writing. A few minutes later, the jurors' conference room door opened and, per a statement taken from a man standing in the hallway, a voice from the room called for the bailiff.

As the court's bailiff reached the door, at least one of the people in the hallway stated he heard the same voice say, "We have agreed."

"Please remain here, while I go tell the judge and counsel," the bailiff was said to have responded, and the door was again closed, as he hurried off down the hall.

A messenger was dispatched to Judge Hargrave's house. Another was sent to the Sheriff's office to have the prisoner brought to the courthouse, and a third was ordered to alert the counsel for the prosecution and the defense.

At ten minutes past eleven, all were assembled at the courtroom, except the State's counsel. The jailer, William Wunderlich, brought in the prisoner, Edward Leyer, who was accompanied by his wife and children. Leyer occupied his accustomed seat within the bar, his facial expression remaining unemotional.

Near him sat two of his counsel, Messrs. Bisch and Richardson. There were roughly a dozen spectators in the courtroom, and around the clerk's desk were gathered a number of court officers.

The jury, preceded by a bailiff, was conducted into the courtroom and after taking their seats, the foreman, Mr. Eli W. Good, arose with a paper in his hand.

"Have you agreed upon a verdict, gentlemen?" asked the judge.

"We have."

"Mr. Clerk, receive the verdict and let it be read."

Mr. Good then delivered the written verdict to Major Walker, Circuit Clerk of Vanderburgh County, who read it aloud: "We, the jury, find the defendant, Edward Leyer, guilty of murder in the first degree, as charged in the indictment, and also find that he be imprisoned in the State prison for the term of his natural life."

After the judgment and sentence were read, the prisoner's face immediately turned pale. Helena, who was sitting on a bench directly behind her husband, rose to her feet and uttered an agonized scream, falling on his neck and sobbing as though her heart would break.

His children, too, began crying and promptly stood up and crowded around him, some crawling onto his lap, joining their tears and lamentations with those of their mother.

Edward maintained his fortitude as well as he could and strove to comfort them. But within moments, there in the dimly lit gloom of the courtroom, the prisoner rose from his chair, with his family clinging to him, and with an uplifted hand declared in German, "I am not guilty. I do not know anything about this crime. I am *not* guilty."

The jurors who understood German translated for those who didn't, leaving some expressionless, while others appeared overcome by the Leyer family's grief and tears. Judge Hargrave ended the embarrassment by quickly ordering the sheriff to adjourn court.

When the officer approached the prisoner to return him to his jail cell, Leyer's wife and children clung to him with agonizing shrieks, and it was only with great difficulty that his family finally released him.

The same scene was repeated when the iron doors of the prison cell closed on Edward Leyer.

***

After the sheriff left, and Leyer's family was escorted out of the jail, an unfamiliar man's voice from the cell across the hall asked, "Are they gonna' hang you?"

Edward got up off his cot and onto his feet, then stuck his arms between the bars and replied, "They gave me life. They stole my freedom for a crime I didn't commit."

"Are you gonna' fight it?"

"I must. I'm not guilty of this crime. I did nothing wrong."

***

"Helena."

Slowly opening her eyes, Edward Leyer's wife recognized her friend and neighbor standing before her in the darkness, lit only by a nearby streetlamp.

"Mrs. Rithmire."

"My dear, you must've been sitting on this bench for a long time. It's past *midnight*. You need to get home. You and your children need some sleep."

Helena looked from side to side and realized she was still sitting in front of the jail. Mina's head was lying in her lap and the boys were sitting silently, leaning against her and each other.

Helena lamented, "I don't know what to do. I don't know where to go."

"Rudolph asked me to check on you. Come, my dear, let's get you home."

After helping the children to their feet, she opened a blanket she had brought with her and wrapped it around the grief-stricken woman's shoulders.

Helena weakly stood and followed her friend's lead, the two walking arm-in-arm with the children in tow.

Chapter 31

Edward found himself alone in his cell, the shadows having gathered around him, as he was left to face the dreadful sentence just pronounced against him.

At half-past midnight on Sunday, Franz Basan, a German-speaking jailer, entered Edward's cell and told him, "I need you to get up now. I'm going to clean out your cell. Stand over there and don't move, understand?"

After doing what he was told, moving to a far corner of the cell and standing still, Edward asked, "What's that for?" as the jailor began to remove the mattresses and the glass bottle in which a piece of a candle had been placed.

"It's the rule," the jailor answered indirectly. "We must clean out the cell whenever a man's been handed down a long sentence."

Hid under the mattress, Franz found two ragged bits of glass, sharp and deadly. Without uttering a word, he held them up in the dim light for Edward to see.

With a somewhat defensive tone, Edward said, "Oh, you needn't do that. I'm an innocent man, and I'll be here when you come for me. No need to fear for me."

Franz, ignoring the prisoner, tossed the mattress and pillow into the corridor before bringing in replacements. Next he laid neatly folded replacement linens on the mattress. "Leyer, you have a wife and family. The court may have taken your liberty, but your wife and children are still yours. Don't make life harder on them than it already is."

Edward sat on his cot and lowered his head, "I don't know how I can live without them."

At 1 o'clock, Franz nodded and moved to leave Edward to his thoughts, turning the metal bolts in the heavy doors on his way out.

At 5:30 the same morning, Jailor Wunderlich entered the jail to make an early round, accompanied by Officer Basan. As the two men stood looking upon Leyer, Franz whispered, "He had a rough night, but he finally fell asleep a few hours ago."

Upon leaving the jail out the back door, Wunderlich paused when he heard a sound as if someone was heaving or vomiting. Attaching no importance to it, he went out and fed the horses, returning afterwards to serve breakfast to the inmates.

As he approached the back door, Officer Basan rushed up and said, "Quick, come inside! Something's the matter with Leyer!"

Hurrying into the cell block, the jailor and his night officer found Edward lying on his bed, which was discolored with blood.

"Open the cell!" Wunderlich barked, tightly clenching the bars.

After entering, he nudged Leyer's arm to wake him.

With a nervous smile, the prisoner held up his left arm, around the wrist of which was bound a rag, also saturated with blood.

"Franz, bring me some light," Wunderlich called out, as he removed the rag and beheld the sight of a deep gash across the wrist, about an inch from the hand, extending from one side to the other, laying bare the bone itself.

"There's two more cuts above the large one," Franz pointed out as he brought the candle closer.

"He certainly didn't lack courage or determination," Wunderlich said. "Obviously figured he'd sever the main artery, but didn't realize that was being protected by the two larger bones of his forearm."

Officer Basan moved the candle near the floor, saying, "Here," after which he bent over the side of Edward's cot and picked up a sharp piece of glass, still wet with blood.

Within thirty minutes of being summoned by the jailor, Drs. Compton and Ross soon came and gave Leyer's wounds proper attention. "The prisoner, it seems," Dr. Compton said, as he cleaned the prisoner's wrist with alcohol, "had repented himself of his intention after making the wound… and had bound it up in such a manner as to reduce the severity of the effects."

While Edward sat upright on his cot with his back against the wall, watching the doctor wrap his wrist with white gauze, Wunderlich asked, "Where did you get the shard to cut yourself? Officer Basan thoroughly cleaned this cell last night."

"I'd broken a bottle containing some medicine and had hidden a piece under some dirt in one corner of the cell before it was cleaned out. I didn't want to live anymore. I would rather die than spend my life in prison for a crime I didn't commit."

Speaking directly to Wunderlich, Dr. Ross interjected, "The quickness with which your prisoner had bound up the wound showed he was not overly anxious to die. When he made the ugly gashes, the pain must have been so extreme as to make him deathly sick."

"That was the vomiting sound I heard when I went to feed the horses," the jailor mumbled, as he frowned and cut his eyes toward the prisoner.

Once the doctors and jailor had left, Edward suddenly heard Margaret calling out from her cell, "My German brother, hear the words of God and repent for what you have done! The Good Book tells us, 'The Lord is close to the brokenhearted and saves those who are crushed in spirit.'"

Edward flipped onto his side, facing the wall, then used his hands to hold his pillow in place to cover his ears. "*Please, woman,* he whispered aloud, *I don't care to hear your mad rantings today. Leave me alone with my fate.*"

"Hear me!" she called out louder, shaking the bars fiercely with her hands. "The righteous person may have many troubles, but the Lord delivers him from them all. Listen to the words of God, German brother, salvation is coming!"

As she loudly hummed an old spiritual song, Edward pulled the pillow over his ears even more tightly and began a slow rocking motion, his body moving to and fro on his cot, until he fell fast asleep.

Chapter 32

Early the next morning, Dave Whittaker, the lead reporter from *The Evansville Journal*, came to the jail and was shown to the prisoner's cell. Edward lay in bed with a blanket pulled over him to his chin, his bandaged hand and forearm lying motionless by his side.

As the reporter stood just outside his cell and withdrew a pen and notepad from his pockets, Leyer stared at him for a moment and then lifted himself up quickly to a sitting position in his bed.

"What did you say to the judge last night?" Whittaker asked, stepping closer to Edward's cot just outside the bars of the cell.

"I said, before God I am innocent, and *I am*. It's mighty hard to make a man suffer for what he has not done. They say I bought arsenic, but I never bought any. If I had poisoned the cistern, would I stay here? I had my pockets full of money and could have gone away with my son, Herman. I did not know anything of the cistern being poisoned. I do not know if my boy did it. If he did, my wife knows of it. She brought him here to this city. I've tried to get her to tell me the truth, *and* whether or not he is guilty. She would not say. I told General Shackelford to see my wife this morning and talk *good* to her… get her to tell all she knows. I do not know where my boy is, but I *will* find him when I get out of here."

"Of those who have followed your trial, a few men do not agree with the guilty verdict, and believe you were pronounced a guilty man before the jury took the case. Do you believe you *are* a victim of prejudice?"

"In Evansville, I lived in a community of German immigrants. Here, I was with people I could understand and who understood me. In Grier Township, I was hated because I'm German, even though I consider America my home."

"I dare say, Mr. Leyer, if you *are* truly innocent as you say, a gross injustice has been committed against you *and* your family."

After leaving Edward behind in his jail cell, Whittaker then went to see the jury's foreman, Eli W. Good, Esq. at his office in Washington Block to discover, if possible, the jury's deliberations. He had heard word the delay in the verdict was caused by a wavering between the death penalty and the more merciful imprisonment for life, and further that the jury's first ballot had resulted in a unanimous verdict of *guilty,* but the next ballot, as to the degree of punishment, had not been resolved. Apparently, several votes had been cast for the death sentence, so a battle between Edward's life and death began.

Pen and notepad in hand, Whitaker took a seat in front of the jury's foreman and said, "My purpose in speaking with you, Mr. Good, is to learn all I can about how the jury arrived at the more lenient sentence of life in prison for Edward Leyer."

"I cannot tell you anything about it, sir. When we entered the room, the jury all agreed the deliberations should never be divulged, and I cannot say anything."

"Many think the jury should have passed the death sentence."

"I don't know about that. I think the jury did nothing less than its full duty. The evidence was mostly circumstantial, and in that case, a door should be left open to correct a mistake. Besides, mercy is never lost, and if the man should ever be able to establish his innocence, it's not impossible to amend the sentence."

"What was your impression as to the conduct of the trial?"

"The trial occupied ten days and discovered some of the most interesting theories I've ever heard developed in court. As to the conduct of the case, the result spoke volumes, and the prosecution deserves credit for the manner in which they placed every point before the jury. The defense also deserves credit, if for no other reason than for saving their client's life."

"Thank you, Mr. Good. I have what I need."

"One last thought, Mr. Whittaker. If perjury was committed, as I believe it may have been, this man deserves a new trial."

***

Dave Whittaker sat quietly as his copy editor read through his notes. Finally, breaking the silence, the newspaper's chief asked, "Tell me, can you give me a-... a general description of this man? Paint me a picture."

"Leyer, the convicted man, is 53 years of age and a man of what I'd say was an unusually repulsive personal appearance. Round-shouldered, shuffling in his gait, and unclean in his dress, he, at first sight, kills sympathy. If you've read DeQuincy's account of 'Three Celebrated Murders,' you'll remember his description of the murderer of the Mar family as a man whom nature had so molded as to fit him perfectly for the work his soul delighted in. His hair was thin, and his head peaked and misshaped. The eyes were dull and glassy, and *the light of love and mercy seemed to have gone out forevermore* in them. His face was thin and sallow, and the blood vessels were so arranged that it was impossible for him to blush or pale. That *very* description would fit Edward Leyer."

Chapter 33

While visiting the county jail to discuss the appeal process with his client, Edward Leyer, Col. Victor Bisch was summoned to the cell of the inmate, "Stamp" Wellington, who had given evidence that Leyer had confessed to him he had poisoned the cistern, the one used by the family of Fred Cook.

"What is it, Wellington?" Col. Bisch asked as he approached the cell door.

"I want to make a confession."

"I'm listening."

"First, I must know, if a man had sworn to false testimony, such as the confessions of Leyer, at the insistence of the husband of Mrs. Cook under some arrangement, could he be prosecuted for swearing falsely?"

"Swearing falsely on the stand is *perjury*, which is punishable by the court, but it is to every man that he ought to tell the whole truth, regardless of consequences."

"Let me think about it, then," Wellington said, turning away from the colonel and promptly sitting down at the foot of his bed, staring down at his knees in an obvious state of reflection.

***

Gen. Shackelford handed a brandy glass to Col. Bisch before sitting in his wing tipped chair. Both men swirled the Cognac in the glass to warm it by the heat of their hands. "Pray continue, Colonel."

Col. Bisch shifted on the couch before saying, "That was yesterday, and then this morning, I was once again in Leyer's cell when I received word that Wellington wished to speak with me. However, I was informed that the jailer, William Wunderlich, said Judge Hargrave had given him instructions to allow no one to talk to or to communicate with Wellington. Therefore, acting under the orders of Judge Hargrave, Wunderlich prevented me from seeing Wellington."

"This man, Wellington," Gen. Shackelford added, "is a convicted thief on his way to the penitentiary for the third term. His father and grandfather before him were thieves, and both had served stints in the State prison."

"Wellington twice called for me to see him," Col. Bisch said, "but I made no advances or overtures to visit him. To do so would be contempt of the court. Stamp Wellington's testimony was the chief reliance of the prosecution, *and* during his brief conversation with me, he had plainly indicated not only had he sworn to a lie, but *also* he had been procured to swear to a lie. Leyer is entitled to whatever benefit he might derive from this confession of Wellington's, according to the ideas of justice and fair play.

"But the Court ruled otherwise, and there are laws punishing people for contempt of courts, even when the courts are beneath contempt. So, I left Wellington to himself, and the law was vindicated, whether justice had been done or not."

***

On Monday morning, April 2, 1877, the court met in regular session with Judge William P. Hargrave on the bench. The attorneys for Edward Leyer filed their written motions for a new hearing of the case. There was no argument on either side. Accordingly, the motion was overruled, and the prisoner was brought into court and received the sentence arrived at by the jury. His counsel submitted a motion to appeal to the Indiana State Supreme Court and was granted thirty days to perfect their arguments. The grounds for a new trial, as urged by Leyer's attorneys, were that the judge erred in the instructions to the jury, erred in permitting the counsel for the prosecution to discuss Leyer's character and not allowing the defense to reply, and erred in not permitting character witnesses for the defense to be presented.

Upon hearing these grounds for a new trial, as presented by the defense, Judge Hargrave ordered that Leyer be taken to the State Penitentiary in Jeffersonville, Indiana, within the week to begin serving his life sentence.

Part 4

Last Wish

Please Lena, honor my final wish. Leave this state, and keep our family together.

- Edward Leyer

Chapter 34

A LIFE FOR A LIFE!

"On Horrors Head Horrors Accumulate."

Edward Leyer Summoned Before a Higher Court.

The Tragic Death of a Man Sentenced for "A Deed to Make the Heavens Weep"—His End in a Prison Cell.

The Mystery Surrounding His Death—His Wife Suspected of Administering Poison.

A week later, on Tuesday, April 10th, 1877, while the attorneys of Edward Leyer, the now *convicted* poisoner, were engaged in preparing his appeal to the Supreme Court of the State, the prisoner himself took his final appeal directly to The Almighty.

Around 5 o'clock in the afternoon, there was a sudden commotion at the jail when people in the street observed Drs. Compton and Muhlhausen hurrying into the gloomy reception waiting for them in the county jail. Finally, Dr. Muhlhausen emerged, and then by word of mouth, the news rapidly spread, Edward Leyer was dead.

Once again, Dave Whittaker, the reporter from *The Evansville Journal*, visited the jail a few minutes afterward and found the yard and the entrances blocked with a crowd of people, all of whom demanded admission, in vain. The jail yard and courthouse were filled with a curious throng, anxious to get a glimpse of the body. Sheriff Wunderlich arrived straightaway and escorted the reporter and Dr. Achilles, the chemist whose testimony in the case was an integral part of the trial, to the cell of the deceased convict.

When Mr. Whittaker reached the jail and was admitted, Leyer's cell was surrounded by men and boys looking through the bars and craning their necks to glimpse the body, which could hardly be distinguished in the gloom and darkness of the cell. A constable stood guard at the half-open door, and the head of the iron cot had been drawn to the open cell door, in order to let the last rays of the dying day fall through the barred windows on the countenance of the dead convict.

Mr. Whittaker began writing in his notepad what he observed for his article's publication in the morning edition: *The face was as pallid and white as the sheet on which the lifeless body lay. The breast had been bared to allow the physicians to find whether there was any life remaining in the body. It lay in a natural position, the hands resting alongside in a natural way. The appearance of the body resembled that of a man in a sound sleep, rather than a lifeless corpse.*

Whittaker's notes continued, *The only person near Leyer when the last gasp left his body was a prisoner trustee named William Sortner, who I found leaning against the wall of a nearby cell conversing through the bars with another inmate awaiting his trial.*

"What do you know of Leyer's death?" Whittaker asked.

"Well," Sortner replied, "I was in the corridor outside Leyer's cell when he threw up his hands and gasped and fell back dead."

"Did you see him before that?"

"Oh, yes. He complained frequently of being unwell and never slept soundly. I used to hear him muttering and groaning in his sleep."

"What would he say?"

"It was always the same thing; *I am innocent! God help me. I wish I could die!*"

After further conversation, Whittaker wrote, *Sortner stated that Leyer always acted very confused; no one in the jail could understand him. He seemed to have lost all hope and would lie for hours on his cot without moving. That being, even though he received a great deal of attention from his family, who visited him daily.*

The reporter then returned to Leyer's cell where he interviewed Sheriff Wunderlich.

"Leyer had complained of feeling a little badly the day before," the Sheriff explained. "At supper, Monday night, his wife brought him some oyster soup, coffee, meat and other eatables. Leyer ate, though sparingly, and left some of the soup and coffee in the dishes, which I personally took care of and preserved.

"This morning, not much attention was paid to him. The jailor, in his rounds, thought him asleep. He drank more coffee at breakfast. At dinner time, his wife offered him food and drink, but he refused it and was very tired and stupid. I was called in and tried to arouse him. I asked Leyer if he might want a physician, but the prisoner shook his head and asked in a drowsy way if it was nine o'clock. I said it was. It was past nine o'clock, actually, and nearly one.

"Then Leyer said to me, 'If it's 1 o'clock, you'd better call Dr. Kennedy.'

"Not suspecting any dangerous situation, I ate my dinner and then summoned Dr. Kennedy, who found Leyer in a fever, gave him some simple remedies, and took his departure. At half-past four, the jailor discovered the prisoner was in critical condition and warned me, to which I quickly summoned Drs. Compton and Muhlhausen, who arrived to find him dead."

As reported by Whittaker, *Rumors were flying about in the crowd that Leyer had committed suicide—having procured lethal poison in some unknown manner—or had been murdered by poison that had been administered in the soup the night before, and from the effects of which he had immediately fallen into a semi-drowsy condition, then perished. Regarding the latter, Sheriff Wunderlich had thoughtfully preserved and sealed portions of the remaining soup and coffee as evidence for chemical analysis.*

Dr. Achilles was summoned to gather the preserved evidence and to evaluate the scene for possible causes of death. When the chemist arrived, Sheriff Wunderlich conducted him through the crowd and into the jail, where in the corridor, a knot of men was gathered at Leyer's cell door, waiting for the coming of the coroner's jury who would take charge of the death investigation.

The report Whittaker filed the next morning, paraphrased below following his interview of Dr. Achilles—which occurred soon after he'd emerged from the jailhouse—indicates some measure of what transpired during the chemist's visit.

The jail-cell door was opened, and Dr. Achilles stepped forward into the dark, gloomy place, the dead man's ghastly face being the first sight the doctor had of the now-deceased prisoner. Edward's countenance was upturned with his eyes tightly closed, the rest of the body stretched out upon the low pallet, extended back into the cell. His hands were folded across his chest, and Leyer's bedclothes were bunched up to his middle.

Dr. Achilles called for a lamp, but none could be obtained. The day was so far spent, there was no daylight, so the few matches that were procured were lighted, one after another. The chemist quickly examined Leyer's heart, eyes and mouth. Rather abruptly, Dr. Achilles stood upright, declared he'd concluded his examination, and the little group of curious onlookers followed him into the corridor and then out onto the jailhouse porch.

"Are there indications of poisoning?" asked Mr. Whittaker.

"None," the chemist answered quietly. "None of corrosive poison. The mouth gives no sign of it."

"Would the indications appear so soon after death?" asked a bystander.

"They would appear *before* death, even."

The crowd waited some fifteen minutes before the coroner's jury came with the coroner. As they entered the cell block where Edward Leyer's dead body lay, the group was temporarily distracted by the prisoner Margaret Powell, who was exhorting an imaginary audience of sinners in a loud, piercing tone, occasionally pausing to sing a verse or two of the well-known hymn, *Swing Low, Sweet Chariot*. A portion of the small crowd gathered in front of her door, and through the bars she could be seen singing and marching up and down the cell like a caged beast. Soon after the spectators began looking in, Margaret began flailing her arms, stomping her feet and throwing her head back as she sang out quite loudly, her exhortations rising to a fevered pitch.

Then, quite abruptly, she lowered her voice, stopped her singing and said, "Why do you flee the law? You can't escape from it? It ain't in the courthouse alone. The law's in your homes and on your hearths; it's in your hearts, and you take it home wit' you. If you've done anything wrong, don't try to run from it, for the law is the law, and wit' you *all* the time!"

The law was with Leyer, Whittaker wrote in his notebook, using shorthand as he listened to Margaret's rant. *It had followed him through all the tortuous windings of a mysterious and horrible crime. He had been convicted, and the lunatic's ravings had a dramatic effect when delivered there with the corpse of an illustration not twenty feet away. It was a passing sermon and was impressive to the watchers.*

A few minutes before 6 p.m., the jurors were sworn in, and Mr. J. P. Elliott elected foreman. The coroner directed them to examine all the circumstances of his death and state in their verdict the cause, and whether or not caused by himself or any other person. They then examined the body, discovering no bruises or marks. And after arranging some details for the regular inquest, the jury retired to the circuit courtroom and adjourned to meet again at 7 o'clock the following morning.

Chapter 35

That morning, *The Evansville Journal*'s reporter, Mr. Whittaker, called upon the law office of Gen. Shackelford and Mr. Richardson, in which an interview with the latter was solicited and granted.

Mr. Richardson was one of the counsels for Leyer and had frequent interviews with the prisoner before and after his sentence. The peculiarity of the case, as well as Leyer's manner, interested Whittaker, and he was anxious to know the real facts concerning the Cook poisoning.

"I never found him changed," said Mr. Richardson. "He was always the same – protesting his innocence *so earnestly* there was no mistaking it. When he received his sentence, I went to see him in jail. He had great hopes of obtaining a new trial, and not until Judge Hargrave refused to grant it did he appear to lose hope.

"When I spoke to him about carrying the case to a higher court, he was impatient about the time he would have to wait. I assured him when the trial did come, the decision of the jury would be reversed, as I am confident it would have been. I urged him to keep up his spirits and, when he was taken to Jeffersonville, to bear in mind it would not be for long and he must keep up his courage.

"But he would say, 'If I ever go to the penitentiary, I will never come out alive. I am over fifty years old now, and this imprisonment has weakened me more than all my troubles.'

"I never saw anyone exhibit such affection for his family. When his children visited him in jail, he would take them in his arms and embrace them ardently again and again, with tears streaming from his eyes. He could not have been a bad man at heart. The love he displayed for his family showed a disposition that could *not* have been found in one who was so wicked as Leyer was painted."

"How do you believe Leyer met his doom?" Whittaker asked.

"Until the coroner's inquest is complete, I cannot express a professional opinion. The rumors that his death resulted from poison have grown more numerous, and a hundred tongues glibly express a belief the wife must have been instrumental in her husband's death. Some say it was done at his request. Others hint perhaps he was about to confess something that would implicate the wife, and the poison had been administered to prevent an unpleasant exposure. Fortunately, the tin buckets in which the coffee and oyster soup had been brought to the jail by the wife have been seized and sealed by the Sheriff, and a detective has been hired to dog her tracks and see that she does not flee the city. I must say, what a *remarkable* turn of events."

Mr. Whittaker immediately dispatched to interview Edward Leyer's wife, Helena, whom he found out the police had also been ordered to place under surveillance. As he approached her front door, an officer stepped out who said Mrs. Leyer had just left home and had gone toward the jail. The reporter then turned back in search of her, and was eventually informed she was in the office of Victor Bisch, Esq., one of the counsels for her husband's defense. Again Mr. Whittaker bent his steps to that place and arrived at the door, through the plate glass of which a view of the entire interior could be had.

Looking through the glass, he saw a stoic-looking German boy about nineteen years old sitting motionless in a chair near the door, gazing out into the street. Whittaker surmised it was Rudolph Leyer, the dead man's cousin and a witness who had figured extensively in the case. As the reporter first glanced around the room, he could see no one else present.

Then, as he looked through the lower portion of the glass into the corner of the room next to another door, Whittaker could see a woman sitting on a chair beside a sofa. Her head rested on the arm of the couch, with her arms folded behind her neck, silent and motionless, as though she were dead. But soon, a sob and an upsurge of grief shivered through her seemingly lifeless body, and then the reporter entered the office.

Rudolph Leyer turned in his seat and stared briefly at Mr. Whittaker, who somewhat solemnly asked if he knew the whereabouts of Mrs. Leyer. The boy pointed to the motionless woman, who didn't look up or speak a word. When Rudolph leaned over and touched her arm, she straightened herself up in her chair, as the reporter drew up his chair and prepared to question her.

Pulling out his notepad and pencil, Mr. Whittaker paused and gazed at the woman before him, clothed in a poor calico dress, collarless and untidy. Before speaking with her, he wrote his first impression. *She's so thin and pale, and those deeply furrowed wrinkles on her brow surely haven't been helped by all the troubles and losses she and her family have recently endured.*

"Did you take Mr. Leyer some supper last night?"

"Yes," Helena answered simply, with a questioning look.

Her eyes were weeping and red, he recorded in his notes. *Her mouth was quivering, and her short hair was messy and unkempt. Her voice was trembling and broken when she first spoke. Her face assumed a quiet expression that recalled more forcibly the likeness of the woman who had stood by her husband so firmly and faithfully during all his troubles.*

"What kind of soup was it?"

"Oyster soup with crackers and a little coffee."

This story came from a heart in which neither fraud nor murderous intentions had any habitation, he wrote.

"How did you come to take it to him?"

"Well, you see, I was with my husband yesterday, and he felt badly. I asked him if he was sick; he said he had caught a cold, and it hurt him. So I told Edward I would remove his boots, which would probably make him feel easier. He wanted some milk soup with a few oysters and crackers in it. I went to Mr. Weisheimer's store and gave five cents for the milk, ten cents for the oysters, and the children got a few crackers. I made the soup myself and took it to my husband, but he didn't eat it all. That's when Edward said he didn't want hot coffee anymore; he wanted it cold. So I took back the balance of the soup and this morning, the children ate what was left."

"Did you give your husband anything else?"

"Well, Edward *did* ask me for fifty cents to buy some whiskey, so I gave a silver half-dollar to Mr. Wunderlich to buy it. My husband then asked me for five dollars to buy some things he needed. I told him-..." Helena then began choking and her voice broke down. "I had no money that much. I got money no longer. I am now poor."

"Did he get the whiskey?"

"I don't know. I gave Mr. Wunderlich the money."

"Did you see your husband today?"

"Yes, I saw him today at dinner. The children brought him coffee this morning at breakfast, and I brought coffee at dinner. He was sleepy and would not talk. I again asked, 'Are you sick?' But he only say, 'Ugh.' I could not do anything, so I told the jailor I would go away. But before I left, I gave Dr. Kennedy's medicine to Edward. They were powders. I mixed it in a spoon with my finger and gave it to him, then told the jailor I would come back at night. He said I could come back in two hours. So I left at four o'clock and went home. When I started back a little while ago, I met a man, a policeman, I think, but am not sure. He asked me, 'Do you know that Edward Leyer is dead?'

"'No,' I said. 'I was at the jail a little time ago, and he was *not* dead.'"

"'He's dead now!' said the man."

Mr. Whittaker leaned back in his chair, as Helena bowed over on the sofa again. *This is not the grief of a murderess*, he wrote. *This woman is genuine.*

Mr. Whittaker then asked, "I've been told you said to the officer when he told you of your husband's death, 'What, so soon?'"

"No, I did not. I said I was there just a little while ago." Pausing and staring down at her lap, her hands shaking, she solemnly added, "I went to the jail, but they would not let me in. I have not seen him since I left him at 4 o'clock."

"How long have you been married to Mr. Leyer?"

"Twenty-three years I'm married."

"What's your age?"

"I'm 53 years old. My husband is three months younger than me. I was born in September, and he in December. His birthday was the night the mob went to the jail in Boonville."

"One last question, ma'am. How long have you been in America?"

"We came to America twenty-one years ago."

The reporter then stood up and thanked her. As he left the office, Helena fell on the sofa again, folded her arms over her head, and was motionless.

Mr. Whittaker paused after stepping outside, pulled his notepad out and wrote his final thoughts. *The story was told plainly and without any attempt at effect. She was earnest and expressed it vehemently but occasionally broke down. Her grief was the grief of separation after a companionship of 23 years. She has truly been a devoted wife, by any stretch of the word.*

Helena's allusion as to how she received the news of her husband's death led Mr. Whittaker to Officer William D. Harmon, the man to whom he figured she was referring. "I found them at their home on Upper Main Street," explained the officer, "and rapped at the door for admission. A little girl drew the window curtains to one side and, seeing me, ran back. I then proceeded around to the rear porch, where I met Mrs. Leyer coming toward me. I announced the death of her husband and received her response of, 'What, so soon?' with a great deal of astonishment.

"When I asked if she was expecting his death, Mrs. Leyer replied, 'Oh, no, but Edward has been so unwell that I did not expect him to recover.' She said this with much coolness and an apparent attempt to act surprised, so it seemed to me. His wife did not shed any tears, but wrung her hands and exhibited signs of uneasiness. These movements may have been feigned, or they may have been natural. I do not pretend to judge."

When Mr. Whittaker, after this exchange, stood up to leave, Officer Harmon added, "I hear her actions in the jail, when she went to view the dead body of her husband, were equally confusing. They say she showed no feeling; none whatsoever.

"But who am I to judge the grief of a woman who was just widowed? Who can tell the pent-up anguish that may have filled her heart? Who knows but what in the solitude of her own home, surrounded by children – orphaned by the consequences of the law – she wept bitter tears and grieved with her little ones the death of her husband?"

Chapter 36

At 7 o'clock that same evening, the coroner's jury reassembled at the courthouse and a large crowd of spectators and physicians were present. The proceedings were quickly inaugurated, and the testimony was as follows:

The first witness, Dr. J. W. Compton, stated he visited the convicted prisoner Edward Leyer 20 minutes after 5 o'clock earlier that same day, and pronounced him dead. "He looked like a man asleep. Certain poisons paralyze the heart, or death might have occurred from natural causes."

Jailor William Wunderlich was called to the stand and testified he'd informed his brother, Sheriff Chris Wunderlich, at 12:40 P.M. that Leyer was very sick. "I was told his wife had been with him and offered him food, but she could scarcely wake him. I then entered his cell, took him by the shoulder and shook him, and called him by name, at which point he opened his eyes and looked at me. I asked him if he was sick. When he said his chest pained him, I asked him if he wanted a doctor. He replied no, but then asked me if it was 9 o'clock. I told him it was quite a bit past nine, nearly one o'clock.

"By 4:30 P.M., one of the guards told me Leyer was dying. I immediately went for a doctor and found Dr. Compton in his office on Main Street. On our way back to the jail, we saw Dr. Muhlhausen in the pharmacy, and I called him in, as well. Dr. Compton then examined the body and quickly pronounced him dead."

Jailor Wunderlich stopped his testimony upon seeing Col. Bisch enter the room and take a seat.

Then, looking back toward the jury, he continued, "Last Sunday week, after Leyer cut his wrist, I went in to see him and asked him why he did it. He said he was tired of living and wanted to die. Then, once he reflected a bit, said he didn't want to put me to any inconvenience. So for my sake, he stopped the flow of blood by wrapping the wrist tightly.

"In the evening of the same day, when his wife came, the prisoner requested to see me. I went in with her and talked with him and his wife. Leyer appealed to her, proclaiming he was innocent and that Gen. Shackelford had been in to see him, saying there was no question but that some member of the Leyer family had put the poison in the cistern *and* that if he had done it, the general wanted to know it. He added, if Leyer *didn't* do it, to tell, if he knew, who did.

"Mr. Leyer then said, 'Lena, you know I didn't do it, and if you know who did, why don't you say so? Tell it all in the presence of Mr. Wunderlich.' Mrs. Leyer refused, saying she'd told Gen. Shackelford all she knew and only told the truth, and that she wouldn't lie for anybody, not even for her own father. I then asked her if the children were present when she talked to Gen. Shackelford, and she just said, 'No.' I should add Mrs. Leyer made them leave the room while this conversation was going on."

When Col. Victor Bisch was called upon to testify, the cusp of his testimony focused on the desperation of Leyer's health while locked in jail. "During all my interviews, he complained of his confinement, made solemn declarations of his innocence, and desired to be tried at the earliest date. Very frequently, almost every visit, he complained of the delay of the proceedings, asserting his right to be free, and repeating most earnestly the request to be tried, so as to be restored to his family. Mr. Leyer repeatedly said that confined as he was and being unwell, he was afraid he could not stand it. He claimed to be suffering and physically unable to stand his enduring imprisonment."

At the conclusion of Mr. Bisch's testimony, Sheriff Wunderlich brought before the jury two tin buckets, bound with cloth bands and sealed, which he said contained part of the coffee and soup furnished to Leyer by his wife.

Foreman Elliot then, at twenty minutes past nine, delivered the articles into the hands of Dr. Kennedy, the county physician, and directed him to make an analysis of them, as well as to re-examine the body of Leyer and perform an autopsy of it, if necessary. Dr. Kennedy was then asked to report the result of the investigation as early as possible.

The jury then adjourned till 9 o'clock the next morning, at which time, they were told, the inquiry would be resumed.

After the adjournment, Dr. Kennedy and several other physicians held a postmortem in the courthouse's lower hall. The eyes of Edward Leyer's cadaver were examined, and his pupils were found to be neither dilated nor contracted. Froth was issuing from his mouth; otherwise, the examining physicians discovered nothing unnatural about the corpse.

When the chest was opened and the heart removed and examined, it showed no peculiar changes, and seemed perfectly free from clotted blood. Next, the abdomen was opened, and Dr. Compton noted the stomach and intestines were very much distended with gas. The doctors proceeded to take out and seal—for Dr. Achilles' later analysis—the stomach, portions of the liver and duodenum, one kidney and the bladder.

Leyer's skull was then opened and the brain was taken out. The *dura mater* and *pia mater* were determined to be slightly distorted. Beyond that, Dr. Compton and the examining medical team found there was nothing worthy of note or unnatural in the condition of Edward Leyer's body.

Interestingly however, the brain's weight was fifty-seven and one-half ounces, which is unusually large. An ordinary male adult brain never weighs more than fifty-three ounces, and generally from forty-eight to fifty ounces. None of the doctors present speculated on this anomaly.

This group of doctors did not ascertain the cause of Edward Leyer's death, and therefore it would be necessary to await Dr. Achilles' analysis results, which could not be made before noon, and would probably not be completed by that time.

Mrs. Leyer remained under police surveillance until the inquest could be concluded.

Mr. Whittaker's column in the morning edition kept his readers on edge, as the drama continued to unfold: *The fact that the heart and brain were healthy would give great color to the suspicion of poisoning, as there must have been something, yet undiscovered, to produce the death so suddenly.*

To those who believe his death to be a cowardly act of suicide, I say this: Suicide is not a confession. It can easily be conceived how death is preferable to imprisonment for life, even to a man in the vigor of youth. Here was an old man, fifty-three years of age, with hope, had he enjoyed good health, running out with the sands of his life. At fifty-three and incarcerated, he had little to look forward to, even when his life was his own. At fifty-three, under such a sentence as Leyer's, what hope can live with the prison walls in sight! Whether innocent or guilty, there is a choice between death and imprisonment at such an age, and if it should be proven that Leyer is a suicide, those who believed him innocent would still believe it. As he stands before God, the question will be asked, was he guilty; he cannot deceive eminence.

Chapter 37

WAS HE POISONED?

The Second Day of the Leyer Inquest.

Waiting for the Chemist's Report—The Funeral of the Deceased.

The Letters Left with the Sheriff—His Affecting Farewell to his Wife and Children.

He Proclaims his Innocence on the Verge of Eternity.

The Mystery of the Cook Poisoning Still Unsolved—Is Suicide Confession, or is Leyer the Victim of Circumstances—A Thrilling Case.

It would not be an exaggeration to say the tragedy of Edward Leyer's death in jail on Tuesday, April 10, 1877, caused quite a stir throughout the city. Per the *Evansville Daily Journal*, his demise was one of the main topics of public conversation within a matter of hours.

The coroner's jury met at nine o'clock in the morning on Wednesday, April 11th and continued the examination of witnesses as follows:

Upon being called for further testimony, Dr. Kennedy explained he had been summoned to the prisoner on Tuesday, whereupon he observed Leyer was suffering from a cold, but nothing worse. "He appeared to be very stupid. I asked him if he had taken anything. There was a lady present, I suppose his wife. She said no, he had taken nothing but a bowl of soup. I asked if he had eaten much of it. She said he had eaten right smart and had requested that she get him some oysters. I gave her chloride of ipecac and potash in three or four powders, and showed her how to mix and administer them to her husband. Mrs. Leyer thanked me and I took my leave."

William Wunderlich was called back to the stand and testified he had observed Mrs. Leyer bring her husband some soup and coffee.

"Then, about 4:45 in the afternoon, I was called to Leyer's cell by one of the guards, because he believed the prisoner was dead. I took my keys and went into Mr. Leyer's cell, then stood there about three minutes. The whole time, he didn't seem to breathe, but then all at once, he drew a long, last breath. My first thought was of the times he swore he would never go to prison, and now I believed him."

Following his brother's testimony, Sheriff Wunderlich took the stand and said, "I have a letter here handed me by Dr. Kennedy, who found it lying next to the corpse. It's written in a difficult German dialect, but I can translate it. The letter, which is addressed to me, reads:

"*Mr. Chris Wunderlich:*

I express my thanks to you. You and your brother William have tried to cheer me, but it was impossible. My heart is broken down by the disgrace. I suffer terribly. I am very ill. I do not believe that I can live longer. I pray to God and Jesus Christ for strength and help, yet I cannot survive. Again, my thanks for your kindness, and further, I beg you to carry out this, my Last Will: Give to my wife, Lena, my body and the papers which you have from me, because she is the only heir. Please sign my Will, that she alone is the inheritor of my paternal and fraternal inheritance. Think not that I sought my own destruction. No. If I die, I die naturally. I beg day and night to be rescued from this earth. I have now, for six days, eaten scarcely anything, and still, there is purging that breaks me down. I believe this is all. Once more, be all greeted. Amen, Edward

"I have some other letters, which were handed me the morning Leyer tried to commit suicide, following his conviction, by cutting his wrist. These letters were written by him and contain statements somewhat similar to those in the letter I just read. In them, he proclaims his innocence and his Final Will, as though he expected every day to be his last. I'll file these letters with the coroner's office following this hearing."

Next, Dr. Kennedy was recalled and began by stating, "Last night, I removed Leyer's body to the courthouse and had a table prepared for a postmortem. I then finished the postmortem, assisted by Dr. Hodson, with Drs. Compton, Achilles and Owen all being present. We found nothing upon the body sufficient to cause death. The brain was somewhat congested, which might be caused by some opiates, or a long sleep would produce about the same. His stomach, part of a kidney, a piece of liver and bladder are in Dr. Achilles' possession."

Dr. George Hodson and Dr. J. W. Compton, both of whom assisted in the postmortem, were then called to testify, each noting similar observations to Dr. Kennedy's. At the conclusion of their statements, it was clear all agreed with Dr. Compton's conclusion: "If death was produced by poison, Prof. Achilles's analysis should identify it."

Once again, William Wunderlich was called to the stand for further questioning. "Well, on Monday between 12 noon and 1 o'clock, Mrs. Leyer brought her husband some egg pie or cake in a basket. I didn't notice at any time Leyer feared eating or drinking anything his wife brought him. He seemed to want her to confess everything she knew, but she seemed reluctant. So he asked for a preacher to come on Tuesday afternoon to administer a healing sacrament to them. She then whispered something in his ear. Leyer pulled back and said he had been honest, and that she should say the truth in front of me. Mrs. Leyer then said to her husband she had told Gen. Shackelford everything she knew, and the general had told her to keep her mouth shut. At that point, Mrs. Leyer promised her husband she would bring a preacher, but didn't do it."

The jury investigating Edward Leyer's mysterious death comprised of the following citizens: J. P. Elliot, who acted as the foreman, Nathan Gross, J. F. Lindley, John Dannettell, Jr., Louis Bittrolff and H. W. Lauer. Upon conclusion of the day's testimony, the coroner, Mr. Little, instructed the jurymen to exercise patience.

"Gentlemen, public opinion as to Mr. Leyer's guilt or innocence is very much divided. The community seems to have generally acquiesced in the verdict of conviction, but Edward Leyer's untimely and possibly circumspect death in jail has made him a martyr, and many now doubt his guilt. It was only the doubt, however, that suicide generally raises; many will take it as evidence of guilt and many as proof of innocence.

"That he died violently or by suicide is believed in many quarters, while others believe his wife interfered to prevent a probable confession in that summary way. But public opinion cannot settle upon floating innuendos, and you, the coroner's jury, best uncover the facts. This inquest is now adjourned to await the result of the chemical analysis."

The following morning, Thursday, April 12th, the investigation resumed, and a reporter for the *Evansville Daily Journal* wrote in his article the following day, *The coroner's jury in the Leyer case deserves the utmost credit for the cautious and sensible manner they maintained while the investigation was conducted. They did not rush at conclusions, did not hurry the proceedings, but with all the facts and probabilities before them, patiently considered the matter in all its phases, analyzed every point, produced it in its regular order, and prepared to render a just and sensible verdict.*

There was scarcely a trace of doubt among the physicians called in and present at the postmortem and inquest that Edward Leyer died of poison. Yet, according to the doctors' testimonies, based on their collective examinations of the body on Tuesday, made while still warm, no signs of corrosive poisoning were revealed. It was pointed out these usually developed in discolorations and contortions, none of which were found. The pupils of the eyes were neither dilated nor contracted noticeably; the effect of narcotic poisons was thus absent.

As explained by Dr. Kennedy during his testimony, "The examination was hastily made in a dark cell and cannot be considered conclusive. The postmortem revealed that his body was sound and healthy, and no natural disease could have produced it. Corrosive poison would have left recognizable traces; narcotics would have operated more stealthily. We expect to find poison in the analysis."

In a newspaper article summarizing the ongoing investigation into Leyer's death, it was noted Prof. Achilles had been busy all day with Dr. Compton conducting the analysis of the food articles from the prisoner's last meal, as well as the organs removed from his body postmortem. Dr. Compton conveyed to the reporter the utmost care was being taken that the result should be declared with mathematical directness. With this objective in view, the reagents were all tested or prepared personally by the chemist, all of which was tedious work and required time.

When asked by Mr. Whittaker, *Evansville Daily Journal* reporter, about the progress of the chemical analysis he was performing, Prof. Achilles courteously informed him, "We have found no mineral poisons. I have analyzed every article in my possession and the portions of the body, and there are no traces of mineral poisons, such as arsenic."

"You have found no traces?"

"Mineral poisons are absent from the samples taken.

"I have also tested for the presence of hydrocyanic acid, a poison neither organic nor inorganic, but partaking of both. If administered, there is a chance of not finding it and quite possibly it would leave no trace. Hydrocyanic acid is a volatile poison that sometimes produces convulsions, but may act as a sedative and produce symptoms similar to those recorded in Leyer's death. It is a poison so deadly that a fraction of a grain will cause death. If the action is sedative, this is evidence that it has not been inflammatory, and there would be no signs of that kind in the stomach. The poison itself can only be discovered by the peculiar odor it causes, resembling the fragrance of peach blossoms. The fact is, Leyer had been accustomed to the use of hydrocyanic acid in the preparation of hardening iron to make files and was thoroughly acquainted with all its effects and properties, as testimony was presented he had previously admitted to a number of people."

Mr. Whittaker turned the page as he feverishly transcribed the professor's explanation, using his reporter's shorthand.

"On the other hand," Prof. Achilles stated, "the death may have resulted from despondency or from a culmination of slow fright, in either of which cases there would be no sign of disease or rupture of the organs, but the body would appear perfectly natural and healthy."

"Have you tested for organic poisons?"

"No. I should explain, however, we did not expect to discover mineral poisons; no symptoms were pointing to their presence. The test was made merely to make assurance doubly sure. We have not yet tested for narcotic poisons. If there are any present, I think they will prove to be of that class. I will not ascertain before tomorrow morning."

When asked, Professor Achilles estimated he would be ready to report the result of his analysis in the morning at nine o'clock, when the inquest was to resume.

Chapter 38

Wednesday morning, while sitting with her children on the couch in their small, rented house on Main Street, Mrs. Leyer listened to Rudolph as he read from the Bible, Romans 8:38.

"For I am convinced that neither death, nor life, nor angels, nor rulers, nor things present, nor things to come, nor powers, nor height, nor depth, nor anything else in all Creation, will be able to separate us from the love of God in Christ Jesus, our Lord."

Rudolph skipped through a few pages until he came to 'The Great Commandment' in the Book of Matthew, whereupon he read aloud, "Thou shalt love thy Lord thy God with all thy heart, and with all thy soul, and with all thy mind, and thou shalt love thy neighbor as thyself."

Mina's head was nestled against her mother's shoulder, when she suddenly interrupted the reading. "Mama, must we love the people who hurt Papa?"

Helena leaned her cheek against the top of her daughter's head. "First, we have to forgive them, Mina," she replied in almost a whisper, a single tear sliding down her cheek, disappearing into the little girl's hair. "It will be a long time before I can forgive, my dear. And I don't know if I will ever-..."

"Mama?" Mina asked, lifting her head.

"Yes, darling, I'm sorry. God *does* expect us to love everyone, and forgive as we've been forgiven, but it's very hard when they've taken everything from us."

As she glanced over and saw the emotionless faces of her boys and Rudolph, Helena noticeably flinched when the solemn room's brief silence was interrupted by a loud rapping at their front door. Rudolph started to rise from his chair, but Helena stood and laid a hand on his shoulder to stop him.

"No, Rudolph, I'll see who it is. Take the children into the kitchen, please."

Slowly pulling the door open to a small crack, Helena asked, "Yes, what is it?"

A tall, thin man dressed all in black, with sunken eyes and a melancholy look, stood outside on the stoop. Bringing his gloved hand to his mouth, he politely cleared his throat, "Many pardons for disturbing you so early in the morning, Mrs. Leyer," he said with a raspy voice, "We have brought your husband's body. His last wish, as written in his letter, was to spend one night under your roof."

Helena brought her fingers to her mouth and gasped, but took a deep breath and nodded to the man. Pulling the door open, she glanced at the two muscular men standing behind him, holding the pine coffin. "Yes, thank you. Please bring him in."

The men carefully set the coffin on a coffee table. "I'm sorry for your loss," said the undertaker.

The other two men removed their hats and nodded respectfully before exiting. Solemnly, Helen nodded back.

Closing the door behind them, Helena heard a tiny whimper from Mina, who was standing in the kitchen doorway, staring at the pine box that held her father's lifeless body. Hurrying toward the children, she took Mina's hand in hers and squeezed it gently. "It'll be alright. Papa has come home for one more night with us."

Rudolph walked over to the coffin and laid his hands on it.

"Open it," Helena said, stepping up beside Rudolph.

"*What?*"

"Please, open it, Rudolph. I can feel his presence, but I need to see him one more time." Looking back to the kitchen door, she reminded the children, "Stay in there until I call for you."

Slowly, Rudolph pried the lid open. As the room's dim light revealed the body within, Helena recognized her husband's mouth, but his head was entirely bandaged above the nose and his skin was pale. Black thread had been used to sew his lips together.

After touching the white bandage encircling his head and moving it slightly upward, she cried out, "No, no! They cut him open!"

Suddenly her eyes rolled back and Helena fainted straight away. Catching her as she fell forward, Rudolph gently eased her to the floor. Quickly, he laid the coffin's lid back in place, as the other children watched nervously at the kitchen door.

"Stay where you are! Don't come in here! Your Mama will be fine."

Kneeling beside her, Rudolph called out Helena's name repeatedly to rouse her, a little louder with each attempt. Finally, she opened her eyes and burst into tears.

"Rudolph. My poor husband! My poor Edward!"

Rudolph sat down next to her and gave a comforting embrace. "I suppose they wanted to know how he died."

Helena lifted her apron to wipe away her tears before saying, "You can't find a broken heart with an autopsy."

Shortly after dinner, August went to the town magistrate to apply for a burial certificate. "Our mother fainted when our father's body was brought home, and she was suffering so much we thought it best to bury him as soon as possible."

The funeral took place at 10 o'clock, Thursday, April 12, 1877, with the bodily remains being conveyed to Oak Hill Cemetery, followed by several carriages containing the family, neighbors and friends of the deceased.

Helena, dressed in black, stood silently with her family at the gravesite after the short service, a thin veil covering her face, so onlookers would not see her woeful eyes, bloodshot from days of crying. The morning fog had created a gloomy, gray atmosphere for the service, but as it began lifting, a few rays of sun peeked through the clouds. Helena continued staring reflectively into the deep hole that held the pine box containing the remains of the man she loved.

Finally turning to her left, she saw her boys and Rudolph standing silently near the grave. Moments later, a smile arose on the face of Edward Leyer's widow upon hearing them begin to tell stories of their family's good times with him.

Swiveling her head to see where Mina had gotten off to, Helena saw her emerging from behind a large oak tree with a handful of tiny, yellow wildflowers.

Kneeling down alongside the deep hole, she tossed the flowers onto the coffin's lid. Helena smiled when she overheard Mina say, "These are for you, Papa. I love you."

When Mina stood up, her mother stepped forward, put her arm around her and pulled her close.

"My dear child," she whispered.

Then, looking down at the plain wooden box that contained her husband, she said, "You're at peace now, my love. No more pain. No more fear. I promise you, I will do whatever I must to keep our family together. Go with God."

Hearing a low muttering in the distance, she saw two men talking by some trees. When Rudolph walked over to her, he subtly gestured their way and said, "Those are the gravediggers.

They're waiting to fill the grave in."

Giving them a nod, which they respectfully returned, Helena gathered Rudolph and her children and started slowly walking home. As they walked away, Mina continued to turn around every few steps, looking back at the grave, tears streaking down her rosy cheeks.

Chapter 39

In the afternoon of Wednesday, April 11th, John K. Miller, a reporter for *The Evansville Courier and Press*, approached Sheriff Wunderlich for his consent to enter the jail and see what Wellington had to say regarding the trial of Leyer and its subsequent result. When the permission was granted, the turnkey was roused from his cot in the hall to open the iron doors leading into the jail corridors.

Proceeding without a guide onto the upper terrace, Mr. Miller reached the cell of Wellington who, in answer to the reporter's request, came to the bars of the door.

"I want to know from you, Wellington," Mr. Miller asked, "whether you intended to communicate some important facts to Col. Bisch when he was here the other day."

"Well, I don't know how important they were, but I was going to tell him something."

"I would very much appreciate it if you would tell it to me, Sir. The whole thing is over now. Leyer is dead, and you can't harm him further."

"Yes, but making a statement might hurt me. I don't care to go to jail for perjury. I know the law – two to fourteen years."

"There's a good deal of excitement in town about the verdict returned in the case, Mr. Wellington. What's your opinion of it?"

"My opinion is that he was not guilty."

"Okay, so when did he make that confession to you about poisoning the well?"

"He might have made it while we were in jail in Boonville. But I won't tell you any more than that."

"When did the sheriff hear it?"

"I told Taylor, the sheriff, a few days after the mob came, after Leyer and the other boys were brought down here. Ya' see, I wasn't taken down with them, and so had the run of the whole jail. They didn't lock me up. A few days later, Fred Cook and his brother-in-law were there. I didn't know who they were until after they had gone, when Taylor told me. The pair of 'em was in the kitchen when I came in to eat my supper. The sheriff told me to go back, as he wanted to talk to them. They never asked me anything about the confession then."

"Did Cook ever offer you any bribe to testify?"

"That ain't a fair question. I won't say whether I was bribed."

"Well, will you say whether your testimony was true or false?"

"No, it's no use trying to get me to answer that. I won't say what Cook did or didn't do. But I could tell you things about that case you have no idea of."

"Did you tell Cook of Leyer's confession?"

"No, I told Mrs. Taylor, the sheriff's wife, and she told Mr. Taylor, and he told Cook."

"What inducement did Cook hold out to you?"

"I don't want to answer that."

"Well, has Cook done anything for you since he was told of the confession?"

"No, he hasn't. On the contrary, he hasn't treated me as he oughta' have done."

"Have you seen Cook since you've been in jail here?"

"Yes. He and Sheriff Taylor came in the night after I was brought here."

"Did you say anything to him at that time about Leyer's confession?"

"No, I didn't, but I told him I needed some clothes, as those I had on were dirty and didn't belong to me. I didn't want to come from Jeffersonville in the prison suit."

"What did he say?"

"Nothing but, '*Well...*'"

"Mr. Wellington, don't you think you had better tell all the circumstances as they occurred?"

"I don't know. It might get me into further trouble, and I don't want to be sent to the penitentiary for fourteen years for perjury."

"Why, there's no danger of that! Any harm has been done already, and you'd do *better* to tell what inducements were offered you to give the testimony you did regarding the confession."

"If I told you, people would think I was bribed and should tell what I know – that is, if I know anything."

"When was your first conversation with Cook?"

"It was in January. I was eating my dinner in the jail's kitchen. Mrs. Taylor was also there. Cook came in, and then Mrs. Taylor went upstairs and left me with him."

"Well, what was your conversation with him at the time?"

"I don't think I oughta' tell that."

"What were you doing in jail at the time?"

"I was there waiting for my trial."

"Did Cook say he would use his influence to get you off?"

"I won't answer that question, but you can go to John Taylor, prosecuting attorney of Warrick County, and he might tell you what Cook did or tried to have done."

"Did Cook endeavor to get the prosecuting attorney to nullify your case?"

"I won't say whether he tried that, y'know, to get a change of venue for me or a new trial... or a continuance of my case."

Shuffling his feet for a moment, he gripped the jail cell bars and turned to face the reporter more directly. "Now let me ask *you* a question."

"Go ahead."

"I want to ask you, if you were in my position, and a man should come out of the blue and promise to help you, what would *you* have done if you'd thought you had a chance to get clear of your difficulties?"

"Well, I don't know, but I think I would have done as you probably did."

"Well, suppose the man did not keep his promise. What then?"

"Have you heard from Cook *at all* since he was here to see you?"

"No, I haven't. So, whadaya' think they'd do with a man for bribing—or *attempting* to bribe—anyone to perjure himself?"

"I wish you the best, and a good day, Mr. Wellington," the reporter said as he walked from the prisoner's cell.

After interviewing Wellington, Mr. Miller wrote up his piece and published his conclusion that very day in *The Evansville Courier and Press*:

Wellington had something he wished to tell, but was apprehensive that it would make matters the worse for him, and he was also apprehensive of danger from another quarter. His anxiety to get back to Jeffersonville, where he thought he would be in no trouble, and his desire to be in more comfortable quarters seemed uppermost on his mind. So he spoke in the highest terms of his future residence. He said he would get good food there, clean clothing, and would receive kind treatment. Wellington, we should judge, would not stop at anything to save himself, but now that he found all hope was gone from the source which he most expected it, his moments for reflection were bringing a troublesome and bitter reward. Leyer's death, and the prominent part which he had assumed in the terrible drama so lately enacted, was restoring the details of it to his keen remembrance. The day was not distant when a true statement of the facts would be laid before the public and when the guilty and innocent actors of the tragedy would receive their condemnation or reward, as far as this world is concerned.

As he appeared at the door, Wellington seemed to be about five-feet-eight or nine inches tall, slender, with a good head covered with auburn hair, a rather pleasant face, steel-blue eyes, an aquiline nose and a very high forehead. His language was good. He seemed to thoroughly understand the awkward position he was placed in. His experience taught him, as he said, never to give testimony against anyone as long as he lived.

There was a woman living on Main Street with five of her six children, whose lives had been darkened for all times to come by the shadow of Wellington's testimony. It was hardly probable he would derive much comfort when he reflected on the disaster and ruin he caused by being a partial instrument in what he brought to their home.

Chapter 40

STILL IN DOUBT.

Conclusion of the Coroner's Inquest in the Leyer Case.

The Report of Dr. Achilles—He Found No Indications of Poison—Other Testimony.

"DEATH FROM UNKNOWN CAUSES."

The coroner's jury in the Leyer case reassembled at the courthouse Friday morning, April 13th, at nine o'clock, to hear the report of the chemist, Dr. Achilles, and to conclude their deliberations in the case.

Before calling upon Dr. Achilles, Col. Victor Bisch and Sheriff Wunderlich were questioned concerning Edward Leyer's handwriting and they each determined the letters found on his person were written by him.

Dr. Achilles then made quite a lengthy report of his analysis, beginning with his explaining to the jury the tests he had applied in every case, then closing by saying he had failed to find poison in either any parts of the body or in any of the substances submitted to him by the jury.

He explained, "My opinion is that it is not impossible for a person to die of incidental causes, leaving no trace after death. But if Edward Leyer died from hydrocyanic acid, although none was found or could be found at the time of the analysis, that would not alter the opinion. My reasons for this are that the suddenness or circumstances of death strongly indicate poison. I incidentally learned that this man was acquainted with hydrocyanic acid and its deadly purposes. In fact, he knew that a small quantity of this poison would kill. It acts as a sedative poison, lowering the body's energies and only occasionally causing spasms and convulsions, and generally, the symptoms nearly correspond to those of the deceased.

"Whether it was taken by Leyer himself or was given to him by other parties remains to be shown. Strong suspicion falls on the food or drink provided to him by his wife. This theory is strengthened by the fact that Leyer was as familiar with poisons and what effect they would have upon the body as most any physician. Moreover, while in the file business, he had to make use of hydrocyanic acid for the purpose of hardening the iron. On many occasions, Edward Leyer was seen at his workbench with his face masked, and when questioned as to why he used it, replied it was necessary to protect him from the effects of the poison.

"The fact that no poison was found in the stomach would not be proof of its not having been there," concluded Dr. Achilles, "because it is apt to become volatile even at common temperature and the smallness of the dose. I give you this opinion for what it's worth. I did not find the poison and cannot say it was there."

Dr. Kennedy was then recalled and presented the following testimony. "Taking into consideration all the circumstances connected with the postmortem, the visits I made, and the analysis of the stomach, I would say this man's death resulted from hydrocyanic acid. When I visited him at two o'clock on the afternoon he died, I made as thorough an examination as possible, and failed to find anything the matter with him, except a cough he complained of. His pulse was rather quick and full. I asked him if he had been taking anything, and he answered he had not. I made up my mind that he had, or else was playing off on me.

"I gave some expectorant powders to his wife and then left, and from the postmortem, we found his heart in a healthy condition, and his lungs, liver and kidneys apparently sound. We could find nothing indicating sickness or that he had been ailing whatsoever. Upon examining the brain, I found the blood vessels somewhat injected and dark, which might be caused by the hydrocyanic acid, as I was informed he was using it in his business, and was well-informed as to the effect of it. He must have taken a small dose of it after I left him, if taken at all. One minimum portion or drop would be sufficient to do the work. I was somewhat convinced he had taken that, as his eyes showed rather a glaring appearance at the postmortem."

After Dr. Kennedy concluded, Dr. Compton then testified. "I'm of the opinion Edward Leyer died from natural causes. If he died from poison, I can conceive of no other than that of hydrocyanic acid. After witnessing all the chemical tests and seeing them made scientifically from good reagents, and no poison being discovered, I am compelled to think there was none taken. We have numerous instances on record, and some under my personal observations, where soldiers in poor health have desired to return to their homes and families. Applications for furlough were made through subordinate officers who gave cheering accounts of the success of such applications. But, when the same would reach headquarters, the authorities did not sympathize with the soldier's condition and hopes and, through some technicality, would deny the request. The news having been carried back to the soldier, hope departed, and general depression would follow. The soldier died suddenly without any disease to which death could be attributed.

"Here was this man, Leyer, in feeble health for years, suddenly arrested and charged with a terrible crime. The stress must have produced a severe shock to his nervous system. Then followed the remarkable trial. A host of witnesses appeared on the stand testifying strongly against him, almost or quite an equal number testifying in his favor. His life in jeopardy, his liberty endangered, the influences of *hope* and *fear* alternately acting upon his already debilitated nervous system, and finally his sentence, yet a feeling of hope for a new trial bracing him up. The effort for a new trial resulted in an appeal to the Supreme Court.

"The result necessitated probable incarceration in the state prison for one or two years before his case would be reached in the court. This information coming to him, together with the thought of his final separation from his wife and family, the hope which had sustained him to this point, left him, and he died from the depression which naturally followed. It is, therefore, my opinion this man died from a broken heart.

"There is yet, however, another influence not mentioned. Very able counsel prosecuted this man, and his character was so severely denounced as almost to break him down on the witness stand. On the other hand, equally able and earnest attorneys defended him, and the alternation of hope and despair was constant throughout the long trial. These influences must have had a strong effect on the nervous system and vitality of the deceased. Either way, he died a broken man."

After final deliberation, the coroner's jury then published their conclusion in a report to the coroner: *The autopsy was completed at about half past ten o'clock or six and a half hours after death, and it does not seem probable the presence of poison could have escaped the notice of the physicians, had Leyer really died from its effects. Those who testify that, in their opinion, Leyer died from the effects of the acid admit there was no trace of its presence, but think the letters he left indicate he died by his own* hand and he must have died of hydrocyanic acid. *This analysis seems to be an exceedingly arbitrary view of the matter. Leyer had been accustomed to the use of this acid in his business; therefore, because no trace of poison was found, it was this poison that killed him? This line of reasoning is without logic. An autopsy showed the vital organs were all healthy, and the death was likely caused by nervous prostration brought on by fright.*

The jury, therefore, finds we have procured all the information possible on the matter and return a verdict of "death from causes unknown to the jury."

***

Gen. Shackelford pulled a half-full bottle of brandy from his bottom left drawer and poured two fingers into each of two glasses. After handing one to Col. Bisch, he sat across the table and warmed the brandy, swirling it in his glass.

"Whatever may have been his faults," Bisch said, "Leyer's letters showed him to be a man of a morbidly sensitive nature. The trial was a severe test of all his powers, and when the verdict of the jury struck down hope, it's not surprising he gave up all will to live. He was an old man with but a few years before him, even had his liberty been restored. To him, separation from his wife and children for the remainder of his life was worse than death. It was living despair."

"Aye," Shackelford said after taking a sip from his glass. "It's not strange such a fate wore out his vitality. Life cannot exist without hope, and hope died within Leyer's breast when he heard the *guilty* verdict pronounced against him."

Both men paused, silently sipping their brandy.

Eventually, Shackelford spoke up, "Throughout the trial, you and I never discussed Leyer's guilt or innocence."

"He was our client. We believed him innocent to offer a just defense."

"Aye, but it's over now. The poor soul took the final appeal to the highest court. I told him and Mrs. Leyer a few days back that, in my opinion, if he didn't poison the cistern, then I believe someone in his household surely did."

After swirling his own brandy glass and contemplating his fellow litigator's comments, Bisch finally said, "Wellington has all but confessed to perjury for his account of Leyer's confession in the Boonville jail. Without Leyer's confession, all that remains to the prosecution is circumstantial."

"Aye."

"They accuse him now of suicide by use of hydrocyanic acid. He was familiar with that form of acid's deadly, virtually undetectable and untraceable characteristics, yet he was convicted of murder using arsenic, a much more easily detectable and traceable poison. I will offer you another scenario, but it's so-... *calculating* that I dare not bring myself to discuss it without the aid of this brandy."

Shackelford leaned forward and sat his glass on the table. "Pray, continue."

"Mr. Cook left on a hunting trip, and when he returned, the cistern was poisoned, and his wife and children had drank of it for several days. What if he had expected to come home to find them dead?"

"You propose that Cook poisoned the water before leaving?"

"Had he done so, he would have had the perfect alibi. His family would have died while he was out of state."

"But why would he have done such a horrible thing to his own family?"

"Who knows why men do these things, General, but it seems to happen all too often. And indeed, it helps keep us in business! But the misdeed failed to claim a single victim by the time Fred Cook returned. Instead, doctors and neighbors swarmed his house and spoke in hushed tones about a crime. He had to quickly cast the blame on *someone* other than himself. The obvious perpetrator would be an ill-mannered neighbor who hated him with a passion. But he knew there was no evidence against Leyer that would hold up in court, so he rallied a mob to lynch him before an alibi of his making could be established. With Leyer's death, it would have been a simple matter to construct the motive and means that would have justified the killing."

"Umph! You still lack Cook's motive."

"Cook has been keeping company with one," Bisch replied, as he flipped a couple of pages in his pocket notebook, "Mary A. Irons. He hired her to care for his daughters after the passing of his wife. Miss Irons is nearly half the age of Mr. Cook, at sixteen years. Perhaps he was just as familiar with her before Mrs. Cook's death."

"But there's no evidence of a relationship, romantic or otherwise."

Bisch put the notebook back in his pocket. "You asked for a motive. Love and hate are the most powerful of all motives, General."

"Aye."

***

Meanwhile, Sheriff Chris Wunderlich, and his brother, Jailor William Wunderlich, sat at a table in the Corn Husk Diner, reading and rereading Edward Leyer's letters, as they were printed in *The Evansville Journal*, March 12, 1877.

"Was he the victim of circumstantial evidence or a shrewd and cunning assassin?" the sheriff asked.

"He was rude and uneducated, but he had the soul of a man and the heart of a Christian. Listen to this from one of his letters: *My God, thou knowest I am innocent. Innocent, I was thrown into prison by a band of thieves and murderers. Oh, my kind God, I beg Thee forgive them.*

"His last prayer was not for the protection of his wife and children, but for the forgiveness of his enemies – those who charged him with murder and who violently assailed the prison in which he was being held."

"True," William replied. "The mob would have hung him. The law crucified him upon the cross of mortification and despair."

Sheriff Wunderlich folded his newspaper and laid it on the table. "Was he the victim of a base and cowardly conspiracy, or was he the just recipient of God's judgment? Was he a brilliant serial killer, who had mastered the use of deadly poisons to the extent that the best of the scientific and medical community couldn't detect its use in his victims? Or was he an illiterate *Dutchman* so hated by his neighbors they would band together to bring about his demise?"

Chapter 41

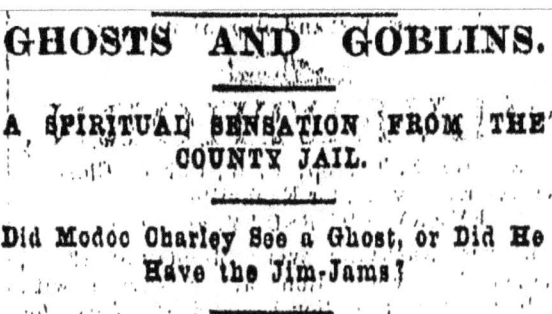

Dave Whittaker, the lead reporter from *The Evansville Journal*, sat across his editor's desk as he tried to convince him of the newsworthiness of his research.

"In the weeks and months following Edward Leyer's death, some of the most vivid ghostly encounters ever reported in the county came to light. The jailor, William Wunderlich, bore testimony to the tales told to him of supernatural encounters that began soon after Leyer unexpectedly died in his cell."

"Mr. Whittaker, you understand the reputation of this paper is at stake? If you wish to write tabloid news, *The Journal* may not be the place for you."

"Yes, sir, but I assure you I only recorded the stories as told to me and make no claim as to their authenticity. This is human interest at its best. I believe our readers will enjoy it!"

"Go ahead then, read me what you have."

Lifting the page filled with his shorthand notes, he read aloud, "If there is any doubter in the belief of ghostly appearances in Evansville, he has an excellent opportunity to investigate the subject, and the county jail offers the best field research. The prison inmates were agitated over what they swore were ghostly visits from the spirit of Edward Leyer, who died under such sudden and mysterious circumstances as to heighten the belief in spiritual unrest. It was said by several witnesses, including Wunderlich, Leyer had threatened to haunt the jail before he died, and if the prisoners interviewed were telling the truth, he is clearly engaged in keeping his word.

"The popular superstition regarding the appearance of ghosts, particularly when following shortly after a person's death, seems to prevail mostly among the unschooled and lower classes, and it was from these classes the jails drew the large majority of their inmates. The lack of formal education may, to some degree, account for their fears and apparent communication with the ghostly visitors; but being uncultured is not always to be relied upon to breed superstition, if superstition it is. Some very learned and intelligent men have believed in ghosts and the re-appearance of the spirits of persons, either those recently passed or long dead. However, the fact remains a number of the inmates currently incarcerated in the Evansville County Jail suspect it of being haunted, and told some lively stories.

"After Edward Leyer's postmortem, several supernatural appearances seemed to have revived the talk of ghosts. One of the prisoners assured Wunderlich that late one night, he had seen the figure of a man standing in the corner of the jail in front of Leyer's cell, gazing fixedly and with an impression of melancholy about him at the bars of the door. He said the figure resembled Edward Leyer. The prisoner was greatly alarmed and conveyed in both tone and sense of conviction his sincere belief in the vision that had appeared to him."

The reporter, glancing up from his notes and seeing his editor was still attentive, continued: "Charley Modoc, confined in the jail and sent up for larceny, has remained kept in Edward Leyer's cell for some time. One night, when Wunderlich was at the jail door very late, he heard alarming cries from Modoc, and entering the jail, hurried over to his cell.

"When Wunderlich entered, the prisoner stood in one corner in abject fear, shivering like one stricken with palsy. Upon being interrogated, Modoc said the ghost of Leyer had appeared to him and dragged the cover from his bed. After soothing the man and attempting to convince him it was just a dream, the jailor retired, but waited. In a few minutes, he heard Modoc yell wildly, *Help! Help!*

"Opening the door, he rushed to the cell, and again the prisoner was cowering and shivering with fear. He said the ghost had reappeared, torn the cover from the bed a second time, and flung it into a corner. Then, the specter pointed to the mattress and said, *See! See! There's blood on it!*"

***

"All this sounds rather extraordinary, Mr. Whittaker. Go on."

"Yes, sir. Perhaps the most bone-chilling account was given by two prisoners, Baker and Simmons, who shared a cell directly across the hall from Leyer's. Two days after his death, before the corpse had been buried, the men offered their testimony to the jailor, Wunderlich.

I woke around 1:00 a.m., said Simmons, and noticed the light from a candle in Leyer's cell. After approaching the bars of my cell, I saw a man sitting on the cot, the very one where Leyer had drawn his last breath. I shook Baker to wake him, and whispered for him to come see.

'They must have brought someone in after dark,' Baker replied. *'Go back to sleep.'*

But before I returned to my cot, I spoke to the man in the cell across the hall, asking him, 'What's your name?'

Baker sat up in his cot and we both stared as the man turned his head toward us. With a thick German accent, he said, 'I'm not dead.' Then, the figure turned to lie down on his bed, after which the candlelight faded into darkness.'

"But according to Wunderlich, that wasn't the end of it. When morning came, after a restless night, Baker and Simmons stood at their cell door looking across the hall into an empty cell. When the guard made his morning rounds, he confirmed to them no new prisoners had been processed in overnight."

"That sends a chill down my spine," the editor said. "It seems as though it may be Leyer's spirit was just as confused by his death as anyone."

Chapter 42

While chatting in the office of Mr. John Decker, the township trustee, Gen. Shackelford said, "Though weeks have passed, I'm still shaken by the outcome of the Edward Leyer case."

"Speaking of which," Decker said, "I've wanted to tell you something about Leyer, whom you knew all too well. I was acquainted with him during his time here in the area, and at one point had close business relations with him. I always regarded him as a very peculiar man and actually felt suspicious of him. But somehow, he became attached to me, as much as a man of his unusual character could be to anyone. Once, while apparently in a communicative mood, he related his life experience to me. He said he was born in Germany and that his father was an educated man who had charge of a hospital. Leyer himself had received a very fair education and had a hereditary liking for the science and analysis of drugs. His desire and curiosity in this direction were fully satisfied by being granted unrestricted access in the hospital, where he had a rich opportunity to experiment and study to his heart's content. It seems he followed his bent in this direction only during his residence in Germany, for he turned his attention to mechanics on his arrival in this country.

"But what I wanted to tell you especially was Leyer said he had the *secret of life* in his possession, which would prove a fortune to someone who knew how to use it. This secret, he told me, was a compound of drugs he could administer to persons, and it would kill them, for all intents and purposes. Physicians could examine them, and they would pronounce them dead, and an autopsy would not reveal anything in the way of poison. *But* Leyer said he also possessed an antidote, which would bring the person back to life, if given within forty-eight hours. Taken in connection with the number of deaths charged to him, I believe he must have experimented with his drugs on some of his workmen."

Gen. Shackelford sat up in rapt attention, his mouth slightly ajar. "I bid you, please continue."

"It is my belief he took the drug himself, once he saw prison life staring him in the face, after a life sentence had been passed upon him. I think he had arranged the whole matter with his wife, and she was to administer the antidote. For if you'll remember, he not only died suddenly, but on his corpse was found a letter earnestly requesting the authorities to send his body to his wife and let it remain under her roof at least one night before burial. But this the prison officials did not do. Instead, they sent the body to a medical postmortem, where it was thoroughly examined as to the cause of death. The stomach was removed, and chemical tests were made, but no poison was discovered. The brain was also dissected, but nothing unusual was discovered, except that it was slightly above the usual weight. I have never said anything to anyone about this before, simply because it never occurred to me to do so, and I only recall it now in connection with your close association with the case. The whole thing was so remarkable, I could not help but remember my chat with this uniquely curious man-... or *ghoul*, whatever you may call him."

In response to Decker's story, Gen. Shackelford asked, "Is it possible the doctors ended the existence of a man who was attempting the perfect prison escape?"

"General, I study cases of misdiagnosed death with passion. History records *countless* times that persons have been supposedly dead, when in fact, they were not. Numerous instances are on record where parties have been placed in their coffins, and at some point during the funeral procession, life again reasserted itself. So numerous are these instances that it has given rise to the common expression – *a lively corpse*.

"Why, tomorrow night on the stage of the Evansville Opera House, one of Shakespeare's grandest plays will be enacted – a play that commemorates and renders sacred love, the noblest passion of the human breast – in which the fair Juliet, in order to escape the tyranny of her hardhearted and inhuman parents, *and* to fly to the arms of her loved one, takes a sleeping potion, and so dead does she become that frantic parents, loving friends and skillful physicians proclaim the fact that her fair spirit has winged its way to the better land; so dead, that when the brave Romeo comes into her presence, his great love – a love that should seek and find all stings – cannot find enough of spirit left in that fair frame on which his great love could fasten, to proclaim the fact that she was not dead, but asleep."

"Tradition and history teach us," Shackelford added, "that men frequently have been supposed to be dead, when in truth, they were under the influence of some powerful narcotic. Since the trial, the medical brethren have been having fun at the expense of the legal fraternity, because of their ignorance of the influence and effect of certain poisons and their wild theories. Today, the tide turns by the lawyers suggesting to the doctors he was not dead, but was asleep. May it not be true the idea entered Leyer's head that he could take some opiate that would, for a time, arrest the functions of life, and leave him apparently dead? Could this be why his wife cried out and fainted dead away when she laid eyes on the mutilated corpse?"

"The doctors," Decker replied, "say he showed no signs of death from any natural cause. The symptoms of his supposed last illness indicate the influence of some powerful narcotic. There is no question *now,* but that he is dead. After a painful, yet skillful analysis, the doctors proclaimed him dead. They can now say, as a certain doctor once said, in a county not far removed from this, when called by a coroner's jury to testify as to the death of a certain subject, felt his wrist, looked at his tongue, opened his eyes, pinched him, shook him, kicked him, took out his heart, held it with forceps, and then said, *I'll be dammed if he ain't the deadest man I ever saw.* Couldn't the Evansville doctors say as much now, in regard to Edward Leyer?"

Shackelford shook his head. "This makes a comment made by Dr. Kennedy on the stand during the coroner's inquest particularly gruesome, in light of this conversation."

"What was that?"

"While describing the autopsy of Leyer, which took place in the late hours following his death, Dr. Kennedy noted that, upon the removal of his stomach, it seemed unusually warm to him when he held it in his hands."

Chapter 43

"A young boy brought this letter for you, Mr. Bisch. I think he's one of the Leyer children."

"Thank you, Anna," Col. Bisch said, as he accepted the letter from his secretary. Opening it, he read:

Dear Mr. Bisch,

I have no one on this earth whom I can trust. I turn to you to give me advice and assistance on caring for and feeding my poor children. I can't help but sell everything, including my husband's work clothes. I received 7 dollars and 50 cents from Shackelford. With what I got from Sheriff Taylor, I paid for the coffin and some flowers to pay my respects to my husband. My God! What should I feed the poor children? I sent my Eddy to see Trustee Fisher. The same sent me an answer that I should go to Warrick County, where they murdered my husband and orphaned the children. Oh, Mr. Bisch, I'm close to desperation. My children are starving! I can't believe it. I don't mind if I have to go hungry; if only the poor children don't have to go hungry. I want to serve, but I can't go out. Give me and my son work. I want to take over the plague house. Go after Dr. Ogden and Dr. Harvey. The latter is no longer here. Write to him, and you will hear that I can run the plague house with honor, even with the children. Then, if there are sick people, I may have an apartment and money to support my children. I am convinced that no complaint will come against me. Let my worst enemy have no reason to slander me. I will do everything I can to feed myself and my family legally, so my children do not die of starvation. I will not bother the trustee again. Fisher should not point me back to my husband's robbers and murderers. Oh, Mr. Bisch, have mercy on a poor woman who is close to despair! My strength is leaving me! I can't come myself! God have mercy on me!

Maria Helena Leyer.

***

Hearing a knock at the door, Helena walked from the kitchen toward the front of the house to see who was calling. Opening the door, she said, "Mr. Bisch, hello."

"Mrs. Leyer, I'm very sorry to disturb you so early in the morning. May I come in?"

"Yes, naturally. You received my letter?"

"I did. Is there somewhere we can talk?"

Helena gestured behind her and led him to a table in the kitchen, where he sat in a somewhat wobbly wooden chair across the table from her.

"Mrs. Leyer, you know I steadfastly believe in your husband's innocence."

Shifting in her chair, she nodded and rested her chin on her hands.

Leaning forward, his fingers interlaced on the scuffed-up tabletop, he lowered his voice and said, "I regret, though, that the county prosecutor does not share my certainty. I have just come from Mr. Hatfield's office, and need to inform you he holds fast to Herman's conviction. As you know, both Herman and Edward were convicted of murder in the first degree. We can ask for a new trial, but there are no guarantees. Now, *please* don't tell me you know where Herman is hiding, or if he is yet alive. Just, if you are able, convey this message to him. He has been convicted of murder and will be treated as such by the State of Indiana if he ever returns."

Tilting his head and raising one eyebrow, he asked, "Do you understand what I'm telling you, Mrs. Leyer?"

With her eyes beginning to tear up, she dipped her head in acknowledgment to the colonel, then began nervously wringing her hands.

"There's more, Mrs. Leyer-... Helena."

Col. Bisch leaned in even closer to her and spoke quite solemnly. "Mr. Hatfield told me this morning the State of Indiana is preparing charges against *you*. They are considering a second-degree murder charge for the death of your husband."

Bowing her head, she immediately began sobbing into her hands, the colonel looking away uneasily. Several moments later, when her crying diminished, Helena took a deep breath and composed herself, sitting up straight in her chair. Then, pulling a handkerchief from her apron pocket, she wiped her wet cheeks and eyes.

Suddenly she blurted out, "This can't be! I had nothing to do with Edward's death! This state killed him!"

The colonel quickly agreed, "I know, I know, and I don't think they have a case against you. But I have to warn you that, based on the autopsy report of your husband, the prosecutor does *not* believe he died of natural cause."

Standing up abruptly, Helena began pacing back and forth across the kitchen floor. "Mr. Bisch, what now? Will they kill us one by one, until we're all gone?"

"I *have* thought earnestly of your situation, and every scenario leads me to the same conclusion."

Pulling a small coin purse from his pocket, he sat it on the table and said, "Here are twenty dollars. Please take this and use it to leave Evansville. Leave Indiana, Helena, as your husband requested in his letters. Tell no one, not me, not even your closest friend, when you're leaving or where you're going. The constable has a man who watches you, so give no inclination of your impending departure. Leave quietly in the dead of night."

Staring into the colonel's eyes, she bent over and picked up the purse. After studying it carefully, she managed a constrained smile and said, "Thank you, Col. Bisch. It's so kind of you to warn me and offer money to help."

Then, after slipping the money into her apron pocket, Helena began pacing again and nervously asked, "And when they find me, then what?"

"Off the record, Mr. Hatfield assured me he does not intend to pursue you. But Herman is a different story. There's a bounty on his head, which means he'll be hunted. If caught, he'll be returned to Indiana to serve his sentence. There will be no trial. He has already been convicted and sentenced, Helena. Plus, the fact that he fled will make it virtually impossible for him to get a new trial."

"Then there's no choice. I-... *we* must leave Indiana!"

Chapter 44

Two days later, well after midnight, Helena peeked through the closed curtains, looking up and down Main Street for any sign of activity. Stepping gingerly across the floor, she shook Rudolph's shoulder, who was sleeping on the sofa.

"Rudolph," she whispered. "Rudolph, wake up."

"What is it?" he groaned, only half awake.

"I need you to get up."

"Why? What time is it?"

"It's quite late. But I need you to come in the other room before the children stir, so we can talk."

Sitting at the dinner table, with a single candle burning between them, Helena quietly said, "We're leaving Indiana tonight. I want you to take us to the Old Henderson Road Ferry, so we can make sure we're not being followed. We can't tell anyone where we're going, not even the children. Hitch the horse to the wagon and pull it to the back door. Make as little noise as possible."

While Rudolph prepared the wagon, Helena packed food and clothing for the long trip ahead. Once she and Rudolph carried all the goods out back to the wagon—with only the light of the moon to guide them—they created an area in the bed of the wagon with blankets for the children to rest during their late-night getaway out of Evansville.

With the wagon loaded, Rudolph and Helena hurried back inside to wake the children.

Nudging her boys as they slept, she said, "I need you to wake up. I'll explain later, but for now, you must trust me."

"Mama, what's wrong?" Mina asked, sleepily rubbing her eyes as she stumbled into the room. "It's so dark outside."

Once all the children were awake, they gathered in the living room.

"We're leaving Evansville," Helena whispered, looking into the faces of her children. "We have food, our clothes are in the trunk, and we have blankets for all of you to lie on in the wagon. These are the only things we're taking, you understand? Everything else stays. Now let's get settled in the wagon quickly, and we must all be quiet. No talking."

"But where are we going?" Eddy asked.

"I can't tell you, not just yet," she said, gesturing to herd her family toward the back door. "You'll all find out when we get there."

"Are we coming back?" August asked.

"No, dear. But I'll explain everything once we're out of Evansville."

One by one, the children climbed onto the wagon and covered themselves with blankets. With everyone settled and Helena perched beside Rudolph, he gripped the reins and began guiding their horse through the backstreets until they reached the edge of town.

Two lanterns swung loosely from the sides of the bench to help guide them through the darkness. Five miles out of town, on Old Henderson Road, Albert tugged on the back of his mother's dress and said, "I hear a horse coming, Mama."

"I hear it, too." Touching Rudolph's arm, she said, "Stop the wagon."

"What? Why? We're nearly to the ferry!"

"Don't argue with me, Rudolph. We won't beat the horseman, not in this cart. It's too dangerous to try to run at night. *I'm* the one they want! Let me off and you keep going."

"No! We can make it! We need to stay together!"

"Do as I say, Rudolph! If they arrest me, I need to know you and the children will be safe in Kentucky!"

Stepping down from the wagon after it stopped, Helena took one of the two lit lanterns. Rudolph snapped the reins, leaving her alone on the road.

Turning around, she watched as the galloping horse grew nearer, until its hooves pounding the dirt were all she could hear.

As he approached Helena standing beside the road with a lantern, Officer Chris Vogt pulled his mare to a quick stop. Looking down at her from his horse, he asked, "Where are you off to now, Mrs. Leyer?"

Standing still and not saying a word, she stared at the horse panting heavily in the night air.

"I asked you a question, Mrs. Leyer. I've been tasked with knowing your whereabouts."

While continuing to offer no response to the officer, Helena was not surprised when out of the darkness, Mina came up alongside her and wrapped her mother's arm around her neck.

Undaunted, Officer Vogt said, "I don't want your children, ma'am. But you've gotta' accompany me back to Evansville, until the law has no more business with you."

Suddenly, Eddy appeared and stood next to his mother, and without uttering a word took the lantern from her.

"I'll place you under arrest if I must," he said.

One after the other, the lantern illuminated the remaining children as they approached and stood next to their mother in front of the horse-mounted officer: August, Richard and Albert.

"Mrs. Leyer, I'm warning you!"

Lastly, Rudolph walked past the family to stand between Helena and the horseman.

After slapping his pistol that hung in its holster, Officer Vogt barked, "Consider yourself a fugitive from the law, Mrs. Leyer! The men who return you to Evansville won't be as pleasant as me!"

Then he turned his horse and galloped back toward Evansville.

***

When they rode off the ferry after crossing the Ohio River and entered Henderson, Kentucky, Helena breathed a loud sigh of relief.

Gazing back over her shoulder, she took one last look at what she could see of Indiana, now a darkened landscape of ghostly gray and black shadows, illuminated only by moonlight.

As Rudolph drove the horse-drawn wagon down the hard-packed dirt road, he saw tears streaming down Helena's face, though she continued wiping them away with her fingers as quickly as they arose. Rudolph remained stoic, staring face-forward, long into the early morning hours.

***

Sometime after sunrise on the first day in June, Helena said to Rudolph, "Pull to the side of the road and stop the wagon."

Guiding the horse to the side of the dusty road, he pulled hard on the wagon's brake.

Spinning around on the bench and facing her children—who were all sitting up in the wagon bed, their legs still covered with blankets—she said, "Alright, children, it's time for me to explain."

After Rudolph tied the reins to the wagon and turned around on the wooden bench, Helena said to the children, "This is very important, and I need you to listen carefully. We are now in the state of Kentucky. Indiana is on the other side of the river, miles from here. None of us can ever cross back into Indiana again. We're going to Louisville to start a new life and to find your brother."

Mina sat up and called out, "Herman?"

"No! You must never say that name again for as long as you live!"

As Helena reprimanded her young daughter, Mina drew back and retreated to August's shoulder.

Upon seeing Mina's stunned expression, Helena softened her tone. "None of you, not even you, Mina, can ever forget what I'm about to tell you. Before today, I couldn't tell anyone we were leaving Indiana, but this was your father's last request. No one, friend or stranger, can know where we're going.

"Herman has adopted my father's name, Charles Distler. *All* of us will be using the last name 'Distler' from now on. I never want to hear any of you say the names of Herman or Leyer. If you do, it could destroy our family, and we would be torn apart. So please don't ever forget this. Our last name is *Distler*. We'll practice it over and over until it feels natural."

"We can't tell our friends?" August asked.

"No, never... *no one* can know."

"But, Mama!" Eddy whined.

"I'm sorry, Eddy. I know this is painful. But if any living soul discovers who we are or where we are, Charles and I will be found and taken back to Indiana, where we will suffer the same fate as your father's. I promised him I would keep this family together, no matter the cost. This is the way it has to be."

After pausing momentarily, she asked, "So, Mina, what's your name?"

"Mina Distler?"

"That's right. And what's your oldest brother's name?"

Mina thought for a moment and then smiled. "Charles Distler?"

"Good, very good. Distler was my maiden name. If you're ever asked, you were born in Louisville, Kentucky. I will be using my real first name from now on. Your parents are Edward and Maria Distler. Your father, Edward Distler, died of consumption. I know it seems like a lot to remember, but we'll eventually learn… and live by it."

"Maria is a pretty name," Mina said with a grin.

"Thank you, dear."

"But why do you and Charles have a new first name and not the rest of us?" August asked.

"Indiana wants to arrest Herman Leyer and Helena Leyer on the same lies that killed your father. For our sake, you must never say those names, not even amongst yourselves. *No one*, not your wives, children, or grandchildren, can know who we were. We must put that part of our lives behind us and start over. Now I want each of you to swear to this on my life."

One by one, the children repeated, "I promise, Mother."

"Good!" Turning back around on the bench, she said loudly enough for them all to hear, "Now, I want each of you to practice your new name for the rest of the trip."

***

At half-past three on the first Sunday in June, their wagon stopped at the bottom of the steps to Saint Peter's Episcopal Church in Louisville, Kentucky. The Distler children looked around in awe at the big, bustling city.

Maria remained staring intently at the crowd of people on the church's front steps, until Rudolph tapped her on one arm and pointed at a young man sitting on a bench.

"There! Over there!"

Stepping down from the wagon, she hurried toward the short, poorly dressed man, who was seated beside the stone stairs leading to the church's front entrance, and cried out, "Charles! Charles Distler!"

Finale

Public sentiment remained divided. Even the papers of the day were firm in opposing views. *The Evansville Journal*, dated April 16, 1877, found no room for doubt.

THE LEYER CASE.

The interest in this case does not seem to lessen, but the question of his guilt or innocence is universally discussed. The great majority of the community take no stock in the belief of his innocence. Prof. Achilles is attacked upon his analysis, and accused of having conducted it in an improper manner. Prof. Achilles is amply able to take care of himself, and will no doubt do it; but we may remark in passing, that he enjoys a high reputation as an analytical chemist, and therefore most probably richly deserves it.

Prof. Achilles' opinion as to the cause of Leyer's death has brought down upon him the wrath of the partisans of innocence, who would make Leyer out an unfortunate angel. Prof. Achilles' opinion outside of the chemical view, is supported by all the natural appearances in the case

If he was an innocent man, his wife must have known it and his son, and no prison on earth could have held him one year, for truth is mighty and will prevail, or crushed to earth will rise again. He had no reason to be dependent, under any circumstances. The opinion of the lawyers was somewhat divided as to the proof in the case, some of them thinking that it was not proven to the strict legal standard. With this doubt it was extremely probable that the Supreme Court of the State would have ordered a new trial, and he had a better opportunity to escape than before.

No; he was a guilty man and knew there was no escape for him with that crime upon his heart, and he settled the question the quickest way.

Yet *The Evansville Courier and Press*, dated April 13, 1877, took a softer stance, given the admission of perjury by the prisoner, Wellington.

> THE COURIER'S belief in the innocence of EDWARD LEYER is now shared by a large majority of the people. Who the guilty party is still remains in doubt. It is a cruel, heartless thing, however, to charge that Mrs. LEYER poisoned her husband; to torture the language of his letters into a cunning attempt to shield his wife and children from suspicion. Shame on the wretch who thus early begins to weave about those who are left of this stricken family the same web of circumstantial evidence that has murdered EDWARD LEYER! THE COURIER does not understand why the officers of the law have ceased to investigate the case further. *Why do they not get* WELLINGTON'S *statement before he is taken back to the penitentiary?* He has made public the fact that he knows the truth about the case and that what he said on the trial was not the truth. He has told Col. BISCH that he had a confession to make exposing a certain person or persons who bribed him to swear falsely. Why, we repeat,

do not the proper officers of the law take his statement? If EDWARD LEYER was innocent, the State at least owes it to his wife and children that his good name shall be restored, and should show as much zeal in relieving his memory of disgrace as it exercised in visiting upon him the vengeance of the law. Let WELLINGTON be assured that he will not be punished for telling the truth and clearing up the mystery.

The Leyer Letters

HIS FAREWELL LETTERS.

Ten letters in total were found in Edward Leyer's Evansville cell. One was written to the jailor as read in Chapter 37. The remaining nine are as follows. The letters, handwritten in German, were translated and published in the Evansville Courier and Press, April 12, 1877, for the English reader.

The letters were written on different dates. Many are titled *My Last Will*, as if he believed that day would be his last, yet some of the letters were written before the trial began, as though he had a premonition of the outcome.

MY LAST WILL
Evansville, March 7, 1877
My Most Beloved Wife and My Dear Children:
When this writing reaches you, you stand before me, and it is not permitted that my eyes see you. My heart has ceased to beat. But my beloved, the last pulse was for you, the last sigh, the last word was 'my beloved dear wife and children.' Oh, you cannot imagine, Lena, how I have suffered until now from hemorrhage. I have not thought to live through it, and since then have spit blood

continually. Then, my dearest, I've been innocent to suffer the mortification so long. Yes, my God, Thou knowest I am innocent. Innocent, I was thrown into prison by a band of thieves and murderers. Oh, my kind God, I beg Thee to forgive them. Oh, Heavenly Father! Thou art the witness of my innocence. Give to all people the knowledge that he who lays here – this Edward Leyer – on his death bed, that I, innocent, have died from pain and mortification. Then I beg you to fulfill my last request, to give my dead body to my beloved wife and children. Thine through eternity, my wife,
 Edward

 MY LAST WILL
 Evansville, March 12, 1877
Beloved Dear Wife and Children:
You all know I am innocent; that we in our lives have never had more than one five cents' worth of arsenic in the house, and besides that, have had nothing to do with poison... but that was a long time ago, the second year our shop was by Reitz & Haney's. Therefore, my dearest wife, I can calmly step before the judgment seat of God; because He, my God and Jesus Christ, are the witnesses I am innocent. Therefore I can die calmly. But one request, my heart-beloved wife – let my dead body rest one night with you under one roof. Then conduct it to the grave. Take the county coffin – the county grave – add to the coffin two or three dollars. That is all I wish. Then, beloved wife, leave Indiana. It has robbed you of your innocent husband and our poor children of their father. And upon finding yourself a new home, my beloved, be to the children a true mother. Be true to yourself wherever you are. My spirit shall surround you, that nothing wicked shall harm you. In eternity thine,
 Edward

I AM INNOCENT
Evansville, March 15, 1877
Dear Beloved Wife:
You stand by my dead body. I could not endure the mortification longer. Honor, all that is dear to man, is gone. By this, all our earnings, which by industry and hard work were earned for our children, all is gone. Oh, dear wife, I hope you know my endeavor was only to make you happy. For that, I have worked on ceaselessly. Oh, my God, today I am before Thy judgment seat, but Thou knowest I am innocent, that no arsenic was in my house. Oh, dear heavenly Father, Thou seest in the future, it is known to Thee. Thou art my witness they have prosecuted me, even though I am innocent. Thou knowest, my God, that only by my diligent hand and hard work I wished to secure my living, and that the cistern poisoning is but a slander to ruin me, which this band tried to do for years. Beloved dear wife, do as I direct. It is the last that I can advise you. Leave this state. Go forth from it. Be to the children a dear mother. Hold them to all that is good, because this state has robbed you of your husband and the children of an innocent father. Oh thou, my God, protect my children and my beloved wife. Take them all in Thy charge, my Heavenly Father, because I cannot more. Oh, my God, it is hard, being innocent, to suffer and die, to take leave of my beloved ones for eternity. Oh, separation! Oh, how parting gives pain! Oh, my Heavenly Father, before Thy judgment seat, I now stand, but innocent, and my entire house is innocent.

MY LAST WILL
Evansville, Indiana, March 16, 1877
To My Dear Wife and Children:
This my last will, my beloved Lena, my heart's beloved wife: I give you herewith full power that you are the inheritor of all my property that comes from my side, from my parents, brothers or relations. You can do with it as you choose, because you have

been to me a brave wife and to the children a good mother. Let this be signed in this place by those present, my heart's beloved wife.

Your ever-loving, Edward Leyer

MY LAST WILL
Evansville, March 18, 1877
Beloved Dear Wife:
Oh, dear heart, Lena! How my heart pains me... how parting from you, my inmost-loved wife, and our precious children, gives pain. I would so willingly have lived and worked for you for years to come; but God has ordered it otherwise. His will be done in Heaven, as also on Earth! But, my dear wife, yonder in the starry heights, there we shall meet again. Oh, my beloved, take my dead body from here; let it remain with you one night under the same roof in your dwelling. Beloved wife, fulfill my request. And again, be to the children a true, brave mother. Be to your husband, your ever-loving Edward, true beyond the grave, and leave this state. Indiana robbed you of all, and yet I was innocent; therefore, leave it as soon as you can.

Yours, ever yours, Edward

MY DECLARATION TO THE PUBLIC
Evansville, March 19, 1877
Dear Fellow Citizens:
I arrived here in 1856; had never been prosecuted for wrongdoing; was never in bad company; those who know me must admit this; but still, I was punished on account of the cistern poisoning. I am innocent, and stand so, as you read this before the judgment seat of God; but so true as God and our Jesus Christ, who shed his blood on the cross for us, I am innocent, and my whole house, because in my house there was no arsenic.

Fellow citizens, it is charged against us, but the future will clear up the mystery later. I hope so because thereby, everyone sees that they have ruined an innocent man and an innocent family – that they have slandered a man who has six children and who for twenty-three years has labored in sweat to nourish his children, to build them a safe path through life. But God has ordered otherwise. My race is run. It is no man's blame that I die so suddenly, only the mortification – the honor which this band of robbers and murderers have stolen from me; therefore, for the last time, I am innocent, so help me, God, because there was no arsenic in my house. I will now tell you what happened to me in the two years and nine months in the country. It is three years ago this month, namely on the 12th day of March 1874, I owned a blacksmith shop and made new wagons. We had to give up the business, not because there was no work, but because the people paid us in fruit and took advantage of me; so, I gave up after the first nine months. Then came the second of April; I had shut my shop and only worked for myself and good friends. On this second of April, I was called by my children out on the street. As soon as I came forward, some people attacked me and said, "Kill the damn Dutchman," but this was for work done. They wished to pay the debt owed to me with murder, however I came safely back into my yard. So it went on until the end of May and until I lost six horses in fifteen months. This was what the thieves and murderers had done to me. Also, a year ago, they had me indicted for slaughtering on Sunday. I was cleared but had to pay the lawyer's fee on this account. Fellow citizens, from the second of April, I have tried to sell my property; I did not wish to dwell among you, and on the second of December, 1876, I received a postal card that conveyed if I would sell cheap, I could now sell for cash. So we sold at this period. I thought not in the least of anything, and as soon as Cook and his mob heard that I had sold, they accused Herman and me of murder. But to close, I repeat, we are innocent. We have had no arsenic, so help me, God.

Ed Leyer

FAREWELL TO MY FAMILY
Evansville, April 1, 1877
Dear Beloved Wife and My Dear Children and Rudolph:
When you see this letter, I shall be no more. Oh, beloved Lena, be strong and leave the State of Indiana. She bereaved you of your husband and your children of their father. And that I am innocent, Judge Hargrave and the twelve jurors had well enough seen and heard. Had they had honor and compassion, they would have seen that Ed Leyer was innocent. I am now before the tribunal of God, before a just judge, before my Almighty God, who knows I am innocent, even if Andrew Butcher swears hundreds of perjuries against me. God will pass judgment on him. The day comes, oh my beloved wife, and I cannot live any longer. No, my honor, the bread of the children, all we have saved by the sweat of our brow in twenty-three long years, this band of robbers have taken, and those twelve jurors, together with Judge Hargrave, have joined hands with them. God, who is the judge over us all, will remind them of it on their deathbed; of the orphans who have been made orphans by them. Therefore, be strong, my beloved wife, for you must watch the flock. Farewell, my dear beloved Lena.

Your Edward

MY LAST WILL AND MY WISH
Evansville, April 2, 1877
Beloved Wife:
Oh, Lena! A thousand thanks! That you have sacrificed for me in such a way. God will reward you for it. Oh! One more request, dear Lena; please don't leave me in the jail. Let my corpse rest with you one more night under the same roof. Living, I could not be with you; in death, they cannot hinder it. Once more, farewell to you all. Over there, above the starry heaven – there, beloved, there we shall meet again.
    Yours, for eternity yours.
    Ed Leyer

I AM INNOCENT
Evansville, April 3, 1877
Beloved Fellow Citizens:
Now you have seen how an innocent man is sentenced. As truly as I stand before the tribunal of God, I have not said in Boonville that my son Herman and I had done the deed in the dark silence of night. The Sheriff, Gurley Taylor, has bought them. Lippert had to say he received arsenic from me. Yes, he was at my house to get arsenic, but we had none, so help me, God. Nor did I sweat. My blood be upon you, Lippert. You will suffer eternal damnation for what you have done to me, an innocent man. You know I was innocent, but God will judge you, because you have made six innocent children orphans.
    Ed Leyer

These letters were not written by an illiterate man. If Leyer died guilty of the crime of which he was convicted, with his mind made up to assert his innocence to the last, the letters he wrote are just what he would have written. Shrewd guilt will, in searching for effect, light upon just such displays that innocence is led into.

On the other hand, if Leyer was an innocent man, he would have written the letters just as he did, fraught with his woes, his mind not in a sane condition, and his declarations having no binding quality.

The tone was that of a man oppressed with unjust punishment. He was forgiving to his jailer, made no charges against his prosecutor, and predicted he would die of a broken heart. The man is dead and gone to eternal account. We can pursue him no further.

If Leyer was guilty, he has been punished. If he was innocent, he has been wronged; then throw the clods on his coffin. In either event, the investigation into this man ceased with his death, and if his son, Herman, was in criminal compact, he was shielded from pursuit given the horror of his father's sacrifice.

Epilogue

General John Hunt Morgan

Following his capture near Salineville, Ohio, by General Shackelford, General Morgan was held in the Ohio State Penitentiary until his escape in late November of 1863, only to resume his position and be placed in command of the Eastern Tennessee region. During a surprise attack by a detachment of Union cavalry on September 4, 1864, he was killed in Greenville, Tennessee, in the garden of the house where he'd been sleeping the night before. General Morgan was buried in the Lexington Cemetery in Lexington, Kentucky.

Brigadier General James Murrell Shackelford

From 1880 through 1888, General Shackelford was the Republican Elector for the State of Indiana. In 1889, President Benjamin Harrison appointed Shackelford the first judge of the United States Court in the Indian Territory that would later become Oklahoma. He died September 7, 1909, at the age of 82, in Port Huron, St. Clair County, Michigan, where in his later years he'd spent his summers. General Shackelford was laid to rest in Cave Hill Cemetery in Louisville, Kentucky.

Frederick Cook

In 1880, Frederick Cook was elected the trustee of Greer Township in Warrick County, Indiana on the Republican ticket. Cook was married twice—the first time on December 2, 1867 to Elizabeth Butcher of Warrick; the second time on April 11, 1878 to Mary A. Irons. Mr. Cook was also twice elected constable of Greer Township. He died March 23, 1884 from typhoid pneumonia, just two days after his second wife, Mary, had succumbed to the same illness. Both were buried in Barnett Chapel Cemetery, Elberfeld, Warrick County, Indiana, near the burial plot of his first wife, Elizabeth.

Maria Distler (Maria Helena Leyer)

Maria Distler never remarried, choosing to live out her remaining years in the company of her children and grandchildren in Louisville, Kentucky. She died on April 28, 1906, twenty-nine years after her beloved, Edward had passed away. Maria was buried in Cave Hill Cemetery in Louisville, Kentucky.

Charles Distler (Herman Leyer)

Charles Distler lived out the rest of his life in Louisville, Kentucky. Never again did he venture across the Ohio River to set foot in Indiana. He worked his entire career as a machinist for the railroad. In 1880, Charles married Mary Prinz, who died a year later. The couple had no children. In 1885, he married Barbara Kastner, and together, they had five children. However, the first two, twin boys, died in their first year of life.

Charles took the family secret to the grave. His death certificate listed his father as W. A. Distler and mother as Lena Leyer. A lifelong member of the Freemasons, Charles died on January 1, 1942, and was buried in Cave Hill Cemetery in Louisville, Kentucky.

A Final Note from the Author

The Distler children never revealed the secrets of their past. I wish to acknowledge Glenda Distler and Wanda Distler Engel for their genealogical research that first uncovered this tragic thread of family history. Glenda, Wanda and my husband, Greg Distler, are just a few of the many great-grandchildren of Charles H. Distler (Herman Leyer).

www.ingramcontent.com/pod-product-compliance
Lightning Source LLC
Chambersburg PA
CBHW051527020426
42333CB00016B/1821